Wiley 11th Hour Guide for 2015 Level II CFA Exam

Thousands of candidates from more than 100 countries have relied on these Study Guides to pass the CFA® Exam. Covering every Learning Outcome Statement (LOS) on the exam, these review materials are an invaluable tool for anyone who wants a deep-dive review of all the concepts, formulas and topics required to pass.

Originally published by Elan Guides, this study material was produced by CFA® Charterholders, CFA® Institute members, and investment professionals. In 2014 John Wiley & Sons, Inc. purchased the rights to Elan Guides content, and now this material is part of the Wiley Efficient Learning suite of exam review products. For more information, contact us at info@efficientlearning.com.

Wiley 11th Hour Guide for 2015 Level II CFA Exam

WILEY

Contents

Derivatives

Portfolio Management

Foreword

Wiley 11th Hour Guide for 2015 Level I CFA Exam is a concise and easy to understand review book that is meant to supplement your review for the CFA Level I exam. It becomes extremely difficult to go through the entire curriculum in the last few weeks leading up to the exam so we have condensed the material for you. You must remember though, that this book is not meant to be a primary study too for the exam. It is designed to help you revise the material in an efficient and effective manner so that you can be confident on exam day.

About the Author

Basit Shajani, CFA, founded online education start-up Élan Guides in 2009 to help address CFA candidates' need for better study materials. As lead writer, lecturer, and curriculum developer, Basit's unique ability to break down complex topics helped the company grow organically to be a leading global provider of CFA Exam prep materials. In January 2014, Élan Guides was acquired by John Wiley & Sons, Inc., where Basit continues to serve as director of CFA content. Basit graduated magna cum laude from the Wharton School of Business at the University of Pennsylvania with majors in finance and legal studies. He went on to obtain his CFA charter in 2006, passing all three levels on the first attempt. Prior to Élan Guides, Basit ran his own private wealth management business. He is a past president of the Pakistani CFA Society.

STUDY SESSION 1: ETHICAL AND PROFESSIONAL STANDARDS

CODE OF ETHICS AND STANDARDS OF PROFESSIONAL CONDUCT
Cross-Reference to CFA Institute Assigned Reading #1 & 2

All CFA Institute members and candidates enrolled in the CFA Program are required to comply with the Code of Ethics and the Standards of Professional Conduct (Code and Standards). The CFA Institute Bylaws and Rules of Procedure for Proceedings Related to Professional Conduct (Rules of Procedure) form the basic structure for enforcing the Code and Standards.

The Rules of Procedure are based on the following two principles:
1. Fair process.
2. Maintaining confidentiality of process.

The CFA Institute Board of Governors is responsible for implementing the Professional Conduct Program (PCP) through the Disciplinary Review Committee (DRC).

The CFA Institute Designated Officer, through the Professional Conduct staff, carries out professional conduct inquiries. Circumstances which can initiate an inquiry include:

- Information disclosed on the annual Professional Conduct Statement.
- Written complaints received by Professional Conduct staff.
- Questionable conduct as publicized by the media or any other source.
- A violation report submitted by a CFA examination proctor.

Once an inquiry is initiated, the Professional Conduct staff undertakes an investigation which can include:
- Requesting a written explanation.
- Interviewing related person(s).
- Collecting any supporting documents.

The information collected is reviewed by the Designated Officer, who may conclude that:

1. No disciplinary action is needed
2. A cautionary letter needs to be issued
3. Proceedings need to be continued.

If it is concluded that there has been a violation of the Code and Standards, the Designated Officer can propose a disciplinary sanction. The member or candidate has the right to accept or reject the decision. A rejection would require the matter to be referred to a hearing by a panel of CFA Institute members. Sanctions by CFA Institute may include condemnation by peers, consequences for current or future employment or suspension from the CFA program.

The adherence of investment professionals to ethical practices benefits all market participants.

- Clients are reassured that investment professionals they hire prioritize their interests.
- Investment professionals benefit from the more efficient and transparent operation of the market that integrity promotes.

Sound ethics is fundamental to capital markets and the investment profession as it increases investors' confidence in global financial markets. Ethics is also of paramount importance because of the interconnectedness of global financial markets, which gives rise to the issue of market sustainability. It is imperative that top management foster a strong culture of ethics not just among CFA charter holders and candidates but among all staff members who are involved directly or indirectly with client relations, the investment process, record keeping, and beyond.

However, new challenges continually arise for members and candidates in applying the Code and Standards. This is because ethical dilemmas are not unambiguously right or wrong and require a bit of judgment.

The CFA Institute Code of Ethics plays an integral role in maintaining the integrity of CFA Institute members and upholding professional excellence. All CFA Institute members and CFA candidates must abide by this code and are encouraged to notify their employers of any violations. Violations may result in disciplinary sanctions by CFA Institute, which may include revocation of membership, candidacy in the CFA program and the right to use the CFA designation.

The Code of Ethics requires all members and candidates to:

- Act with integrity, competence, diligence, respect, and in an ethical manner with the public, clients, prospective clients, employers, employees, colleagues in the investment profession, and other participants in the global capital markets.
- Place the integrity of the investment profession and the interests of clients above their own personal interests.
- Use reasonable care and exercise independent professional judgment when conducting investment analysis, making investment recommendations, taking investment actions, and engaging in other professional activities.
- Practice and encourage others to practice in a professional and ethical manner that will reflect credit on themselves and the profession.
- Promote the integrity of, and uphold the rules governing, capital markets.
- Maintain and improve their professional competence and strive to maintain and improve the competence of other investment professionals.

Standards of Professional Conduct:

I. Professionalism
   A. Knowledge of the Law
   B. Independence and Objectivity
   C. Misrepresentation
   D. Misconduct

II. Integrity of Capital Markets
   A. Material Nonpublic Information
   B. Market Manipulation

III. Duties to Clients
   A. Loyalty, Prudence and Care
   B. Fair Dealing
   C. Suitability
   D. Performance Presentation
   E. Preservation of Confidentiality

IV. Duties to Employers
    A. Loyalty
    B. Additional Compensation Arrangements
    C. Responsibilities of Supervisors

V. Investment Analysis, Recommendations and Actions
    A. Diligence and Reasonable Basis
    B. Communication with Clients and Prospective Clients
    C. Record Retention

VI. Conflicts of Interest
    A. Disclosure of Conflicts
    B. Priority of Transactions
    C. Referral Fees

VII. Responsibilities as a CFA Institute Member or CFA Candidate
    A. Conduct as Participants in CFA Institute Programs
    B. Reference to CFA Institute, the CFA Designation, and the CFA Program

The best way to prepare for Ethics is to thoroughly read the Standards themselves, along with related guidance and examples.

CFA INSTITUTE RESEARCH OBJECTIVITY STANDARDS
Cross-Reference to CFA Institute Assigned Reading #3

When designing policies and procedures for implementing the CFA Institute Research Objectivity Standards, firms should strive to achieve the following objectives:

A. To prepare research reports, make investment recommendations, and take investment actions; and develop policies, procedures, and disclosures that always place the interests of investing clients before their employees' or the firm's interests.

B. To facilitate full, fair, meaningful, and specific disclosures of potential and actual conflicts of interest of the firm or its employees to its current and prospective clients.

C. To promote the creation and maintenance of effective policies and procedures that would minimize and manage conflicts of interest that may jeopardize the independence and objectivity of research.

D. To support self-regulation through voluntary industry development of, and adherence to, specific, measurable, and demonstrable standards that promote and reward independent and objective research.

E. To provide a work environment for all investment professionals that supports, encourages, and rewards ethical behavior and supports CFA Institute members, CFA charterholders, and CFA candidates in their adherence to the CFA Institute Code and Standards.

CFA Institute Research Objectivity Standards

1.0 Research Objectivity Policy

Requirements

Firms must have:

a. A formal written policy on the independence and objectivity of research (Policy) that must be:
   i. made available to clients and prospective clients (both investing and corporate); and
   ii. disseminated to all firm employees;

b. Supervisory procedures that reasonably ensure that the firm and its covered employees comply with the provisions of the policy and all applicable laws and regulations; and

c. A senior officer of the firm who attests annually to clients and prospective clients to the firm's implementation of, and adherence to, the Policy.

2.0 Public Appearances

Requirements

Firms that permit research analysts and other covered employees to present and discuss their research and recommendations in public appearances must require these employees to fully disclose personal and firm conflicts of interest to the host or interviewer and, whenever possible, to the audience.

3.0 Reasonable and Adequate Basis

Requirements

Firms must require research reports and recommendations to have a basis that can be substantiated as reasonable and adequate. An individual employee (supervisory analyst who is someone other than the author) or a group of employees (review committee) must be appointed to review and approve all research reports and recommendations.

4.0 Investment Banking

Requirements

Firms that engage in, or collaborate on, investment banking activities must:
  a. Establish and implement effective policies and procedures that:
     i. segregate research analysts from the investment banking department; and
     ii. ensure that investment banking objectives or employees do not have the ability to influence or affect research or recommendations;
  b. Implement reporting structures and review procedures that ensure that research analysts do not report to, and are not supervised or controlled by, investment banking or another department of the firm that could compromise the independence of the analyst; and
  c. Implement procedures that prevent investment banking or corporate finance departments from reviewing, modifying, approving, or rejecting research reports and recommendations on their own authority.

5.0 Research Analyst Compensation

Requirements

Firms must establish and implement salary, bonus, and other compensation for research analysts that:
  a. Align compensation with the quality of the research and the accuracy of the recommendations over time; and
  b. Do not directly link compensation to investment banking or other corporate finance activities on which the analyst collaborated (either individually or in the aggregate).

6.0 Relationships with Subject Companies

Requirements

Firms must implement policies and procedures that manage the working relationships that research analysts develop with the management of subject companies.

Research analysts must be prohibited from:
  a. Sharing with, or communicating to, a subject company, prior to publication, any section of a research report that might communicate the research analyst's proposed recommendation, rating, or price target; and
  b. Directly or indirectly promising a subject company or other corporate issuer a favorable report or a specific price target, or from threatening to change reports, recommendations, or price targets.

7.0 Personal Investments and Trading

Requirements

Firms must have policies and procedures that:

a. Manage covered employees' "personal investments and trading activities" effectively.
b. Ensure that covered employees do not share information about the subject company or security with any person who could have the ability to trade in advance of ("front run") or otherwise disadvantage investing clients.
c. Ensure that covered employees and members of their immediate families do not have the ability to trade in advance of or otherwise disadvantage investing clients relative to themselves or the firm;
d. Prohibit covered employees and members of their immediate families from trading in a manner that is contrary to, or inconsistent with, the employees' or the firm's most recent, published recommendations or ratings, except in circumstances of extreme financial hardship; and
e. Prohibit covered employees and members of their immediate families from purchasing or receiving securities prior to an IPO for subject companies and other companies in the industry or industries assigned.

8.0 Timeliness of Research Reports and Recommendations

Requirements

Firms must issue research reports on subject companies on a timely and regular basis.

9.0 Compliance and Enforcement

Requirements

Firms must:
a. Have effective enforcement of their policies and compliance procedures to ensure research objectivity;
b. Implement appropriate disciplinary sanctions for covered employees, up to and including dismissal from the firm, for violations;
c. Monitor and audit the effectiveness of compliance procedures; and
d. Maintain records of the results of internal audits.

10.0 Disclosure

Requirements

Firms must provide full and fair disclosure of all conflicts of interest to which the firm or its covered employees are subject.

11.0 Rating System

Requirements

Firms must establish a rating system that:
a. Is useful for investors and for investment decision-making; and
b. Provides investors with information for assessing the suitability of the security to their own unique circumstances and constraints.

STUDY SESSION 2: ETHICAL AND PROFESSIONAL STANDARDS—APPLICATION

TRADE ALLOCATION: FAIR DEALING AND DISCLOSURE
Cross-Reference to CFA Institute Assigned Reading #7

The CFA Institute Standards of Professional Conduct require members to not only disclose trade allocation procedures fully, to adopt such trade allocation procedures that treat clients in an equitable manner. This means that members should adhere to allocation procedures that ensure that investment opportunities are allocated to all clients in an appropriate and fair manner.

To ensure that adequate trade allocation practices are followed, the CFA Institute Standards of Practice Handbook suggests that members and their firms should:

- Obtain advance indications of client's interest for new issues.
- Allocate new shares by client rather than by portfolio manager.
- Adopt a pro rata or similar objective method or formula for allocating trades.
- Treat clients fairly in terms of both trade execution order and price.
- Execute orders timely and efficiently.
- Keep accurate records of trades and client accounts.
- Periodically review all accounts to ensure that all clients are being treated fairly.

CHANGING INVESTMENT OBJECTIVES
Cross-Reference to CFA Institute Assigned Reading #8

When managing pooled investment funds, it is extremely important for portfolio managers to adhere to the investment strategy stated in the fund's prospectus. This enables investors:
- To judge the appropriateness and suitability of the fund for themselves; and
- Protects them from style drift and exposure to investment strategies, asset classes, and risks other than those explicitly stated.

A material deviation from the fund's stated objectives, if not approved by shareholders, is a violation of Standard III (C.2) – Suitability, and Standard V (B.1) – Communication with Clients and Prospective Clients

In order to abide by the CFA Institute Standards, portfolio managers should take the following steps:

- Determine the client's financial situation, investment experience, and investment objectives. This information should be updated at least annually.
- Adequately disclose to clients the basic format and general principles of the investment processes by which securities are selected and portfolios are constructed.
- Conduct regular internal checks to ensure that portfolio characteristics meet the account's investment mandate, or the stated investment strategy in the case of pooled funds.
- Notify clients and investors of any potential changes in the investment objectives or strategies of the managed portfolios, including the impact of the change on the portfolio, and secure documented authorization of the change in strategy from the client.

STUDY SESSION 3: QUANTITATIVE METHODS FOR VALUATION

CORRELATION AND REGRESSION
Cross-Reference to CFA Institute Assigned Reading #9

Scatter Plots

A scatter plot is a graph that illustrates the relationship between observations of two data series in two dimensions.

Correlation Analysis

The correlation coefficient measures the direction and extent of the linear relationship between two variables. It lies between -1 and +1.

- A positive correlation coefficient implies that the two variables generally move in the same direction.
- A negative correlation coefficient implies that the two variables generally move in opposite directions.
- A correlation coefficient of zero indicates that there is no linear relationship between the two variables. In this case, the value of one variable tells us nothing about the value of the other.
- If all the points on a scatter plot illustrating the relationship between two variables lie along an upward-sloping straight line, the correlation between the two variables would be +1 regardless of the slope of the line.
- If all the points on a scatter plot illustrating the relationship between two variables lie along a downward-sloping straight line, the correlation between the two variables would be -1 regardless of the slope of the line.

The correlation coefficient is easier to interpret than sample covariance because it is a simple number, while covariance is expressed in units squared.

Calculating and Interpreting the Correlation Coefficient

In order to calculate the correlation coefficient, we first need to calculate covariance. Covariance is a similar concept to variance. The difference lies in the fact that variance measures how a random variable varies with itself, while covariance measures how a random variable varies with another random variable.

Properties of Covariance

- Covariance is symmetric i.e., $Cov(X, Y) = Cov(Y, X)$.
- The covariance of X with itself, $Cov(X,X)$ equals the variance of X, $Var(X)$.

Interpreting the Covariance

- Basically, covariance measures the nature of the relationship between two variables.
- When the covariance between two variables is *negative*, it means that they tend to move in opposite directions.
- When the covariance between two variables is *positive*, it means that they tend to move in the same direction.
- The covariance between two variables equals zero if they are not related.

$$\text{Sample covariance} = \text{Cov}(X, Y) = \sum_{i=1}^{n}(X_i - \bar{X})(Y_i - \bar{Y}) / (n-1)$$

n = sample size
X_i = ith observation of Variable X
$\bar{X}$ = mean observation of Variable X
Y_i = ith observation of Variable Y
$\bar{Y}$ = mean observation of Variable Y

The numerical value of sample covariance is not very meaningful as it is presented in terms of units squared. Covariance is standardized by dividing it by the product of the standard deviations of the two variables. This standardized measure is known as the sample correlation coefficient (denoted by r) and is easy to interpret as it always lies between −1 and +1, and has no unit of measurement attached.

$$\text{Sample correlation coefficient} = r = \frac{\text{Cov}(X, Y)}{s_X s_Y}$$

$$\text{Sample variance} = s_X^2 = \sum_{i=1}^{n}(X_i - \bar{X})^2 / (n-1)$$

$$\text{Sample standard deviation} = s_X = \sqrt{s_X^2}$$

Computed correlation coefficients are only valid if the means and variances of X and Y, as well as the covariance of X and Y, are finite and constant.

Limitations of Correlation Analysis

- It is important to remember that the correlation is a measure of linear association. Two variables can have a very strong non-linear relation and still have low correlation.
- Correlation may be an unreliable measure when there are outliers in the data. Analysts must evaluate whether outliers should be included in the data when calculating and interpreting correlation.
- Correlation does not imply causation.
- Correlations may be spurious, in that they may highlight relationships that are misleading. The term "spurious correlation" is used to refer to relationships where:
  - Correlation reflects chance relationships in a data set.
  - Correlation is induced by a calculation that mixes two variables with a third.
  - Correlation arises from both the variables being directly related to a third variable.

Uses of Correlation Analysis

- Investment analysis (e.g. evaluating the accuracy of inflation forecasts in order to apply the forecasts in predicting asset prices).
- Identifying appropriate benchmarks in the evaluation of portfolio manager performance.
- Identifying appropriate avenues for effective diversification of investment portfolios.
- Evaluating appropriateness of using other measures (e.g. net income) as proxies for cash flow in financial statement analysis.

Testing the Significance of the Correlation Coefficient

To test whether the correlation between two variables is significantly different from zero:

$H_0: \rho = 0$

$H_a: \rho \neq 0$

$$\text{Test-stat} = t = \frac{r\sqrt{n-2}}{\sqrt{1-r^2}}$$

n = Number of observations
r = Sample correlation
n – 2 = Degrees of freedom

The value of sample correlation (r) required to reject the null hypothesis decreases as sample size (n) increases:

- As n increases, the degrees of freedom also increase, which results in the absolute critical value (t_{crit}) for the test falling.
- The absolute value of the numerator (in calculating the test statistic) increases with higher values of n, which results in higher t-values.

Note:
- All other factors constant, a false null hypothesis ($H_0: \rho = 0$) is more likely to be rejected as we increase the sample size.
- The smaller the size of the sample, the greater the value of sample correlation required to reject the null hypothesis of zero correlation.
- When the relation between two variables is very strong, a false null hypothesis ($H_0: \rho = 0$) may be rejected with a relatively small sample size.
- With large sample sizes, even relatively small correlation coefficients can be significantly different from zero.

Uses of Correlation Analysis

- Investment analysis (e.g. evaluating the accuracy of inflation forecasts in order to apply the forecasts in predicting asset prices).
- Identifying appropriate benchmarks in the evaluation of portfolio manager's performance.
- Identifying appropriate avenues for effective diversification of investment portfolios.
- Evaluating the appropriateness of using other measures (e.g. net income) as proxies for cash flow in financial statement analysis.

Linear Regression with One Independent Variable

Linear regression is used to make predictions about a dependent variable (Y) using an independent variable (X), to test hypotheses regarding the relation between the two variables and to evaluate the strength of this relationship. The regression computes the line of best fit that minimizes the sum of the regression residuals (the sum of the squared vertical distances between actual observations of the random variable and predicted values of the variable based on the regression equation).

$$\text{Regression equation} = Y_i = b_0 + b_1 X_i + \varepsilon_i, i = 1, ..., n$$

b_1 and b_0 are the regression coefficients
b_1 = Slope coefficient
b_0 = Intercept
ε = The error term that represents the variation in the dependent variable that is not explained by the independent variable.

Classic Normal Linear Regression Assumptions

1. The relationship between the dependent (Y) and the independent variable (X) is linear in the parameters, b_1 and b_0.
2. The independent variable, X, is not random.
3. The expected value of the error term is zero: $E(\varepsilon) = 0$
4. The variance of the error term is constant for all observations $(E(\varepsilon_i^2) = \sigma_\varepsilon^2, i = 1,..., n)$. This is known as the homoskedasticity assumption.
5. The error term is uncorrelated across observations.
6. The error term is normally distributed.

An unbiased forecast is one where the expected value of the forecast error equals zero.

The Standard Error of Estimate

The standard error of estimate (SEE) is used to measure how well a regression model captures the relationship between the two variables. It indicates how well the regression line "fits" the sample data and is used to determine how certain we can be about a particular prediction of the dependent variable (Y_i) based on a regression equation. The SEE basically measures the standard deviation of the residual term (ε_i) in the regression. The smaller the standard deviation of the residual term (the smaller the standard error of estimate), the more accurate the predictions based on the model.

$$SEE = \left(\frac{\sum_{i=1}^{n}(Y_i - \hat{b}_0 - \hat{b}_1 X_i)^2}{n-2}\right)^{1/2} = \left(\frac{\sum_{i=1}^{n}(\hat{\varepsilon}_i)^2}{n-2}\right)^{1/2}$$

The Coefficient of Determination

The coefficient of determination (R^2) tells us how well the independent variable explains the variation in the dependent variable. It measures the fraction of the total variation in the dependent variable that is explained by the independent variable.

Calculating the Coefficient of Determination

1. $R^2 = r^2$

   The coefficient of determination equals the correlation coefficient squared. This calculation only works in linear regression i.e., when there is only one independent variable.

2. $$R^2 = \frac{\text{Explained variation}}{\text{Total variation}} = \frac{\text{Total variation} - \text{Unexplained variation}}{\text{Total variation}}$$
   $$= 1 - \frac{\text{Unexplained variation}}{\text{Total variation}}$$

Hypothesis Tests on Regression Parameters

$$\text{Test statistic} = t = \frac{\hat{b}_1 - b_1}{s_{\hat{b}_1}}$$

The critical t-value (t_{crit} or t_c) is determined with n-2 degrees of freedom.

In testing whether the regression coefficient equals a particular hypothesized value, the null hypothesis is rejected when the absolute value of the test statistic is greater than t_{crit}.

Confidence Intervals for Regression Parameters

$$\hat{b}_1 \pm t_c s_{\hat{b}_1}$$

- If the hypothesized value of the parameter (b_1) lies within the interval (which is based on the observed value of the parameter, $\hat{b}_1$), we fail to reject the null hypothesis.
- If the hypothesized value of the parameter (b_1) lies outside the interval (which is based on the observed value of the parameter, $\hat{b}_1$), we can reject the null hypothesis.

Confidence Intervals versus Hypothesis Tests

- In a confidence interval, we aim to determine whether the **hypothesized value of the population parameter** lies **within** a computed interval (where the interval is based around, or centered on the **estimated parameter value from sample data**) with a particular degree of **confidence (1-α)**. The confidence interval represents the "fail-to-reject-the-null region".

- In a hypothesis test, we examine whether the **estimate of the parameter** lies in the rejection region or **outside** an interval (where the interval is based around, or centered on the **hypothesized value of the population parameter**), at a particular level of **significance (α)**.

Important Notes

- Choosing a lower level of significance increases the absolute value of t_{crit} resulting in a wider confidence interval and a lower likelihood of rejecting the null hypothesis.
- Increasing the significance level increases the probability of a Type I error, but decreases the probability of a Type II error.
- The p-value is the lowest level of significance at which the null hypothesis can be rejected for a null hypothesis, that the true population parameter equals zero.
- The smaller the standard error of an estimated parameter, the stronger the results of the regression and the narrower the resulting confidence intervals.

Analysis of Variance in a Regression with One Independent Variable

Analysis of variance (ANOVA) is used to evaluate the usefulness of the independent variable in explaining the variation in the dependent variable.

The F-statistic is used to test whether the slope coefficient in the regression equals zero (H_0: $b_1 = 0$ versus H_a: $b_1 \neq 0$). It equals the ratio of the average regression sum of squares to the average sum of the squared errors.

$$F = \frac{MSR}{MSE} = \frac{RSS/k}{SSE/(n-k-1)}$$

Degrees of freedom (numerator) = k = 1
Degrees of freedom (denominator) = n − k − 1 = n − 2

The F-test is a one-tailed test. The null hypothesis is rejected if the F-stat is greater than F_{crit}. Rejection of the null hypothesis means that the independent variable significantly explains the variation in the dependent variable.

- If the independent variable does not explain much of the variation in the dependent variable, the F-stat will be relatively small.
- If the independent variable does a good job of explaining much of the variation in the dependent variable, the F-stat will be relatively high.
- For regression analysis with only one independent variable, the F-test duplicates the t-test. In such a regression, the F-stat (F) equals the t-stat (t_{b1}) squared.

ANOVA Table for Simple Linear Regression (k = 1)

Source of Variation	Degrees of Freedom	Sum of Squares	Mean Sum of Squares
Regression (explained)	1	RSS	$MSR = \dfrac{RSS}{k} = \dfrac{RSS}{1} = RSS$
Error (unexplained)	n – 2	SSE	$MSE = \dfrac{SSE}{n-2}$
Total	n – 1	**SST**	

Components of Total Variation

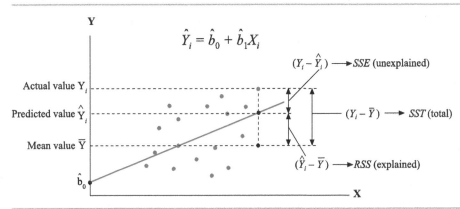

- SST measures the total variation in the dependent variable.

$$SST = \sum_{i=1}^{n}(Y_i - \bar{Y})^2 \rightarrow \text{Total variation}$$

- RSS measures the variation in the dependent variable that is explained by the independent variable.

$$\text{RSS} = \sum_{i=1}^{n} (\hat{Y_i} - \overline{Y})^2 \rightarrow \text{Explained variation}$$

- SSE measures the variation in the dependent variable that is not explained by the independent variable.

$$\text{SSE} = \sum_{i=1}^{n} (Y_i - \hat{Y_i})^2 \rightarrow \text{Unexplained variation}$$

Prediction Intervals

There are two sources of uncertainty when we use a regression model to make a prediction regarding the value of the dependent variable.

- The uncertainty inherent in the error term, ε.
- The uncertainty in the estimated parameters, b_0 and b_1.

$$\text{Estimated variance of the prediction error} = s_f^2 = s^2 \left[1 + \frac{1}{n} + \frac{(X - \overline{X})^2}{(n-1)s_x^2} \right]$$

Once the variance of the prediction error has been computed, the $(1 - \alpha)\%$ prediction interval around the predicted value is estimated as:

$$\hat{Y_1} \pm t_c s_f$$

Limitations of Regression Analysis

- Regression relations can change over time.
- Public knowledge of regression relationships may negate their usefulness going forward.
- If the assumptions of regression analysis do not hold, the predictions based on the model will not be valid.

MULTIPLE REGRESSION AND ISSUES IN REGRESSION ANALYSIS
Cross-Reference to CFA Institute Assigned Reading #10

Multiple Linear Regression

Multiple linear regression allows us to determine the effects of more than one independent variable on a particular dependent variable. The multiple regression equation is given as:

$$Y_i = b_0 + b_1 X_{1i} + b_2 X_{2i} + \ldots + b_k X_{ki} + \varepsilon_i, \, i = 1, 2 \ldots, n$$

where:
Y_i = the ith observation of the dependent variable Y
X_{ji} = the ith observation of the independent variable X_j, $j = 1, 2, \ldots, k$
b_0 = the intercept of the equation
$b_1, \ldots, b_k$ = the slope coefficients for each of the independent variables
ε_i = the error term
n = the number of observations

- In multiple regression, a slope coefficient measures the impact on the dependent variable of a one unit change in the independent variable holding all other independent variables constant. This is why slope coefficients of multiple regressions are also known as partial slope coefficients.
- The intercept and the slope coefficients are all known as regression coefficients. Therefore, there are k slope coefficients in a regression model and $k+1$ regression coefficients.
- The residual term, ε_i, equals the difference between the actual value of Y (Y_i) and the predicted value of Y($\hat{Y}_i$).

$$\hat{\varepsilon}_i = Y_i - \hat{Y}_i = Y_i - (\hat{b}_0 + \hat{b}_1 X_{1i} + \hat{b}_2 X_{2i} + \ldots + \hat{b}_k X_{ki})$$

Confidence Intervals

$$\hat{b}_j \pm (t_c \times s_{\hat{b}_j})$$

estimated regression coefficient $\pm$ (critical t-value)(coefficient standard error)

- The critical t-value is a two-tailed value computed based on the significance level (1 − confidence level) and $n - (k+1)$ degrees of freedom.
- A t-test with a null hypothesis of "equal to zero" at a significance level of α and a confidence interval with a (1-α) level of confidence will always give the same result.

Predicting the Dependent Variable

- Obtain estimates for $\hat{b}_0, \hat{b}_1, \hat{b}_2, \ldots, \hat{b}_j$ of regression parameters $b_0, b_1, b_2, \ldots, b_k$.
- Determine the assumed values for independent variables $\hat{X}_1, \hat{X}_2, \ldots, \hat{X}_k$.
- Compute the value of the dependent variable, $\hat{Y}_1$ using the equation

$$\hat{Y}_i = \hat{b}_0 + \hat{b}_1 \hat{X}_{1i} + \hat{b}_2 \hat{X}_{2i} + \ldots + \hat{b}_k \hat{X}_{ki}$$

All the independent variables in the regression equation (regardless of whether or not their estimated slope coefficients are significantly different from 0), must be used in predicting the value of the dependent variable.

Assumptions of the Multiple Linear Regression Model

- The relationship between the dependent variable and the independent variables is linear.
- The independent variables are not random and no linear relationship exists between two or more independent variables.
- The expected value of the error term is zero.
- The variance of the error term is the same for all observations.
- The error term is uncorrelated across observations.
- The error term is normally distributed.

Hypothesis Tests on Regression Coefficients

The test statistic for each regression coefficient is calculated as:

$$\text{t-stat} = \frac{\text{Estimated regression coefficient} - \text{Hypothesized value of regression coefficient}}{\text{Standard error of regression coefficient}}$$

$$t = \frac{\hat{b}_j - b_j}{s_{\hat{b}_j}} = \frac{\text{Estimated regression coefficient} - \text{Hypothesized value}}{\text{Coefficient standard error of } b_j}$$

Degrees of freedom $= n - (k + 1)$

P-Values

- The p-value for each regression coefficient is the lowest level of significance at which we can reject the null hypothesis that the population value of the coefficient is zero, in a two-sided test.
- The lower the p-value, the weaker the case for the null hypothesis.

Results from Regression with Two Independent Variables

	Coefficient	Standard Error	t-Statistic
Intercept	b_0	$s_{\hat{b}_0}$	$b_0 / s_{\hat{b}_0}$
First independent variable X_i	b_1	$s_{\hat{b}_1}$	$b_1 / s_{\hat{b}_1}$
Second independent variable X_i	b_2	$s_{\hat{b}_2}$	$b_2 / s_{\hat{b}_2}$

Residual standard error	SEE
Multiple R-squared	R^2
Observations	n

ANOVA

Source of Variation	Degrees of Freedom	Sum of Squares	Mean Sum of Squares	F	Significance
Regression	k	RSS	MSR = RSS / k	MSR/MSE	p-value
Residual	n − (k + 1)	SSE	MSE = SSE /n − (k + 1)		
Total	n − 1	**SST**			

Testing Whether All Population Regression Coefficients Equal Zero

Analysis of variance (ANOVA) provides the required information to test whether all the slope coefficients in a regression simultaneously equal zero. The F-test is used to conduct the following hypothesis test:

H_0: $b_1 = b_2 = \ldots = b_k = 0$
H_a: At least one slope coefficient does not equal zero

Information required to perform the F-test

- Number of observations (n).
- Total number of regression coefficients ($k + 1$).
- Sum of squared errors on residuals (SSE or total unexplained variation).
- Regression sum of squares (RSS or total explained variation).

$$F = \cfrac{\cfrac{RSS}{k}}{\cfrac{SSE}{[n-(k+1)]}} = \frac{\text{Mean regression sum of squares}}{\text{Mean squared error}} = \frac{MSR}{MSE}$$

- Degrees of freedom (numerator) = k
- Degrees of freedom (denominator) = n − (k + 1)

If the regression model does a good job in explaining the variation in the dependent variable, the F-stat will be relatively large.

Decision rule: Reject null hypothesis if F-stat > F_{crit}. Note that we use a one-tailed F-test.

Adjusted R^2

The coefficient of determination can be increased by adding independent variables that explain even a slight amount of the variation in the dependent variable to the regression equation. Adjusted R^2 does not automatically increase when another variable is added to the regression as it is adjusted for degrees of freedom.

$$\text{Adjusted } R^2 = \bar{R}^2 = 1 - \left(\frac{n-1}{n-k-1}\right)(1-R^2)$$

- If k is greater than or equal to 1, R^2 is greater than adjusted R^2.
- If a new independent variable (k) is added, adjusted R^2 can decrease if adding the variable only results in a small increase in R^2.
- Adjusted R^2 can be negative while R^2 cannot.

Regression Equation

- Shows the relationship between the dependent variable and the independent variables.
- Can be used to predict the value of the dependent variable, given specific values for the independent variables.
- The significance of the individual regression coefficients is evaluated using t-tests or p-values.
- The t-stat for each regression coefficient is calculated by dividing the value of the coefficient by its standard error.

ANOVA Table

- Lists the regression sum of squares (RSS), sum of squared errors (SSE) and total sum of squares (SST) along with associated degrees of freedom.
- Also includes calculated values for mean regression sum of squares (MSR) and mean squared error (MSE).
- The F-stat can be calculated by dividing MSR by MSE. The F-test is used to test whether at least one of the slope coefficients on the independent variables in the regression is significantly different from 0.
- R^2 (and adjusted R^2) can be calculated from the data in the ANOVA table by dividing RSS by SST. R^2 is used to determine the goodness of fit of the regression equation to the data.
- The standard error of estimate (SEE) can also be computed from the information in the ANOVA table. $SEE = \sqrt{MSE}$

Dummy Variables

Using Dummy Variables in a Regression

Dummy variables in regression models help analysts determine whether a particular qualitative variable explains the variation in the model's dependent variable to a significant extent.
- A dummy variable must be binary in nature i.e., it may take on a value of either 0 or 1.
- If the model aims to distinguish between n categories, it must employ n-1 dummy variables. The category that is omitted is used as a reference point for the other categories.
- The intercept term in the regression indicates the average value of the dependent variable for the omitted category.
- The slope coefficient of each dummy variable estimates the difference (compared to the omitted category) a particular dummy variable makes to the dependent variable.
- If we use n dummy variables (instead of n-1) we would be violating the regression assumption of no linear relationship between the independent variables.

Violations of Regression Assumptions

Heteroskedasticity

Heteroskedasticity occurs when the variance of the error term in the regression is not constant across observations.

Effects of Heteroskedasticity

- Heteroskedasticity does not affect the consistency of estimators of regression parameters.
- However, it can lead to mistakes in inferences made from parameter estimates.
  - The F-test for the overall significance of the regression becomes unreliable as the MSE becomes a biased estimator of the true population variance.

- o The t-tests for the significance of each regression coefficient become unreliable as the estimates of the standard errors of regression coefficients become biased.
  - Typically, in regressions with financial data, standard errors of regression coefficients are underestimated and t-stats are inflated due to heteroskedasticity. Therefore, ignoring heteroskedasticity results in significant relationships being found when none actually exist. (Null hypotheses are rejected too often).
  - Sometimes however, heteroskedasticity leads to standard errors that are too large, which makes t-stats too small.

Types of Heteroskedasticity

- Unconditional heteroskedasticity occurs when the heteroskedasticity of the variance in the error term is not related to the independent variables in the regression. Unconditional heteroskedasticity does not create major problems for regression analysis.
- Conditional heteroskedasticity occurs when the heteroskedasticity in the error variance is correlated with the independent variables in the regression. While conditional heteroskedasticity does create problems for statistical inference, it can be easily identified and corrected.

Testing for Heteroskedasticity- The Breusch-Pagan (BP) Test

The BP test requires a regression of **the squared residuals from the original estimated regression equation** (in which the dependent variable is regressed on the independent variables) on the independent variables in the regression.

- If conditional heteroskedasticity does not exist, the independent variables will not explain much of the variation in the squared residuals from the original regression.
- If conditional heteroskedasticity is present, the independent variables will explain the variation in the squared residuals to a significant extent.

The test statistic for the BP test is a Chi-squared (χ^2) random variable, that is calculated as:

$$\chi^2 = n\mathrm{R}^2 \text{ with } k \text{ degrees of freedom}$$

n = Number of observations
R^2 = Coefficient of determination of the **second regression** (the regression when the squared residuals of the original regression are regressed on the independent variables).
k = Number of independent variables

H_0: The original regression's squared error term is uncorrelated with the independent variables.
H_a: The original regression's squared error term is correlated with the independent variables.

Note: The BP test is a one-tailed Chi-squared test because conditional heteroskedasticity is only a problem if it is too large.

Correcting Heteroskedasticity

There are two ways of correction for conditional heteroskedasticity in linear regression models:

- Use robust standard errors (White-corrected standard errors or heteroskedasticity-consistent standard errors) to recalculate the t-statistics for the original regression coefficients based on corrected-for-heteroskedasticity standard errors.
- Use generalized least squares, where the original regression equation is modified to eliminate heteroskedasticity.

Serial Correlation

Serial correlation (autocorrelation) occurs when regression errors are correlated across observations. It typically arises in time series regressions.

- Positive serial correlation occurs when a positive (negative) error for one observation increases the chances of a positive (negative) error for another.
- Negative serial correlation occurs when a positive (negative) error for one observation increases the chances of a negative (positive) error for another.

Effects of Serial Correlation

Positive (negative) serial correlation:

- Does not affect the consistency of the estimated regression coefficients.
- Causes the F-stat (which is used to test the overall significance of the regression) to be inflated (deflated) because MSE will tend to underestimate (overestimate) the population error variance.
- Causes the standard errors for the regression coefficients to be underestimated (overestimated), which results in larger (smaller) t-values. Consequently, analysts may reject (fail to reject) null hypotheses incorrectly, make Type I errors (Type II errors) and attach (fail to attach) significance to relationships that are in fact not significant (significant).

Testing for Serial Correlation- The Durban-Watson (DW) Test

The DW test-statistic is approximated as:

$DW \approx 2(1 - r)$; where r is the sample correlation between squared residuals from one period and those from the previous period.

- The DW-stat can range from 0 (when serial correlation equals +1) to 4 (when serial correlation equals -1).
- If the regression has no serial correlation, the DW stat equals 2.
- If the regression residuals are positively serially correlated, the DW stat will be less than 2.
- If the regression residuals are negatively serially correlated, the DW stat will be greater than 2.
- For a given sample, the critical DW value (d*) is not known with certainty. We only know that it lies between two values (d_l and d_u). Figure (on next page) depicts the lower and upper values for d* as they relate to the results of the DW test.

Value of Durbin-Watson Statistic

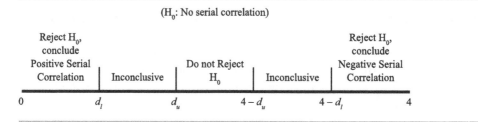

Decision rules for Durbin-Watson tests:

When testing for positive serial correlation:
- Reject H_0 of no positive serial correlation if the DW stat is lower than d_l. Conclude that there is positive serial correlation.
- The test is inconclusive if the DW stat lies between d_l and d_u
- Fail to reject H_0 of no positive serial correlation when DW stat is greater than d_u.

When testing for negative serial correlation:
- Reject H_0 of no negative serial correlation if the DW stat is higher than $4 - d_l$. Conclude that there is negative serial correlation.
- The test is inconclusive if the DW stat lies between $4 - d_u$ and $4 - d_l$.
- Fail to reject H_0 of no negative serial correlation when DW stat is less than $4 - d_u$.

Correcting Serial Correlation

There are two ways to correct for serial correlation in the regression residuals:
- Adjust the coefficient standard errors to account for serial correlation using Hansen's method (which incidentally also corrects for heteroskedasticity). The regression coefficients remain the same but the standard errors change. After correcting for positive serial correlation, the robust standard errors are larger than they were originally. Note that the DW stat still remains the same.
- Modify the regression equation to eliminate the serial correlation.

Multicollinearity

Multicollinearity occurs when two or more independent variables (or combinations of independent variables) in a regression model are highly (but not perfectly) correlated with each other.

Effects of Multicollinearity

- Multicollinearity does not affect the consistency of OLS estimates and regression coefficients, but makes them inaccurate and unreliable.
- It becomes difficult to isolate the impact of each independent variable on the dependent variable.
- The standard errors for the regression coefficients are inflated, which results in t-stats becoming too small and less powerful (in terms of their ability to reject null hypotheses).

Detecting Multicollinearity

- High pair-wise correlations between the independent variables do not necessarily indicate that multicollinearity exists.
- A high R^2 and a significant F-stat (both of which indicate that the regression model overall does a good job of explaining the dependent variable) coupled with insignificant t-stats of slope coefficients (which indicate that the independent variables individually do not significantly explain the variation in the dependent variable) provide the classic case of multicollinearity.
  - The low t-stats on the slope coefficients increase the chances of Type II errors: failure to reject the null hypothesis when it is false.
- Multicollinearity may be present even when we do not observe insignificant t-stats and a highly significant F-stat for the regression model.

Correcting for Multicollinearity

Analysts may correct for multicollinearity by excluding one or more of the independent variables from the regression model. Stepwise regression is a technique that systematically removes variables from the regression until multicollinearity is eliminated.

Problems in Linear Regression and Their Solutions

Problem	Effect	Solution
Heteroskedasticity	Incorrect standard errors	Use robust standard errors (corrected for conditional heteroskedasticity)
Serial correlation	Incorrect standard errors (additional problems if a lagged value of the dependent variable is used as an independent variable)	Use robust standard errors (corrected for serial correlation)
Multicollinearity	High R^2 and low t-statistics	Remove one or more independent variables; often no solution based in theory

Model Specification

Principles of Model Specification

- The model should be backed by solid economic reasoning.
- The functional form for the variables in the regression should be in line with the nature of the variables.
- Each variable in the model should be relevant, making the model "parsimonious".
- The model should be tested for violations of regression assumptions.
- The model should be found useful out of sample.

Model Specification Errors

1. Misspecified functional form
   ○ One or more important variables may have been omitted from the regression. This error would result in estimates of the regression coefficients and their standard errors being biased and inconsistent.
   ○ One or more of the variables may need to be transformed before estimating the regression. For example, if the relationship between the variables becomes linear when one of the variables is presented as a proportional change in the variable, the misspecification may be corrected by using the natural logarithm of the variable.
   ○ The model may pool data from different sources that should not have been pooled.

2. Time-series misspecification results from the kinds of independent variables included in the regression. It causes a violation of the regression assumption that the expected value of the error term equals zero. Time series misspecification can result from:
   ○ Including lagged dependent variables as independent variables to regressions with serially correlated errors. The lagged dependent variable (which serves as an independent variable in the regression) will be correlated with the error term, violating the assumption that independent variables are uncorrelated with the error term. Estimates of regression coefficients will be biased and inconsistent.
   ○ Including an independent variable that is a function of a dependent variable in the regression. In such a case, the particular independent variable would be correlated with the error term.
   ○ Independent variables are measured with error. Once again the independent variable would be correlated with the error term.
   ○ Nonstationarity occurs when a variable's properties (e.g. mean and variance) are not constant over time.

Qualitative Dependent Variables

When trying to predict a qualitative outcome, probit and logit models are generally used.

- The probit model is based on the normal distribution. It estimates the probability that a qualitative condition is fulfilled given the value of the independent variable.
- The logit model is similar except that it is based on the logistic distribution.
- Discriminant analysis yields a linear function (similar to a regression equation) that is used to create an overall score on the basis of which an observation can be classified qualitatively.

Steps in Assessing a Multiple Regression Model

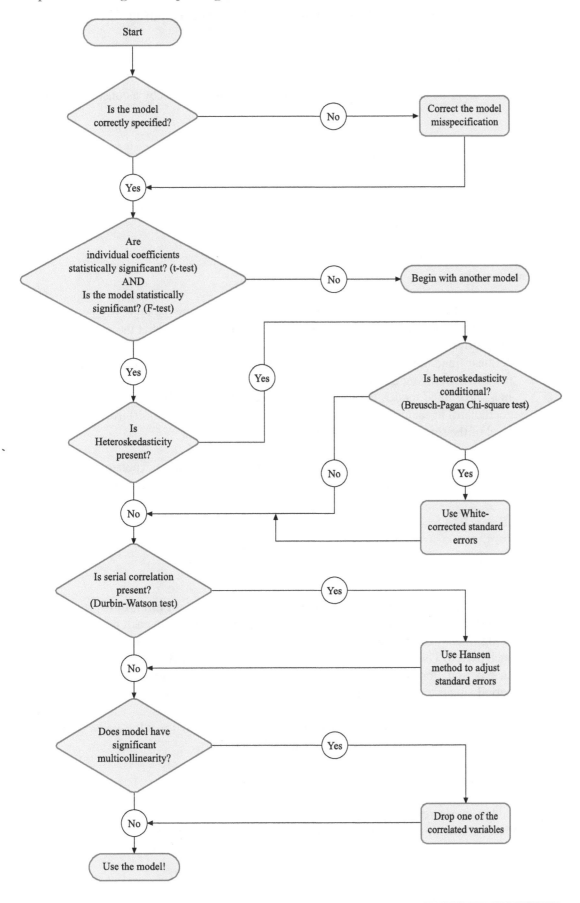

TIME-SERIES ANALYSIS
Cross-Reference to CFA Institute Assigned Reading #11

TREND MODELS

A **linear trend model** is one in which the dependent variable changes by a constant amount in each period.

$$y_t = b_0 + b_1 t + \varepsilon_t, \quad t = 1, 2, \ldots, T$$

y_t = the value of the time series at time t (value of the dependent variable)
b_0 = the y-intercept term
b_1 = the slope coefficient/ trend coefficient
t = time, the independent or explanatory variable
ε_t = a random-error term

- Ordinary least squares (OLS) regression is used to estimate the regression coefficients (b_0 and b_1) and the resulting regression equation is used to predict the value of the time series (y_t) for any period (t).
- A linear trend model is very similar to a simple linear regression model. In a linear trend model, the independent variable is the time period.
- In a linear trend model, the value of the dependent variable changes by b_1 (the trend coefficient) in each successive time period (as t increases by 1 unit) irrespective of the level of the series in the previous period.

Log-linear trend models work well in modelling time series that have exponential growth. Exponential growth is growth at a constant rate ($e^{b_1} - 1$) with continuous compounding.

$$\ln y_t = b_0 + b_1 t + \varepsilon_t, \quad t = 1, 2, \ldots, T$$

Linear Trend Models versus Log-Linear Trend Models

- A linear trend model predicts that $\mathbf{y_t}$ will grow by a **constant amount** (b_1) each period. For example, if b_1 equals 0.1%, y_t will grow by 0.1% in each period.
- A log-linear trend model predicts that $\mathbf{\ln y_t}$ will grow by a constant amount (b_1) in each period. This means that y_t itself will witness a **constant growth rate** of $e^{b_1} - 1$ in each period. For example, if b_1 equals 1% then the predicted growth rate of y_t in each period equals $e^{0.01} - 1 = 0.01005$ or 1.005%.

Also, in a linear trend model the predicted value of y_t is $b_0 + b_1 t$, but in a log-linear trend model the predicted value of y_t is $e^{b_0 + b_1 t}$ because $e^{\ln y_t} = y_t$.

Testing for Correlated Errors in Trend Models

Linear and log-linear trend models must be tested to ensure that the regression error term is not correlated across time periods (observations). This is done by performing the Durban-Watson test, which determines whether the errors are serially correlated.

AUTOREGRESSIVE (AR) TIME SERIES MODELS

An autoregressive (AR) model is a time series that is regressed on its own past values. Past values of the dependent variable itself are used to predict its current value.

First-order AR model:

$$x_t = b_0 + b_1 x_{t-1} + \varepsilon_t$$

pth-order AR model:

$$x_t = b_0 + b_1 x_{t-1} + b_2 x_{t-2} + \ldots + b_p x_{t-p} + \varepsilon_t$$

In order to draw valid statistical conclusions, an AR model must be:

- Covariance stationary, which means that:
  - The expected value of the time series is constant and finite in all periods. The time series has defined mean-reverting level.
  - The variance of observations in the time series is constant and finite in all periods.
  - The covariance of the time series with itself for a fixed number of periods in the past or future is constant and finite in all periods.

- Specified such that the error terms do not exhibit serial correlation.

- Specified such that the error terms are homoskedastic.

Detecting Serially Correlated Errors in an AR Model

The Durbin-Watson test cannot be used to test for serial correlation in an AR model. Therefore, we determine whether the residuals of the time series model are serially correlated by testing whether the autocorrelations of the error terms (error autocorrelations or residual autocorrelations) are significantly different from 0.

- If any of the error autocorrelations are significantly different from 0, the errors are serially correlated and the model is not specified correctly.
- If all the error autocorrelations are not significantly different from 0, the errors are not serially correlated and the model is specified correctly.

Steps in performing the hypothesis test

- First estimate the autoregressive model starting with a first-order AR model
- Calculate the autocorrelation of the model's residuals
- Test whether the autocorrelations are significant

$$\text{t-stat} = \frac{\text{Estimated residual autocorrelation}}{\text{Standard error of the autocorrelation}}$$

- Standard error $= 1 / \sqrt{T}$
- T = Number of observations
- $T - 2$ = Degrees of freedom

Mean Reversion

A time series shows mean reversion if it tends to fall when it lies above its mean and tends to rise when it lies below its mean.

$$\text{Mean reverting level} = x_t = \frac{b_0}{1 - b_1}$$

All covariance stationary time series have a finite mean-reverting level. An AR(1) time series will have a finite mean-reverting level, as long as the absolute level of the lag coefficient (b_1) is less than one.

The chain rule of forecasting is used to make multi-period forecasts. The next period's value (which is predicted by the forecast equation) is used as an input to the equation to determine the value of two periods ahead. Multi-period forecasts are more uncertain than single period forecasts.

Comparing Forecast Model Performance

The smaller the variance of the forecast error from a model, the more accurate the model and the smaller the standard error of the time series regression.

- In-sample forecasts are made using observations from the data used to estimate the model. For time series analysis, in-sample forecasts use data from within the test period.
- Out-of-sample forecasts are made using data from outside the test period. These forecasts are used to evaluate how well the estimated model holds up outside the period used to develop the model.

The out-of-sample forecasting performance of forecasting models is evaluated by comparing their root mean squared error (RMSE), which is the square root of the average squared error.

- The smaller the RMSE, the more accurate the model as a forecasting tool.

Instability of Regression Coefficients

In determining which model to choose, the stability of the regression coefficients must also be considered.

- Using longer time periods brings greater statistical reliability, but there is a greater chance that underlying fundamentals may have changed over the longer time period. Judgement and experience play an important role in determining how to model a time series.

Random Walks

A random walk is a time series in which the value of the series in one period equals the value of the series in the previous period plus an unpredictable random error.

$$x_t = x_{t-1} + \varepsilon_t, \, E(\varepsilon_t) = 0, \, E(\varepsilon_t^2) = \sigma^2, \, E(\varepsilon_t \varepsilon_s) = 0 \text{ if } t \neq s$$

- The error term has a constant variance and is uncorrelated with the error term in previous periods.
- The model is a special case of the AR(1) model with $b_0 = 0$ and $b_1 = 1$
- The expected value of the error term equals 0.
- The best forecast of x is x_{t-1} in every period after t-1

Regression methods cannot be used to estimate an AR(1) model on a time series that is a random walk as it is not covariance stationary because:
- A random walk has an undefined mean reverting level.
- The variance of a random walk has no upper bound.

Since standard regression analysis cannot be used on a time series that is a random walk, first differencing is applied to the time series to convert the data into a covariance stationary time series. This transformation subtracts the value of the time series in the prior period from its current value.

First Difference of Random Walk

$$y_t = x_t - x_{t-1} + \varepsilon_t, \, E(\varepsilon_t) = 0, \, E(\varepsilon_t^2) = \sigma^2, \, E(\varepsilon_t \varepsilon_s) = 0 \text{ for } t \neq s$$

The first-differenced variable (y_t) is covariance stationary:
- It has a mean reverting level of 0.
- Its variance is constant and finite in every period.

Therefore, y_t can be modelled using linear regression. However, since b_0 and b_1 both equal zero, the model is of no use in making forecasts.

Random Walk with a Drift

A random walk with a drift increases or decreases by a constant amount in each period. It has a b_0 that does not equals zero (unlike a random walk).

$$x_t = b_0 + x_{t-1} + \varepsilon_t, \, E(\varepsilon_t) = 0$$

A random walk with a drift also has an undefined mean reversion level as b_1 equals 1. Consequently, the AR model cannot be used to analyze the time series so we must first differentiate it.

$$y_t = x_t - x_{t-1}, \, y_t = b_0 + \varepsilon_t, \, b_0 \neq 0$$

Testing for Nonstationarity

If the slope coefficient of an AR(1) model equals 1, the time series is said to have a unit root. In this case, the time series is a random walk and is not covariance stationary. There are two ways to determine whether a time series is covariance stationary:

Examine the Autocorrelations in the AR Model

A time series that is covariance stationary will typically have:
- Time series autocorrelations that are not significantly different from zero at all lags; or
- Time series autocorrelations that decline towards zero as the number of lags increases.

The Dickey-Fuller Test

This test transfers the AR(1) model into the following form:

$$x_t - x_{t-1} = b_0 + (b_1 - 1)x_{t-1} + \varepsilon_t$$
or
$$x_t - x_{t-1} = b_0 + g_1 x_{t-1} + \varepsilon_t, E(\varepsilon_t) = 0$$

Note:
- The dependent variable is the first difference of the time series.
- If there is a unit root in the AR(1) model ($b_1 = 1$), g_1 will equal 0.
- The independent variable is the first lag of the time series.

H_0: $g_1 = 0$ (the time series has a unit root and is nonstationary)
H_a: $g_1 < 0$ (the time series does not have a unit root and is stationary)

To conduct the test, the t-statistic is calculated in the conventional manner but modified critical values are used. These critical values are larger in absolute value than conventional critical values.

Moving Averages

n-period moving average

$$\frac{x_t + x_{t-1} + \ldots + x_{t-(n-1)}}{n}$$

Plotting the moving average of a series allows us to zero in on long term trends and to remove the effects of seasonal fluctuations (or noise) in the data.

A simple moving average gives an equal weight to all periods. It always lags large movements in the actual data. Consequently, moving averages are not very effective in predicting the future.

MOVING AVERAGE TIME SERIES MODELS

MA(1) model:

$$x_t = \varepsilon_t + \theta\varepsilon_{t-1}, E(\varepsilon_t) = 0, E(\varepsilon_t^2) = \sigma^2, E(\varepsilon_t\varepsilon_s) = 0 \text{ for } t \neq s$$

Note:
- Different weights are placed on the two terms (1 on ε_t and θ on ε_{t-1}) in the MA(1) model unlike the simple moving-average model.

MA(q) model:

$$x_t = \varepsilon_t + \theta_1\varepsilon_{t-1} + \dots \theta_q\varepsilon_{t-q}, E(\varepsilon_t) = 0, E(\varepsilon_t^2) = \sigma^2, E(\varepsilon_t\varepsilon_s) = 0 \text{ for } t \neq s$$

If a MA(q) model fits the time series, the first q autocorrelations will be significantly different from 0, while all correlations beyond that will equal 0.

Determining whether a time series fits an autoregressive or moving-average model:
- For autoregressive time series, the autocorrelations typically start out large and then decline gradually.
- For MA(q) time series, the autocorrelations suddenly drop to zero after the first q autocorrelations.

Seasonality in Time Series Models

Seasonality in a time series may give the appearance that autoregressive time series models cannot be used to perform analysis on the data – the seasonal autocorrelation of the error term would be significantly different from 0. This problem can be solved by introducing a seasonal lag in the model.

Typically, the value of the time series one year before the current period is introduced in the autoregressive model to try to capture the effect of seasonality in the time series. In the case of quarterly data, the fourth autocorrelation of the error term would be significantly different from zero. The modified model may then be presented as:

$$x_t = b_0 + b_1 x_{t-1} + b_2 x_{t-4} + \varepsilon_t$$

If, after introduction of the seasonal lag, none of the autocorrelations are significantly different from zero, the updated model may be used to make forecasts.

Autoregressive Moving-Average Models (ARMA Models)

An ARMA model combines autoregressive lags of the dependent variable and moving-average errors in order to provide better forecasts than simple AR models.

ARMA (p, q):

$$x_t = b_0 + b_1 x_{t-1} + \ldots + b_p x_{t-p} + \varepsilon_t + \theta_1 \varepsilon_{t-1} + \ldots + \theta_q \varepsilon_{t-q}$$

$$E(\varepsilon_t) = 0, E(\varepsilon_t^2) = \sigma^2, E(\varepsilon_t \varepsilon_s) = 0 \text{ for } t \neq s$$

The model has p autoregressive terms and q moving-average terms.

Limitations of ARMA Models

- The parameters of the model can be very unstable.
- There are no set criteria for determining p and q.
- Even after a model is selected, it may not do a good job of forecasting.

Autoregressive Conditional Heteroskedasticity Models (ARCH Models)

Heteroskedasticity occurs when the variance of the error term varies with the independent variable. If heteroskedasticity is present, one or more of the lagged variables in the model may appear statistically significant when they are actually not.

For time series models, ARCH models are used to determine whether the variance of the error in one period depends on the variance of the error in previous periods. The squared residuals from a particular time series model (the model may be an AR, MA or ARMA model) are regressed on a constant and one lag of the squared residuals. The regression equation takes the following form:

$$\hat{\varepsilon}_t^2 = a_0 + a_1 \hat{\varepsilon}_{t-1}^2 + u_t$$

If a_1 is statistically different from 0, the time series is ARCH(1) and the error in period $t+1$ can be predicted using the formula:

$$\hat{\sigma}_{t+1}^2 = \hat{a}_0 + \hat{a}_1 \hat{\varepsilon}_t^2$$

If ARCH errors are found to exist in the model, generalized least squares may be used to correct for heteroskedasticity and to correctly estimate the standard errors of the parameters in the time-series model.

Regression with More than One Time Series

To determine whether we can use linear regression to model more than one time series we must determine whether either of, or both the series contain a unit root. If a series contains a unit root, it is not covariance stationary and any results of regression analysis would not be valid.

The Dickey-Fuller test is used to determine whether the independent variable and the dependent variable have a unit root.

- If neither of the time series has a unit root, linear regression can be used to test the relationships between the two time series.
- If either of them has a unit root, linear regression cannot be used as results may be spurious.
- If both of them have unit roots, we must determine whether the time series are cointegrated.
  - If they are not cointegrated, linear regression cannot be used.
  - If they are cointegrated, the regression coefficients and standard errors will be consistent and they can be used to conduct hypothesis tests.

Two time series are cointegrated, if a long term economic relationship exists between them such that they do not diverge from each other significantly in the long run.

Testing for Cointegration

If the time series used to construct a regression model both have a unit root:

1. Estimate the regression:

$$y_t = b_0 + b_1 x_t + \varepsilon_t$$

2. Test whether the error term (ε_t) has a unit root using the Dickey-Fuller test but with Engle-Granger critical values.
3. H_0: Error term has a unit root versus H_a: Error term does not have a unit root.
4. If we fail to reject the null hypothesis, we conclude that the error term in the regression is not covariance stationary, the time series are not cointegrated and the regression relation is spurious.
5. If we reject the null hypothesis, we conclude that the error term does not have a unit root, it is covariance stationary and therefore the results of the linear regression can be used to test hypotheses about the variables.

Suggested steps in time-series forecasting

The following is a step-by-step guide to build a model to predict a time series.

1. Understand the investment problem you have and make an initial choice of model. One alternative is a regression model that predicts the future behavior of a variable based on hypothesized casual relationships with other variables. Another is a time-series model that attempts to predict the future behavior of a variable based on the past behavior of the same variable.

2. If you have decided to use a time-series model, compile the time series and plot it to see whether it looks covariance stationary. The plot might show important deviations from covariance stationarity, including the following:
    - A linear trend;
    - An exponential trend;
    - Seasonality; or
    - A significant shift in the time series during the sample period (for example, a change in mean or variance).

3. If you find no significant seasonality or shift in the time series, then perhaps either a linear trend or an exponential trend will be sufficient to model the time series. In that case, take the following steps:
    - Determine whether a linear or exponential trend seems most reasonable (usually by plotting the series);
    - Estimate the trend;
    - Compute the residual;
    - Use the Durbin-Watson statistic to determine whether the residuals have significant serial correlation. If you find no significant serial correlation in the residuals, then the trend model is sufficient to capture the dynamics of the time series and you can use that model for forecasting.

4. If you find significant serial correlation in the residuals from the trend model, use a more complex model, such as an autoregressive model. First, however, reexamine whether the time series is covariance stationary.
    Following is a list of violations of stationarity, along with potential methods to adjust the time series to make it covariance stationary:
    - If the time series has a linear trend, first-difference the time series.
    - If the time series has an exponential trend, take the natural log of the time series and then first-difference it.
    - If the time series shifts significantly during the sample period, estimate different time series models before and after the shift.
    - If the time series has significant seasonality, include seasonal lags (discussed in step 7).

5. After you have successfully transformed a raw time series into a covariance-stationary time series, you can usually model the transformed series with a short auto regression*. To decide which autoregressive model to use, take the following steps:
    - Estimate an AR (1) model.
    - Test to see whether the residuals from this model have significant serial correlation.
    - If you find no significant serial correlation in the residuals, you can use the AR (1) model to forecast.

6. If you find significant serial correlation in the residuals, use the AR (2) model and test for significant serial correlation of the residuals of the AR (2) model.
    - If you find no significant serial correlation, use the AR (2) model.
    - If you find significant serial correlation of the residuals, keep increasing the order of the AR model until the residual serial correlation is no longer significant.

7. Your next move is to check for seasonality. You can use one of two approaches:
   - Graph the data and check for regular seasonal patterns.
   - Examine the data to see whether the seasonal autocorrelations of the residuals from an AR model are significant (for example, the fourth autocorrelation for quarterly data) and whether the autocorrelations before and after the seasonal autocorrelations are significant. To correct for seasonality, add seasonal lags to your AR model. For example, if you are using quarterly data, you might add the fourth lag of a time series as an additional variable in an AR (1) or an AR (2) model.

8. Next, test whether the residuals have autoregressive conditional heteroskedasticity. To test for ARCH (1), for example, do the following:
   - Regress the squared residual from your time-series model on a lagged value of the squared residual.
   - Test whether the coefficient on the squared lagged residual differs significantly from 0.
   - If the coefficient on the squared lagged residual does not differ significantly from 0, the residuals do not display ARCH and you can rely on the standard errors from your time-series estimates.
   - If the coefficient on the squared lagged residuals does differ significantly from 0, use generalized least squares or other methods to correct for ARCH.

9. Finally, you may also want to perform tests of the model's out-of-sample forecasting performance to see how the model's out-of-sample performance compares to its in-sample performance.

Using these steps in sequence, you can be reasonably sure that your model is correctly specified.

CURRENCY EXCHANGE RATES: DETERMINATION AND FORECASTING
Cross-Reference to CFA Institute Assigned Reading #12

Spot Exchange Rates

Spot exchange rates (S) are quotes for transactions that call for **immediate delivery**.

When working with bid-ask quotes, to determine whether the bid or the offer rate in the exchange rate quote should be used in a particular transaction:
- First identify the base currency of the exchange rate quote; and then
- Determine whether the client is buying or selling the base currency.

Given bid and ask prices for a particular currency, the bid and ask prices for the other currency in the exchange rate quote can be determined as follows:
- The b/a ask price is the reciprocal of the a/b bid price.
- The b/a bid price is the reciprocal of the a/b ask price.

Currency Cross Rates

A **cross rate** is an exchange rate between two currencies that is derived from each currency's relationship with a third currency.

Cross Rate Calculations with Bid-Ask Spreads

Step 1: Bring the bid-ask quotes for the exchange rates into a format such that the common (or third) currency cancels out if we multiply the exchange rates.
Step 2: Multiply the exchange rates in a manner that maximizes the resulting bid-ask spread. The bid-ask spread is maximized when the bid is minimized and ask is maximized.

Foreign Exchange Spreads

The bid-ask spread that a dealer provides to clients is typically wider than the bid-ask spread observed in the interbank market.

Factors Affecting the Size of the Bid-Ask Spread

The size of the bid-ask spread in the interbank market: The more liquid the interbank market, the narrower the bid-ask spread. Liquidity depends on:
- The currency pair involved
- The time of day
- Market volatility

The size of the transaction: Generally speaking, the larger the transaction, the wider the spread that a dealer will quote to the client.

The relationship between the dealer and the client: Dealers may quote narrower bid-ask spreads to preferred clients based on prospective or ongoing business relationships.

Arbitrage Constraints on Spot Exchange Rate Quotes

The bid-ask quotes provided by a dealer in the interbank market must adhere to two arbitrage constraints:

1. The bid quoted by a dealer in the interbank market cannot be higher than the current interbank offer, and the ask offered by a dealer cannot be lower than the current interbank bid.
2. The cross rate bid quoted by a dealer cannot be higher than the implied cross rate ask available in the interbank market, and the cross rate ask quoted by a dealer cannot be lower than the implied cross rate bid available in the interbank market.

Forward Exchange Rates

Forward exchange rates (F) are quotes for transactions that are contracted (agreed upon) today, but settled at a pre-specified date in the **future** (settlement occurs after a period longer than the two days for spot transactions). Forward exchange rates (just like spot exchange rates) are also quoted in terms of bid and ask prices.

Forward exchange rates are calculated in a manner that ensures that traders are not able to earn arbitrage profits (a condition known as covered interest rate parity).

$$F_{FC/DC} = S_{FC/DC} \times \frac{(1 + i_{FC})}{(1 + i_{DC})}$$

$$F_{PC/BC} = S_{PC/BC} \times \frac{(1 + i_{PC})}{(1 + i_{BC})}$$

Currencies Trading at a Forward Premium/Discount

- If the forward exchange rate is *higher* than the spot exchange rate, the **base currency** is trading at a forward premium. At the same time, the price currency would be trading at a forward discount.
- The forward discount/premium equals the difference between the forward exchange rate and the spot exchange rate.

$$F_{FC/DC} - S_{FC/DC} = S_{FC/DC}\left(\frac{(i_{FC} - i_{DC}) \times Actual/360}{1 + (i_{DC} \times Actual/360)} \right)$$

$$F_{PC/BC} - S_{PC/BC} = S_{PC/BC}\left(\frac{(i_{PC} - i_{BC}) \times Actual/360}{1 + (i_{BC} \times Actual/360)} \right)$$

In professional FX markets, forward exchange rates are quoted in terms of points (pips), which simply represent the difference between the forward rate and the spot rate (forward premium or discount). These points (pips) are scaled so that they can be related to the last digit in the spot quote (usually the fourth decimal place).

Factors Affecting the Bid-Ask Spread in Forward Exchange Rate Quotes

In addition to the factors that affect spreads in the spot market, spreads in the forward market are influenced by the term of maturity of the contract. Generally speaking, spreads tend to widen with longer terms. This is due to:

- Lower liquidity of longer term contracts.
- Greater credit risk in longer term contracts.
- Greater interest rate risk in forward contracts. Forward rates are based on interest rate differentials. Longer maturities result in greater duration or higher sensitivity to changes in interest rates.

Steps Involved in Marking-to-Market a Position on a Currency Forward

- Create an equal offsetting forward position to the initial forward position.
  - Make sure that the settlement dates and the notional amounts of both the contracts are the same.
- Determine the all-in forward rate for the offsetting forward contract.
  - If the base currency in the exchange rate quote should be sold (purchased) in the offsetting contract, use the bid (ask) side of the quote.
- Calculate the profit/loss on the net position as of the settlement date.
  - If the currency that the investor was long on in the initial forward contract has appreciated (depreciated), there will be a profit (loss).
  - If the currency that the investor was short on in the initial forward contract has appreciated (depreciated), there will be a loss (profit).
- Calculate the present value (as of the date of initiation of the offsetting contract) of the profit/loss.
  - Remember to use the appropriate LIBOR rate and to unannualize it (if necessary).

INTERNATIONAL PARITY RELATIONS

Covered Interest Rate Parity

Covered interest rate parity describes a no-arbitrage condition where the **covered** or **currency-hedged** interest rate differential between two currencies equals zero. What this means is that there is a no-arbitrage relationship among risk-free interest rates and spot and forward exchange rates.

$$\text{Covered interest rate parity: } F_{PC/BC} = S_{PC/BC} \times \frac{1 + (i_{PC} \times \text{Actual}/360)}{1 + (i_{BC} \times \text{Actual}/360)}$$

The forward premium (discount) on the base currency can be expressed as a percentage as:

$$\text{Forward premium (discount) as a \%} = \frac{F_{PC/BC} - S_{PC/BC}}{S_{PC/BC}}$$

The forward premium (discount) on the base currency can be estimated as:

$$\text{Forward premium (discount) as a \%} \approx F_{PC/BC} - S_{PC/BC} \approx i_{PC} - i_{BC}$$

- If the risk-free rate on one currency is *greater* than the risk-free rate on another currency, the currency with the higher risk-free rate will trade at a forward *discount* relative to the other currency, such that the benefit of the higher interest rate will be offset by a decline in the value of the currency.

Generally speaking, covered interest rate differentials tend to be close to zero under normal market conditions, which indicates that covered interest parity tends to hold.

Uncovered Interest Rate Parity

Uncovered interest rate parity states that the **expected return** on an **uncovered** or **unhedged** foreign currency investment should equal the return on a comparable domestic currency investment.

$$(1 + i_{DC}) = \frac{(1 + i_{FC}) \times S_{FC/DC}}{S^e_{FC/DC}}$$

The above equality can be used to derive the formula for the expected future spot exchange rate:

$$S^e_{FC/DC} = S_{FC/DC} \times \frac{(1 + i_{FC})}{(1 + i_{DC})}$$

The expected percentage change in the spot exchange rate can be calculated as:

$$\text{Expected \% change in spot exchange rate} = \%\Delta S^e_{PC/BC} = \frac{S^e_{PC/BC} - S_{PC/BC}}{S_{PC/BC}}$$

The expected percentage change in the spot exchange rate can be estimated as:

$$\text{Expected \% change in spot exchange rate} \approx \%\Delta S^e_{PC/BC} \approx i_{PC} - i_{BC}$$

Covered versus Uncovered Interest Rate Parity

- In covered interest rate parity, we consider the **hedged** (against all currency risk) return on the foreign risk-free rate.
  - The investor locks in the **forward exchange rate** today so she is not exposed to currency risk.
  - If covered interest rate parity holds, the **forward premium/discount** offsets the yield differential.
- In uncovered interest rate parity, we consider the **unhedged** (against currency risk) return on the foreign risk-free rate.
  - The investor leaves his foreign exchange position uncovered (unhedged) and expects to convert foreign currency holdings back into her domestic currency at the **expected future spot rate**.
  - If uncovered interest rate parity holds, the **expected appreciation/ depreciation** of the currency offsets the yield differential.

Important:

- Note that under uncovered interest rate parity, the direction of the predicted change in spot rates is counterintuitive. All other factors constant, an increase in interest rates would be expected to lead to an appreciation of the currency, but uncovered interest rate parity implies that the opposite would be the case.

- Uncovered interest rate parity asserts that the **expected return** on the unhedged foreign investment is the same as the return on the domestic investment. However, the **distribution of possible return outcomes** is different. Due to the uncertainty associated with the future spot exchange rate, uncovered interest rate parity is often violated as investors (who are generally not risk-neutral) demand a risk premium for accepting the exchange rate risk inherent in leaving their positions unhedged (uncovered). As a result, future spot exchange rates typically do not equal the forward exchange rate. Forward rates (that are based purely on interest rate differentials to preclude covered interest arbitrage) are therefore, poor (or biased) predictors of future spot exchange rates.

Empirical evidence suggests that:

- Uncovered interest rate parity does not hold over the short and medium terms, but works better over the long-term. Over the short and medium terms, interest rate differentials do not explain changes in exchange rates, so forward rates (that are computed based on interest rate differentials) tend to be poor predictors of future exchange rates.
- Current spot exchange rates are also not good predictors of future spot exchange rates because of the high volatility in exchange rate movements. This suggests that exchange rates do not follow a random walk.

Purchasing Power Parity (PPP)

Purchasing power parity (PPP) is based on the **law of one price**, which states that identical goods should trade at exactly the same price across countries when valued in terms of a common currency.

According to the law of one price, a relative increase (decrease) in prices in one country will result in depreciation (appreciation) of its currency so exchange rate-adjusted prices are constant across countries.

Absolute Purchasing Power Parity (Absolute PPP)

Absolute PPP states that the broad or general price level (GPL) in a country should equal the currency-adjusted general price level in the other country:

$$\text{Absolute PPP: } GPL_{FC} = GPL_{DC} \times S_{FC/DC}$$
$$\text{Absolute PPP: } GPL_{PC} = GPL_{BC} \times S_{PC/BC}$$

Note that absolute PPP assumes that all goods are tradable and that prices indices (used to determine the GPL) in both countries include the same goods and services with identical weights.

$$\text{Absolute PPP: } S_{FC/DC} = GPL_{FC} / GPL_{DC}$$
$$\text{Absolute PPP: } S_{PC/BC} = GPL_{PC} / GPL_{BC}$$

Absolute PPP asserts that the equilibrium exchange rate between two countries is determined by the ratio of their respective national price levels. However, since (1) product-mixes and consumption baskets differ across countries and (2) there are transaction costs involved in international trade as well as trade restrictions, generally speaking, absolute PPP does not hold.

Relative Purchasing Power Parity (Relative PPP)

Instead of assuming that there are no transaction costs and other trade impediments (as is the case with absolute PPP), relative PPP merely assumes that these are constant over time. Relative PPP claims that **changes** in exchange rates are linked to relative **changes** in national price levels, even if the relation between exchange rate *levels* and price *levels* does not hold.

$$\text{Relative PPP: } E(S^{T}_{FC/DC}) = S^{0}_{FC/DC} \left(\frac{1 + \pi_{FC}}{1 + \pi_{DC}} \right)^{T}$$

According to relative PPP, changes in the spot exchange rate can be approximated as:

$$\text{Relative PPP: } \%\Delta S_{FC/DC} \approx \pi_{FC} - \pi_{DC}$$

$$\text{Relative PPP: } \%\Delta S_{PC/BC} \approx \pi_{PC} - \pi_{BC}$$

Relative PPP suggests that the percentage change in spot exchange rate ($\%\Delta S_{FC/DC}$) will be entirely determined by the difference between foreign and domestic inflation. In order to keep relative purchase power constant across countries, currencies of countries with higher (lower) rates of inflation should see their currencies depreciate (appreciate).

Ex Ante Version of PPP

The ex ante version of the PPP is based on relative PPP. While relative PPP asserts that *actual* changes in the exchange rate are driven by *actual* relative changes in inflation, ex ante PPP asserts that *expected* changes in spot exchange rates are entirely driven by *expected* differences in national inflation rates.

$$\text{Ex ante PPP: } \%\Delta S^{e}_{FC/DC} \approx \pi^{e}_{FC} - \pi^{e}_{DC}$$

$$\text{Ex ante PPP: } \%\Delta S^{e}_{PC/BC} \approx \pi^{e}_{PC} - \pi^{e}_{BC}$$

According to ex ante PPP, countries that are expected to see persistently high (low) inflation rates should expect to see their currencies depreciate (appreciate) over time.

Real Exchange Rates

The **real exchange rate** of a currency measures the real purchasing power of a currency in terms of the amount of real goods and services that it can purchase internationally. The real exchange rate ($q_{FC/DC}$) equals the ratio of the domestic price level expressed in the foreign currency to the foreign price level.

$$q_{FC/DC} = \frac{P_{DC} \text{ in terms of FC}}{P_{FC}} = \frac{P_{DC} \times S_{FC/DC}}{P_{FC}} = S_{FC/DC}\left(\frac{P_{DC}}{P_{FC}}\right)$$

The real exchange rate, $q_{FC/DC}$ (purchasing power of domestic citizens) is:
- An *increasing* function of the nominal exchange rate ($S_{FC/DC}$).
- An *increasing* function of the domestic price level (P_{DC}).
- A *decreasing* function of the foreign price level (P_{FC}).

Studies have found that in the long run, real exchange rates tend to stabilize around their mean (mean reversion). Stable or constant real exchange rates in the long run imply that relative PPP holds in the long run.

Historically, it has been observed that:
- Over the short run, nominal exchange rate tend to not follow the path predicted by PPP.
- However, in the long run nominal exchange rates tend to move towards their long run PPP equilibrium values so PPP does serve as a valid framework for assessing the long run fair value of a currency.

The Fisher Effect

The Fisher effect asserts that the nominal interest rate (i) in a country equals the sum of the real interest rate in that country (r) and the expected inflation rate (π^e).

Fisher Effect: $i = r + \pi^e$

Real Interest Rate Parity and the International Fisher Effect

- **Real interest rate parity** asserts that real interest rates will converge to the same level across different countries. It assumes that both (1) uncovered interest rate parity and (2) ex ante PPP hold.

- The **international Fisher effect** asserts that if the real yield spread equals zero in all markets, the foreign-domestic nominal yield spread will be determined by the foreign-domestic expected inflation rate differential.

International Fisher effect: $(i_{FC} - i_{DC}) = (\pi^e_{FC} - \pi^e_{DC})$

Figure 1: Spot Exchange Rates, Forward Exchange Rates and Interest Rates

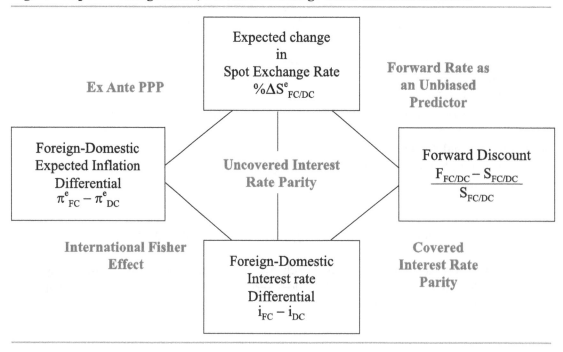

Assessing an Exchange Rate's Equilibrium Level

The IMF uses a three-pronged approach to determine long-term equilibrium exchange rates:

1. The macroeconomic balance approach aims to determine how much exchange rates would need to adjust in order to close the gap between a country's current account imbalance over the medium term and its normal or sustainable current account imbalance.
2. The external sustainability approach aims to determine how much exchange rates would need to adjust in order to ensure that a country's net foreign asset (liability)-to-GDP ratio stabilizes at a particular desired level.
3. A reduced-form econometric model aims to determine the equilibrium path that a country's currency should take based on several macroeconomic variables (e.g. net foreign asset position, terms of trade and relative productivity).

A Model that Includes Long-Term Equilibrium

Another model that is used to predict exchange rates in the long run is based on the assumptions that (1) uncovered interest rate parity holds in the long run and (2) real exchange rates converge to an equilibrium value ($\bar{q}_{FC/DC}$) in the long run. Further, it incorporates risk premia that reflect the perceived sustainability of the country's external balances.

$$q_{FC/DC} = \bar{q}_{FC/DC} + [(r_{DC} - r_{FC}) - (\Phi_{DC} - \Phi_{FC})]$$

According to this model, the real exchange rate can be expressed as:
- A *positive* function of the long run equilibrium real exchange rate, $\bar{q}_{FC/DC}$.
- A *positive* function of the domestic-foreign real interest rate differential ($r_{DC} - r_{FC}$).
- A *negative* function of the difference between the domestic and foreign risk premia ($\Phi_{DC} - \Phi_{FC}$).

The Carry Trade

An **FX carry trade** involves taking long positions in high-yield currencies and short positions in low-yield currencies (also known as **funding currencies**).

Studies have shown that carry trades have earned positive excess returns in most (normal) market conditions. During periods of low turbulence, investors do not see much potential for sudden, substantial, adverse exchange rate movements and are relatively confident of earning excess returns through the strategy. However, in relatively turbulent times (during which asset price and/or FX volatility rise significantly) realized returns on long high-yield currency positions have declined dramatically, and funding costs have risen significantly as well.

Returns of carry trades have not followed the normal distribution; instead the returns distribution has been more peaked with fatter tails that are negatively skewed.
- The peaked distribution around the mean indicates that carry trades typically earn small gains (more frequently that would be expected were the returns normally distributed, which is good).
- The negative skew and fat tails indicate that carry trades have resulted in (1) larger losses and (2) more frequent than implied by a normal distribution. This relatively high probability of a large loss is referred to as **crash risk**.

The primary reason for crash risk is that the carry trade is essentially a leveraged trade.

Managing Downside Risks Associated with Carry Trades

Using volatility filters: Under this approach, the level of implied volatility (implied in equity and currency options markets) is used to determine whether carry trades should be undertaken. If implied volatility rises above (falls below) a certain level, carry trade positions are closed or reversed (opened or initiated).

Using valuation filters: Under this approach, benchmarks based on purchasing power parity are used to determine whether carry trade positions should be opened or closed.
- If high-yield currencies were to become overvalued (undervalued) relative to their prescribed PPP threshold bands, the risk of a significant adverse exchange rate movement i.e., depreciation of the investment currency, would increase (decrease) so investors would close or reverse their positions (leave their positions open).
- If low-yield currencies were to become undervalued (overvalued) relative to their prescribed PPP threshold bands, the risk of a significant adverse exchange rate movement i.e., appreciation of the funding currency, would increase (decrease) so investors would close or reverse their positions (leave their positions open).

The Impact of Balance of Payments Flows

Balance of payments (BOP) accounts are an accounting record of all monetary transactions between a country and the rest of the world.

Current Account Imbalances and the Determination of Exchange Rates

Generally speaking, persistent current account deficits lead to depreciation of the domestic currency. The following mechanisms explain this relationship:

- The flow supply/demand channel
- The portfolio balance channel
- The debt sustainability channel

Capital Flows and the Determination of Exchange Rates

With greater financial integration of the world's capital markets and increased capital mobility, capital flows are now the dominant force in influencing exchange rates, interest rates and asset price bubbles.

Real Interest Rate Differentials, Capital Flows and the Exchange Rate

Relative to its long run equilibrium value ($q_{L/H}$), the real exchange rate ($q_{L/H}$) will rise as:
- The nominal yield spread between high- and low-yield markets ($i_H - i_L$) rises.
- The difference in expected inflation rates in the high-yield market and the low-yield market ($\pi^e_H - \pi^e_L$) declines.
- The difference in risk premia associated with the high-yield market and the low-yield market ($\Phi_H - \Phi_L$) declines.

MONETARY AND FISCAL POLICIES

THE MUNDELL-FLEMING MODEL

The Mundell-Fleming model assumes that there is enough of an output gap in the economy to allow changes in output without having a significant impact on price levels and inflation.

Expansionary Monetary Policy

With flexible exchange rates, expansionary monetary policy will lead to depreciation of the domestic currency as low interest rates cause a flight of capital to higher-yielding markets. Over time, the depreciation of the currency will also increase net exports and reinforce the aggregate demand impact (on investment and consumption spending) of expansionary monetary policy.

With fixed exchange rates, since there will be downward pressure on the currency due to the capital flight triggered by the low interest rates, the monetary authority will have to buy its own currency (using its foreign exchange reserves) in the FX market to keep the exchange rate at the desired (fixed) level. As a result, the monetary base will shrink and domestic credit will dry up, offsetting the desired expansionary affect of the monetary stance.

Expansionary Fiscal Policy

With flexible exchange rates, expansionary fiscal policy will lead to appreciation of the domestic currency as high interest rates stimulate capital inflows.

With fixed exchange rates, since there will be upward pressure on the currency due to the capital inflows triggered by the high interest rates, the monetary authority will have to sell its own currency in the FX market to maintain the exchange rate at the desired (fixed) level. The resulting expansion of domestic money supply will reinforce the aggregate demand impact of expansionary fiscal policy.

Impact of Capital Mobility

With high capital mobility:
- A restrictive (expansionary) monetary policy under floating exchange rates will result in appreciation (depreciation) of the domestic currency.
- A restrictive (expansionary) fiscal policy under floating exchange rates will result in depreciation (appreciation) of the domestic currency.
- If monetary and fiscal policies are both restrictive or both expansionary, the overall impact on the exchange rate will be unclear.

With low capital mobility, the impact of monetary and fiscal policy on the exchange rate comes more from trade flows rather than capital flows. Therefore, with low capital mobility:
- A restrictive (expansionary) monetary policy will lower (increase) aggregate demand, resulting in an increase (decrease) in net exports. This will cause the domestic currency to appreciate (depreciate).
- A restrictive (expansionary) fiscal policy will lower (increase) aggregate demand, resulting in an increase (decrease) in net exports. This will cause the domestic currency to appreciate (depreciate).
- If monetary and fiscal stances are not the same (i.e., one is restrictive while the other is expansionary) the overall impact on the exchange rate will be unclear.

MONETARY MODELS OF EXCHANGE RATE DETERMINATION

Monetary models of exchange rate determination assume that output is fixed and monetary policy's primary impact on exchange rates is through the price level and inflation.

The Monetary Approach with Flexible Prices

This approach is based on the quantity theory of money. If purchasing power parity holds, then the increase (decrease) in domestic price levels relative to foreign price levels that results from a relative increase (decrease) in domestic money supply will lead to a proportional decline (increase) in the value of the domestic currency.

The major shortcoming of the monetary approach is that it assumes that PPP always holds.

The Dornbusch Overshooting Model

The Dornbusch overshooting model assumes that prices are relatively inflexible in the short run, but are completely flexible in the long run. As a result the model predicts that:

- In the long run, since prices are completely flexible, an increase in domestic money supply will lead to a proportional increase in domestic prices and result in a depreciation of the domestic currency.

- In the short run, since prices are relatively inflexible, an increase in nominal money supply translates into an increase in real money supply. As real money supply increases, real interest rates fall, resulting in capital outflows and a substantial depreciation of the domestic currency in nominal and real terms. In fact, the domestic currency would overshoot its long run level, and actually fall to a level lower than predicted by PPP. Eventually, over the long run, as domestic prices and domestic interest rates rise, the nominal exchange rate will recover and approach the level predicted by the conventional monetary approach (in line with PPP) and the real exchange rate will converge towards its long run equilibrium level.

The Taylor Rule and the Determination of Exchange Rates

The Taylor rule is a mathematical rule that can be used to determine the appropriate policy rate for an economy given its neutral rate, its inflation and output targets, and the economy's current deviation from those targets.

The Taylor rule suggests that an increase in base currency inflation implies *appreciation* of the base currency (as higher inflation would induce the central bank to raise real interest rates). On the other hand, the pure monetary/purchasing power parity model suggests that an increase in base currency inflation would lead to *depreciation* of the base currency.

Fiscal Policy and the Determination of Exchange Rates

The **portfolio balance approach** focuses on the long-term exchange rate implications of sustained fiscal imbalances. It asserts that if a particular economy has persistent budget deficits, its persistent demand for financing would eventually lead to (1) investors demanding a higher risk premium to invest in its bonds and (2) domestic currency depreciation.

If the market believes that debt levels are unsustainable, the government may feel pressured into taking one of the following courses of action:
- Monetize the debt
- Reverse the fiscal stance

EXCHANGE RATE MANAGEMENT: INTERVENTION AND CONTROLS

Surges in capital flows can arise due to "pull" and "push" factors.

Pull factors represent a favorable set of developments in the **domestic economy** that attract capital from foreign countries. On the other hand, push factors represent a favorable set of factors in **foreign economies** that drive capital flows abroad.

Objectives of Central Bank Intervention and Capital Controls

- Prevent the currencies from appreciating too strongly in the wake of surges in capital inflows;
- Reduce excessive capital inflows; and
- Enable the monetary authority to pursue independent monetary policy without having to worry about the repercussions of changes in policy rates on capital flows (and the exchange rate).

Emerging Market Responses to Unwanted Surges of Capital Inflows

- If the emerging market (EM) country's currency is **undervalued**, then the appropriate response to a surge in capital inflows would be to let the currency appreciate (as long as it does not overappreciate and compromise the competitiveness of the economy).
- If the EM currency is **fairly valued or overvalued**, the appropriate response would be to intervene in the FX market.
  - If there is **no inflation threat**, then unsterilized intervention is the best option.
  - If **inflation is a threat**, then sterilized intervention would be the way to go.
- If **all of the above fail** to relieve the capital inflow-induced upward pressure on the EM currency, policymakers should consider capital controls.

Evidence on the Effectiveness of Central Bank Intervention

- In the case of **developed countries**, studies have shown that the effect of central bank intervention in the FX market on the level and path of their exchange rates is insignificant.
- In the case of **emerging market currencies**, studies have shown that the effect of central bank intervention in the FX market is relatively more significant but still mixed overall.
  - Intervention has reduced the volatility of EM exchange rates.
  - Intervention has had limited (but more than in the case of developed countries) influence on the level and path taken by exchanges rates.

Evidence on the Effectiveness of Capital Controls

Studies have suggested that capital controls on inflows:
- Make monetary policy more independent;
- Can alter the composition of capital flows;
- Can lower the pressure on the real exchange rate in certain cases.

However, studies have also concluded that capital controls on inflows do not reduce the volume of **net flows**. Further, the larger the magnitude of capital flows and the greater their persistence, the less effective capital controls will be in relieving the upward pressure on the real exchange rate.

Potential Early Warning Signs of a Currency Crisis

- In the period leading up to the crisis, the real exchange rate is much higher than its mean level during tranquil periods.
- The trade balance displays no significant difference in the pre-crisis period versus relatively tranquil periods.
- Foreign exchange reserves tend to decline drastically in the lead up to a crisis.
- There is some deterioration in the terms of trade in the lead up to a crisis.
- Inflation tends to be relatively high in the pre-crisis period relative to tranquil periods.
- The ratio of M2 (money supply) to bank reserves tends to rise in the 2-year period leading up to a crisis, and then declines sharply following the crisis.
- Broad money growth in nominal and real terms rises sharply in the 2-year period leading up to a crisis.
- Nominal private credit growth also rises sharply in the period leading up to a crisis.
- A boom-bust cycle in equity prices generally comes before a currency crisis.
- Real economic activity shows no real pattern before a crisis, but falls significantly following the crisis.

SHORTER-TERM FORECASTING TOOLS

Technical Analysis

- Technical trading rules would have generated significant profits if applied to Forex trading from the 1970s to the early 1990s. However, when applied over the period from 1995-2010, these technical trading rules would not have generated such impressive profits.
- Technical trading rules could still be applied in the early years of a country's floating exchange rate regime to earn excess returns.
- Even though technical trading rules have largely been unsuccessful in enhancing returns, they can play a significant role in controlling risk.

Order Flow, Sentiment and Positioning

FX Dealer Order Flow

Studies have found that:
- There is a strong, positive, contemporaneous correlation between customer order flow and the current trend in exchange rates over short periods (on an intraday or daily basis).
- There is no conclusive evidence on the relationship between lagged order data and future exchange rates so we cannot draw any clear conclusions regarding the predictive value of order flow data.

Currency Options Market

FX traders often use risk reversals to gauge whether the FX market is attaching a higher probability to a currency appreciation or to a currency depreciation. Studies have found that:
- There is a high contemporaneous relationship between the trend in risk reversals and the trend in exchange rates so risk reversals do explain current trends in exchange rates.
- However, there is no statistically significant relationship between lagged risk reversal data and future exchange rate movements so risk reversals cannot be used to predict future exchange rates.

Information on the Size and Trend in Net Speculative Positions

Studies have found that:
- There is a strong, positive and contemporaneous correlation between changes in net positions of speculative accounts and exchange rate movements so changes in net positions of speculative accounts do explain current trends in exchange rates.
- However, changes in net speculative positions cannot be used to predict changes in exchange rates.

ECONOMIC GROWTH AND THE INVESTMENT DECISION
Cross-Reference to CFA Institute Assigned Reading #13

Preconditions from Economic Growth

- Savings and investment
- Financial markets and intermediaries
- Political stability, rule of law, and property rights
- Education and health care systems
- Tax and regulatory systems
- Free trade and unrestricted capital flows

Why Potential GDP Matters to Investors?

One of the primary factors that influence equity market performance is the anticipated growth in aggregate corporate earnings. Growth in potential GDP matters to investors because it places a limit on how fast the economy (and therefore, aggregate corporate earnings) can grow.

Over the short term, growth in stock market prices is a function of (1) the percentage change in GDP, (2) the percentage change in the share of earnings in GDP, and (3) the percentage change in the market price-earnings multiple. However, over the long-term, stock market performance is primarily driven by the growth rate of GDP.

Aside from its impact on equity values, growth in potential GDP is also relevant for fixed income investors through its influence on nominal and real interest rates.

The Cobb-Douglas Production Function

$$Y = AK^a L^{1-a}$$

The Cobb-Douglas production function exhibits the following two important properties:

- Constant returns to scale: This means that if quantities of all inputs are increased by the same percentage, then output would also increase by that same percentage.
- Diminishing marginal productivity of factor inputs: This implies that if we keep on increasing quantities of one of these inputs while holding quantities of the other input constant, the additional output produced will keep declining.

Capital Deepening versus Technological Progress

Growth in output per worker can come from two sources:

Capital deepening: Capital deepening refers to an increase in the capital-labor ratio and is reflected in a movement along the same per-capita production function. The increase in output per worker from increasing the capital-labor ratio becomes relatively insignificant once the capital-labor ratio reaches a relatively high level. This is because the marginal product of capital declines as more capital is added to fixed quantities of labor.

Technological progress: While capital deepening results in a movement along the same per-capita production function, improvements in TFP cause the entire production function to shift upwards. Improvements in technology enable the economy to produce a higher output per worker for a given level of capital per worker. Technological progress can therefore result in a permanent increase in output per worker despite the diminishing marginal productivity of capital.

Developed markets typically have high capital-labor ratios, while developing countries typically have low capital-labor ratios. Therefore:

- Developed countries have relatively little to gain from capital deepening and must rely on technological progress for growth in potential GDP.
- Developing countries on the other hand, have the potential to grow from both capital deepening and technological progress.

Growth Accounting

Solow's growth accounting equation is used to analyze the performance of economies. It is basically the production function written in the form of growth rates:

$$\Delta Y/Y = \Delta A/A + \alpha \Delta K/K + (1 - \alpha)\Delta L/L$$

Uses of the Growth Accounting Equation

- Estimating the contribution of technological progress to economic growth.
- Empirically measure the sources of growth in an economy.
- Measure potential GDP.

Note that potential GDP may also be measured using the labor productivity growth accounting equation, which models potential GDP as a function of (1) labor input quantities and (2) labor productivity.

Growth rate in potential GDP = Long-term growth rate of labor force
+ Long-term growth rate in labor productivity

Natural Resources

- Renewable resources are those that are replenished, such as forests.
- Non-renewable resources are those that are limited in supply and are depleted once they are consumed, such as oil and coal.

Ownership and *production* of natural resources are not necessary for an economy to grow; it is more important for a country to be able to *access* natural resources (e.g. via trade).

Note that the presence of natural resources may sometimes even restrain economic growth, resulting in a "resource curse".

Labor Supply

The potential quantity of labor input in the economy is measured in terms of the total number of hours available for work, which can be estimated as:

Total number of hours available for work = Labor force × Average hours worked per worker

The **labor force** is defined as the working age population (16-64 years old) that is either (1) employed or (2) available for work, but not working (unemployed).

Factors Affecting Labor Supply

- Population growth
- Labor force participation
- Net migration
- Average hours worked

Labor Quality: Human Capital

Human capital refers to the accumulated knowledge and skills that workers acquire from education, training, and life experience. Better-educated and more skilled workers are generally more productive and more adaptable to changes in technology and to other shifts in market demand and supply.

Capital: ICT and Non-ICT

Capital spending can be separated into two categories:
- **ICT investment** is a measure of the impact of the information technology (IT) sector on economic growth. Growth in the IT sector has led to network externalities (i.e., it has enabled people to interconnect and work more productively), which has led to increasing TFP and economic growth.
- **Non-ICT investment** results in capital deepening, and therefore has more of a temporary impact on economic growth.

Generally speaking, there is a high positive correlation between investment in physical capital and GDP growth.

- In the short run, this can be explained by capital deepening.
- Over the long run, this can be explained by a relatively higher portion of capital spending being allocated to ICT investment (which results in improving TFP).

Technology

Improvements in technology result in an upward shift in the production function, and allow economies to overcome limits on growth imposed by diminishing marginal returns to capital. Technological change may be brought about through investment in human capital, and/or new machinery, equipment, and software (especially ICT goods).

- Developed countries tend to spend a higher percentage of GDP on R&D as they primarily rely on innovation and the development of new products and production methods for growth.
- Developing countries tend to spend less on R&D as they (1) can acquire new technology through imitation, and (2) can foster economic growth in the short run through capital deepening.

Public Infrastructure

Investment in public infrastructure such as roads, bridges, municipal water, and dams improves the productivity of private investment.

THEORIES OF GROWTH

Classical Model (Malthusian Model)

This model asserts that growth in real GDP per capita is **temporary**. GDP per capita only grows until it rises above the subsistence level. Once it rises above the subsistence level, real GDP per capita falls due to a population explosion.

This theory predicts that standards of living remain constant over time even with technological progress as there is no growth in per capita output. In the long run, new technologies result in a larger population, but not a richer population.

Neoclassical Model (Solow's Model)

This model is based on the Cobb-Douglas production function. Both labor and capital are variable factors of production and both suffer from diminishing marginal productivity. The neoclassical model seeks to find the economy's equilibrium position, which it asserts occurs when the economy grows at the steady state rate of growth. In this state:

- The output-capital (Y/K) ratio is constant. This ratio is denoted by ψ and calculated as:

$$\frac{Y}{K} = \left(\frac{1}{s}\right)\left[\left(\frac{q}{(1-\alpha)}\right) + \delta + n\right] \equiv \psi$$

- Capital per worker (k = K/L), and output per worker (y = Y/L) grow at the same rate, which is given by:
  - Growth rate in k and y: $\theta/(1-\alpha)$

- Growth is total output (Y) equals the sum of (1) the growth rate in output per worker, $\theta/(1-\alpha)$, and (2) growth in labor supply, n.
  - Growth rate in output (Y) = $\theta/(1-\alpha)$ + n
  - n = $\Delta L/L$ = Growth in labor supply

- The marginal product of capital is also constant, and equals the real interest rate:
  - $MP_K = \alpha Y/K = r$

Important takeaways:
- Even though the capital-labor ratio (k = K/L) is increasing [at the rate $\theta/(1-\alpha)$] in the steady state, which indicates that capital deepening is occurring in the economy, the marginal product of capital remains constant (at $MP_K = \alpha Y/K = r$). This can be explained by growth in TFP offsetting the impact of diminishing marginal returns to capital.
- Further, capital deepening has no effect on the growth rate of the economy in the steady state. The economy continues to grow at a constant rate of $\theta/(1-\alpha)$ + n.

Impact of Changes in Different Variables on the Steady State

Saving rate (s): An increase in the saving rate increases the *levels* of k and y in the new steady state, but it has no impact on the *growth rates* of k and y. They continue to grow at their steady state rates of growth $\theta/(1-\alpha)$ while total output (Y) continues to grow at $\theta/(1-\alpha)$+n.

Labor force growth (n): An increase in labor force growth results in a lower capital-labor ratio and a lower output per worker at the new steady state. There is no impact on the *growth rates* of k and y. They continue to grow at their steady state rates of growth $\theta/(1-\alpha)$, while total output (Y) continues to grow at $\theta/(1-\alpha)$+n.

Depreciation rate (d): An increase in depreciation has the same impact as an increase in labor force growth. The new steady state equilibrium has a lower capital-labor ratio and lower output per worker. There is no impact on the *growth rates* of k and y. They continue to grow at their steady state rates of growth $\theta/(1-\alpha)$, while total output (Y) continues to grow at $\theta/(1-\alpha)$+n.

Growth in TFP (q): An increase in the growth rate of TFP results in a decline in the capital-labor ratio and output per worker. However, output per worker and capital per worker will grow faster going forward.

To summarize:
- Changes in (1) the savings rate, (2) labor force growth rate and/or (3) depreciation rate impact the level of output per worker but do not have a long-term impact on the growth rate of output per worker.
- Only a change in TFP has a permanent impact on the growth rate of output per worker.

ENDOGENOUS GROWTH THEORY

Endogenous growth theory focuses on explaining technological progress (which has proven to be the primary determinant of economic growth in the long run) as opposed to neoclassical growth theory (which treats technological progress as an exogenous variable).

Endogenous theory broadens the definition of capital to include human and knowledge capital and R&D. Investment in physical capital increases output, while investment in R&D results in ideas. The theory asserts that not only do these ideas have a positive impact on the company that comes up with them, but that they have positive externalities and spillover effects as they can be copied by competitors as well. Overall, R&D results in increasing returns to scale across the entire economy as companies benefit from the private spending of their competitors. Therefore, the economy does not reach a steady growth rate (as predicted by the neoclassical model). Instead, saving and investment can generate self-sustaining growth at a permanently higher rate as the positive externalities associated with R&D prevent diminishing marginal returns to capital from setting in. The production function in the endogenous growth model is an upward-sloping straight line given by:

$$y_e = f(k_e) = ck_e$$

Output per worker (y_e) is proportional to the stock of capital per worker (k_e), while c is the constant marginal product of capital.

Takeaways from Endogenous Growth Theory

- Since there are no diminishing marginal returns to capital from the perspective of the economy as a whole, an increase in the savings rate would permanently increase the rate of economic growth.
- Since R&D entails positive externalities, there may be a market failure in the sense that there would be underproduction of R&D from the societal perspective. Therefore, there may be a strong case for government intervention to increase investment in capital in the economy.
- Due to the constant (or sometimes even increasing) returns associated with investment in knowledge capital and R&D, developed countries can continue to grow faster than developing countries. As a result, there is no reason for incomes to converge over time (as predicted by the neoclassical model).

The Convergence Debate

Convergence means that countries with low per capita incomes should grow at a faster rate than countries with high per capita incomes, such that over time, per capital income differences will be eliminated.

- Absolute convergence means that regardless of their particular characteristics, output per capita in developing countries will eventually reach the level of developed countries.

- Conditional convergence means that convergence in output per capita is dependent (or conditional) upon countries having the same savings rates, population growth rates and production functions.

Studies have shown that some of the poorer countries are in fact diverging rather than converging towards the income levels of developed countries. This phenomenon is explained by **club convergence**. Countries with similar structural characteristics (e.g. production technologies, preferences, government policies, etc.) form a club. Within the club, countries with the lowest per capita incomes grow at the fastest rates, while countries outside the club fall further behind. Note that membership of the club is based on the economy exhibiting certain desirable structural characteristics; not on income levels. Poor countries can join the club by making appropriate institutional changes; otherwise they risk falling into a non-convergence trap.

Convergence between developing and developed countries can occur from two sources:

- Capital deepening: Developing countries tend to operate at relatively low capital-labor ratios so the marginal productivity of capital in those countries is still relatively high. On the other hand, developed countries tend to operate at high capital-labor ratios, where marginal productivity of capital is relatively low. Therefore, developing countries can catch up to their developed peers simply through capital accumulation.

- By importing technologies from developed countries, developing countries can achieve faster economic growth and converge to the income levels of advanced economies.

Growth in an Open Economy

Opening up the economy to trade and financial flows has the following advantages:
- Investment is not constrained by domestic savings as the country can finance investments with foreign savings.
- Productivity improves as the country can focus on industries in which it has a comparative advantage.
- Domestic producers can exploit economies of scale as they attain access to larger overseas markets.
- TFP improves as countries are able to import latest technologies.
- Faced with competition from foreign producers, domestic companies strive to produce better products and improve productivity.

Convergence (as predicted by the neoclassical model) should occur more quickly if there is free trade and no restrictions on capital flows.

Classifications of Regulations

- Statutes: Laws enacted by legislative bodies.
- Administrative regulations: Rules issued by government agencies and other regulators.
- Judicial law: Interpretations of courts.

Classifications of Regulators

Regulations can come from government agencies or independent regulators. Independent regulators get their regulatory authority through recognition from a government body or agency. Note that independent regulators do not receive government funding so they are politically independent.

Independent regulators include self-regulatory organizations (SROs). These are private entities that represent their members and regulate them as well. While they may be immune from political pressure, SROs are subject to pressure from their members which can give rise to conflicts of interest. Not all SROs are independent regulators however. Those that are granted authority by government bodies obviously serve as independent regulators, but there are others that get their regulating authority from their members. These members agree to comply with the SROs rules and standards and to enforce them. Note that this authority does not have the force of law.

Reasons for Reliance on Self-Regulation

- Increases overall level of regulatory resources.
- Uses knowledge and expertise of industry professionals.
- Enables the regulator to focus on other priorities while relying on the SRO for front line supervision of members and markets.

Reasons for Decreased Reliance on Self-Regulation

- Privatization of securities exchanges.
- Intense competition.
- Uncertainty regarding effectiveness of self-regulation.
- Internationalization.
- Strengthening of government regulators.
- Trend toward consolidation of financial regulators.
- "Cooperative regulation".
- Pressure to increase efficiency and lower costs.

Economic Rationale for Regulatory Intervention

Regulatory intervention becomes essential due to the presence of informational frictions and externalities.

Informational frictions result in the following issues:

- Adverse selection, where some market participants have access to information that is unavailable to others.
- Moral hazard, where one party will have a tendency to take risks because the costs that could incur will not be felt by the party taking the risk.

Externalities in the context of regulation refer to the provision of public goods. Public goods give rise to the free-rider problem, as consumption of a public good by a person does not preclude another person from consuming it.

Regulatory Interdependencies

The **regulatory capture theory** argues that regulation can often actually advance the interests of the regulated.

Regulatory differences across jurisdictions can result in shift in location and the behavior of entities due to regulatory competition and regulatory arbitrage.

- **Regulatory competition** refers to competition between regulators to provide a regulatory environment designed to attract certain entities.
- **Regulatory arbitrage** refers to practices whereby firms capitalize on loopholes in regulatory systems in order to circumvent unfavorable regulation. It includes cases where companies shop around for locations that allow certain behavior rather than changing their own behavior.

Regulatory Tools

Price mechanisms (taxes and subsidies): Taxes are imposed to discourage certain behaviors (e.g. taxes on cigarettes to deter smoking), while subsidies are imposed to encourage certain behavior (e.g. subsidies for farmers on certain crops to increase domestic production).

Regulatory mandates and restrictions on behaviors: Governments can mandate certain activities (e.g. minimum capital requirements for banks) or restrict certain activities (e.g. insider trading).

Provision of public goods and financing for private projects: Governments can provide public goods (e.g. national defense, transportation infrastructure) or provide loans to individuals and businesses for specific activities that the government wants to promote.

Regulation of Commerce

- Government regulation plays an important role in various aspects of business such as protecting workers' and employers' rights and responsibilities, and consumer health and safety.
- Governments set the legal standards for the recognition and protection of different types of intellectual property.
- Other examples of government regulations covering commerce include company laws, tax laws, bankruptcy laws and banking laws.
- Governments take the steps they deem necessary to support and protect domestic business interests against unfair competition (e.g. by imposing anti-dumping duties).

Regulation of Financial Markets

Regulation of Securities Markets

Securities regulation is generally aimed at protecting investors, creating confidence in markets, and enhancing capital formation. Various aspects of securities regulation include:
- Securities registration requirements to develop investor confidence.
- Regulations geared towards mitigating the principal-agent problem.
- Protecting the interests of retail investors.

Regulation of Financial Institutions

Regulation of financial institutions focuses on protecting consumers and investors, ensuring the safety and soundness of financial institutions, promoting the smooth operation of the payments system, and maintaining availability to credit. Financial regulation also aims to tackle concerns relating to the overall economy such as price stability, unemployment, and economic growth.

Prudential supervision refers to regulation and monitoring of the safety and soundness of financial institutions for promoting financial stability, reducing system-wide risks, and protecting customers of financial institutions. This aspect of financial regulation is critical because a failure of a financial institution can have far-reaching consequences on the overall economy.

The financial crisis of 2008 highlighted two negative externalities that have recently been tackled by financial regulation. These are:
- Systematic risk: The risk of failure of the financial system.
- Financial contagion: A situation in which financial shocks spread from their place of origin to other countries i.e., when faltering economies affect healthier ones.

Increased globalization has led to increased concerns about contagion and regulatory competition.

Antitrust Risk

- In evaluating mergers and acquisitions regulators evaluate whether the merger will lead to monopolization of the market.
- Competition and anti-trust laws also prohibit other types of anticompetitive behavior. Examples of such behavior include exclusive dealings and refusals to deal, price discrimination, and predatory pricing.
- Large companies that operate in multiple markets need to simultaneously satisfy regulators from several countries when faced with antitrust issues.

Costs of Regulation

- Regulatory burden refers to the costs of regulation for the regulated entity. It can be viewed as the private costs of regulation or government burden.
- Net regulatory burden results from subtracting private benefits of regulation from private costs.

When conducting cost-benefit analysis, analysts should consider direct and indirect costs of regulation. Further, there may be "unintended" costs associated with regulations. Sunset provisions require regulators to conduct a new cost-benefit analysis before the regulation is renewed.

Study Session 5: Financial Reporting and Analysis—Inventories and Long-Lived Assets

INVENTORIES: IMPLICATIONS FOR FINANCIAL STATEMENTS AND RATIOS
Cross-Reference to CFA Institute Assigned Reading #15

Inventory Cost Flow Assumptions

FIFO
- Older units are the *first* ones sold.
- Units that are purchased *recently* are included in EI.
- COGS is composed of units valued at *older* prices.
- EI is composed of units valued at *recent* prices.
- FIFO does the best job of reflecting current costs in EI.

LIFO
- Recently acquired units are the *first* ones to be sold.
- Oldest units are included in EI.
- COGS is composed of units valued at *recent* prices.
- Ending inventory is composed of units valued at *older* prices.
- LIFO does the best job of reflecting current costs in COGS.

AVCO (weighted-average cost)
- COGS is composed of units valued at average prices.
- Ending inventory is also composed of units that are valued at average prices.

LIFO is permitted under U.S. GAAP, but not under IFRS. Most U.S. companies use LIFO so that they can save on taxes in an inflationary environment.

LIFO Accounting under U.S. GAAP

U.S. GAAP allows firms to use LIFO, while IFRS does not. During periods of rising prices and stable or increasing inventory levels (as is generally the case), firms prefer to use LIFO because it results in higher COGS, lower net income and consequently lower taxes. Paying lower taxes improves the firm's operating cash flows. On the other hand, LIFO uses older prices to value inventory. Therefore, in a period of rising prices and stable or increasing inventory levels, LIFO results in lower EI and consequently lower current assets on the balance sheet.

- When prices are *rising* during the year and inventory levels are stable or rising:
    - $COGS_{LIFO} > COGS_{AVCO} > COGS_{FIFO}$
    - $EI_{FIFO} > EI_{AVCO} > EI_{LIFO}$

- When prices are *falling* during the year and inventory levels are stable or rising:
    - $COGS_{FIFO} > COGS_{AVCO} > COGS_{LIFO}$
    - $EI_{LIFO} > EI_{AVCO} > EI_{FIFO}$

LIFO versus FIFO when Prices are Rising (with Stable or rising Inventory Quantities)

	LIFO	FIFO
COGS	Higher	Lower
Income before taxes	Lower	Higher
Income taxes	Lower	Higher
Net income	Lower	Higher
Cash flow	Higher	Lower
EI	Lower	Higher
Working capital	Lower	Higher

LIFO versus FIFO Ratios when Prices are Rising (with Stable or rising Inventory Quantities)

Type of Ratio	Effect on Numerator	Effect on Denominator	Effect on Ratio
NP and GP margins	Income is lower under LIFO because COGS is higher	Sales are the same under both	Lower under LIFO
Debt to equity	Same debt levels	Lower equity under LIFO	Higher under LIFO
Current ratio	Current assets are lower under LIFO because EI is lower	Current liabilities are the same	Lower under LIFO
Quick ratio	Assets are higher as a result of lower taxes paid	Current liabilities are the same	Higher under LIFO
Inventory turnover	COGS is higher under LIFO	Average inventory is lower under LIFO	Higher under LIFO
Total asset turnover	Sales are the same	Lower total assets under LIFO	Higher under LIFO

Periodic versus Perpetual Inventory Systems

Periodic inventory system: Under this system, the quantity of inventory on hand is calculated periodically. The cost of goods available for sale during the period is calculated as beginning inventory plus purchases over the period. The ending inventory amount is then deducted from cost of goods available for sale to determine COGS.

Perpetual inventory system: Under this system, changes in the inventory account are updated continuously. Purchases and sales are recorded directly in the inventory account as they occur.

Under the **LIFO** cost flow assumption, in a period of *rising* prices, use of the periodic system for inventory results in a:

- *Lower* value of ending inventory.
- *Higher* value for COGS.

Therefore, gross profit would be *lower* under the periodic system.

- If a company uses FIFO or separate identification for inventory valuation, it would arrive at the same value for COGS and EI under the periodic and perpetual inventory systems.
- Use of LIFO or AVCO may result in different values for COGS and EI under the periodic and perpetual inventory systems.

LIFO to FIFO Conversion

$$EI_{FIFO} = EI_{LIFO} + \text{LIFO reserve}$$

$$COGS_{FIFO} = COGS_{LIFO} - (LR_{ending} - LR_{beginning})$$

During a period of rising prices and stable or rising inventory quantities:

- Net income after tax under FIFO will be greater than LIFO net income after tax by:
  - Change in LIFO reserve $\times$ (1 − tax rate)
- Equity (retained earnings) under FIFO will be greater by:
  - LIFO reserve $\times$ (1− tax rate)
- Liabilities (deferred taxes) under FIFO will be greater by:
  - LIFO reserve $\times$ (tax rate)
- Current assets (inventory) under FIFO will be greater by:
  - LIFO reserve

Increase in LIFO Reserve

In every period during which prices are rising and inventory quantities are stable or rising, the LIFO reserve will increase as the excess of FIFO ending inventory over LIFO ending inventory increases.

Decline in LIFO Reserve

There can be two reasons for a decline in LIFO reserve:
1. LIFO liquidation.
2. Declining prices.

LIFO Liquidation

LIFO liquidation occurs when, during an inflationary period, a firm that uses LIFO sells more units during a given period than it purchases over the period. This causes year-end inventory levels to be lower than beginning-of-year inventory levels.

When a LIFO firm sells more units than it purchases, some of the goods sold are units that were included in beginning inventory. LIFO allocates the oldest prices to inventory, and in some cases these older prices could be outdated by many years. When a company includes older, cheaper stock in its COGS, it severely *understates* its COGS, and LIFO COGS no longer reflect recent, current prices. Consequently a firm with LIFO liquidation *overstates* net income. The higher profits are unsustainable because eventually, the firm will run out of cheaper, older stock to liquidate. The higher net income also comes at the cost of higher taxes that reduce operating cash flow. To postpone these taxes on holding gains on old units of inventory, a LIFO firm must always purchase as many as, if not more units, than it sells.

LIFO liquidation can result from strikes, recessions, or a decline in demand for the firm's product. The irony is that when there is LIFO liquidation, the firm reports surprisingly high profits (due to the realization of holding gains) in hard times when production cuts result in the liquidation of lower cost LIFO inventory.

Analysts must exclude the increase in earnings due to LIFO liquidation from their analysis. COGS must be adjusted upwards for the decline in LIFO reserve, and net income must be lowered.

Declining prices

When prices of the firm's products fall over a given period, the firm will see a decline in its LIFO reserve. If the change in LIFO reserve is negative, $COGS_{FIFO}$ will be *greater* than $COGS_{LIFO}$. FIFO would continue to reflect the latest (and in this case lower) prices in inventory, and will provide the most economically accurate measure of inventory value, while LIFO would continue to reflect current replacement costs in COGS. When the reduction in LIFO reserve is caused by declining prices, no analytical adjustments are necessary.

Inventory Method Changes

Consistency in the inventory costing method used is required under U.S. GAAP and IFRS.

Under **IFRS**, a change in policy is acceptable only if the change results in the provision of more reliable and relevant information in the financial statements.

- Changes in inventory accounting policy are applied retrospectively.
- Information for all periods presented in the financial report is restated.
- Adjustments for periods prior to the earliest year presented in the financial report are reflected in the beginning balance of retained earnings for the earliest year presented in the report.

U.S. GAAP has a similar requirement for changes in inventory accounting policies.
- However, a company must thoroughly explain how the newly-adopted inventory accounting method is superior and preferable to the old one.
- The company may be required to seek permission from the Internal Revenue Service (IRS) before making any changes.
- If inventory-related accounting policies are modified, changes to the financial statements must be made retrospectively, unless the LIFO method is being adopted (which is applied prospectively).

Inventory Adjustments

Under IFRS, inventory must be stated at the lower of cost or "net realizable value" (NRV). NRV is calculated as the selling price minus selling costs. If the NRV of inventory falls below the cost recorded on the balance sheet, the value must be written down, and a loss must be recognized on the income statement. A subsequent increase in NRV would require a reversal of previous write-downs, which would reduce inventory-related expenses in the period that the increase in value occurs. However, the increase in value that can be recognized is limited to the total write-down that had previously been recorded. Effectively, inventory values can never exceed the amount originally recognized.

> Compare cost to NRV.
> NRV = SP - SC

> Compare cost to replacement cost (market)
> where:
> NRV - NP margin
> ≤ replacement cost
> ≤ NRV

U.S. GAAP requires the application of the LCM (lower of cost or market) principle to value inventory. Market value is defined as replacement cost, where the replacement cost must lie within a range of values from NRV minus normal profit margin to NRV. If replacement cost is higher than NRV, it must be brought down to NRV, and if replacement cost is lower than NRV minus normal profit margin, it must be brought up to NRV minus normal profit margin. This adjusted replacement cost is then compared to carrying value (cost) and the lower of the two is used to value inventory. Further, under U.S. GAAP reversal of any write-down is prohibited.

In certain industries like agriculture, forest products and mining, both U.S. GAAP and IFRS allow companies to value inventory at NRV even when it exceeds historical cost. If an active market exists for the product, quoted market prices are used as NRV; otherwise the price of the most recent market transaction is used. Unrealized gains and losses on inventory resulting from fluctuating market prices are recognized on the income statement.

Note:

Companies that use separate identification, FIFO or AVCO are more likely to incur inventory write-downs compared to firms that use LIFO. LIFO uses the oldest costs for measuring ending inventory. In an inflationary environment, these older costs are already relatively more conservative (lower).

Financial Statement Analysis Issues

- A significant increase in unit volumes of raw materials and/or WIP inventory may suggest that the company expects an increase in demand for its products.
- An increase in finished goods inventory with declining raw materials and WIP inventory may signal decrease in demand for the company's products.
- If growth in inventories is greater than the growth in sales, it could indicate a decrease in demand.
- To obtain additional information about a company's inventory and its future sales, analysts should examine the MD&A section, industry-related news and publications, and industry data.

LONG-LIVED ASSETS: IMPLICATIONS FOR FINANCIAL STATEMENTS AND RATIOS
Cross-Reference to CFA Institute Assigned Reading #16

Capitalizing versus Expensing

Effect on Financial Statements	
Initially when the cost is capitalized	• Non current assets *increase.* • Cash flow from investing activities *decreases.*
In future periods when the asset is depreciated or amortized.	• Non current assets *decrease.* • Net income *decreases.* • Retained earnings *decrease.* • Equity *decreases.*
When the cost is expensed	• Net income *decreases* by the entire amount of the cost. • No related asset is recorded on the balance sheet and therefore, no depreciation is charged in future periods. • Operating cash flow *decreases.*

All other factors remaining the same:
- The decision to expense an item as opposed to capitalizing it would give the impression of greater earnings growth.
- The decision to capitalize an item as opposed to expensing it results in higher reported operating cash flow.
- The profitability enhancing effect of capitalizing continues as long as the company's capital expenditures exceed depreciation expense.

Financial Statement Effects of Capitalising versus Expensing

	Capitalizing	Expensing
Net income (first year)	Higher	Lower
Net income (future years)	Lower	Higher
Total assets	Higher	Lower
Shareholders' equity	Higher	Lower
Cash flow from operations	Higher	Lower
Cash flow from investing	Lower	Higher
Income variability	Lower	Higher
Debt to equity	Lower	Higher

Capitalisation of Interest Costs

Under U.S. GAAP and IFRS, companies must capitalize interest costs associated with acquiring or constructing an asset that requires a long period of time to get ready for its intended use. For example, if a company constructs a building for its own use, interest expense incurred to finance construction must be capitalized along with the cost of the building. The interest rate used to determine the amount of interest capitalized depends on the company's existing borrowings, or if applicable, on borrowings specifically incurred to finance the cost of the asset. Capitalized interest costs are included in the cost of the asset and depreciated once the asset is in use. This results in a better "matching" of costs with associated revenues.

If construction and sale of buildings is the core business activity of the firm, and a building is built with the intent of selling it, capitalized interest costs are included along with the cost of construction in inventory as a part of current assets. The capitalized interest is also included in COGS in the period that the building is sold.

Capitalization of interest results in a higher interest coverage ratio (due to lower interest expense) in the year that interest is capitalized, but a lower interest coverage ratio in subsequent years (due to higher depreciation resulting in lower EBIT).

Analytical Issues Regarding Capitalized Interest

- Capitalized interest costs reduce investing cash flows, while expensed interest costs reduce operating cash flows. While this treatment is consistent with accounting standards, analysts may want to examine the impact of classification on reported cash flows.

- To provide a true picture of a company's interest coverage ratio, the entire amount of interest expense, whether capitalized or expensed, should be used in the denominator.

- If a company is depreciating interest that was capitalized in previous years, net income should be adjusted to remove the effect of depreciation on capitalized interest.

- Any interest costs capitalized in the current period should be treated as interest expense. Net income should be reduced by the amount of interest capitalized in the current period.

Capitalisation of Internal Development Costs

Generally, **U.S. accounting standards** require that R&D costs be expensed when incurred. However, they require that certain costs related to software development be capitalized.

- Costs incurred to develop software for sale are expensed until the product's technological feasibility has been established. Once feasibility has been established, associated development costs are capitalized.

- Costs related directly to the development of software for internal use are also expensed until it is probable that the project will be completed and that the software will be used as intended. After that, related development costs are capitalized.

Expensing rather than capitalizing development costs results in:
- Lower net income in the current period,
- Lower operating cash flow and higher investing cash flow in the current period.

The capitalized costs related directly to developing software for sale or internal use include the cost of employees who help build and test the software.

- If current period software development costs *exceed* amortization of prior periods' capitalized development costs, net income would be *lower* under expensing.
- If software development expenditures were to slow down such that current year expenses are *lower* than amortization of prior periods' capitalized costs, net income would be *higher* under expensing.

IFRS requires that expenditures on **research**, or during the research phase of an internal project be expensed rather than capitalized as an intangible asset. The "research phase of an internal project" refers to the period during which the company cannot demonstrate that an intangible asset is being created.

IFRS allows companies to recognize an internal asset from **development**, or the development phase of an internal project if certain criteria are met, including a demonstration of the technical feasibility of completing the intangible asset and the intent to use or sell the asset.

Analytical Adjustments

Adjustments must be made to compare the financial performance of a company that expenses software development costs with that of a peer company that capitalizes these costs. For the company that capitalizes software development costs, an analyst should make the following adjustments:

1. The income statement for the current period should include related software development costs as an expense. Prior period income statements should exclude amortization of previously capitalized development costs.
2. The capitalized asset should be removed from the balance sheet.
3. Operating cash flow should be reduced and investing cash flow should be increased by the amount of development costs that have been capitalized.
4. Ratios that include income, long-lived assets, or cash flow from operations should be recalculated using adjusted values.

Depreciation

There are two primary models for reporting long-lived assets.

The **cost model** is required under **U.S. GAAP** and permitted under **IFRS**. Under this model, the cost of long-lived tangible assets (except land) and intangible assets with finite useful lives is allocated over their useful lives as depreciation and amortization expense. Under the cost model, an asset's carrying value equals its historical cost minus accumulated depreciation/amortization (as long as the asset has not been impaired).

The **revaluation** model is permitted under **IFRS**, but not under **U.S. GAAP**. Under this model, long-lived assets are reported at fair value (not at historical cost minus accumulated depreciation/amortization).

Comparison between Straight Line and Accelerated Depreciation Methods

All other factors remaining the same, a company that uses the straight line method to depreciate its assets will report:

- A lower asset turnover ratio during the early years of the asset's use (due to higher net assets).
- Higher operating profit margin in the early years of the asset's use (due to lower depreciation expense).
- Higher operating ROA in the early years of the asset's use (due to lower depreciation expense) and lower ROA in later years.

Further, a company that uses an accelerated depreciation method will report an improving asset turnover ratio, operating profit margin and return on assets over time.

Depreciation Assumptions

Assumptions of a *longer* useful life and a *higher* expected residual value result in *lower* annual depreciation expense compared to assumptions of a *shorter* useful life and a *lower* salvage value. The subjective nature of these assumptions allows management to manipulate earnings. For example, management could significantly write-down the value of long-lived assets and recognize a hefty charge against net income in the current period. While this would depress earnings in the current year, it would allow management to recognize lower annual depreciation expense going forward, inflate profits, and report impressive growth in profitability. On the other hand, management could also overstate the useful life and the salvage value of an asset to show impressive profits over the near-term, and recognize a significant loss at a later point in time when the asset is eventually retired.

Additional assumptions are required to allocate depreciation expense between (COGS), and sales, general and administrative expenses (SG&A). Including a *higher* proportion of total depreciation expense in COGS *lowers* the gross profit margin and *lowers* operating expenses. However, it does not affect the net profit margin.

When a company determines that a change in a depreciation estimate is required, the change is applied prospectively.

Asset Impairment

An impairment charge is made to reflect the unexpected decline in the fair value of an asset. Impairment recognition has the following effects on a company's financial statements:

- The carrying value of the asset decreases.
- The impairment charge reduces net income.
- Impairment does not affect cash flows because it is a non-cash charge.

Under **IFRS**, an asset is considered impaired when its carrying amount exceeds its recoverable amount. The recoverable amount equals the higher of "fair value less costs to sell" and "value in use", where value in use refers to the discounted value of future cash flows expected from the asset. The impairment loss that must be recognized equals the carrying amount minus the recoverable amount.

Under **U.S. GAAP**, an asset is considered impaired when its carrying value exceeds the total value of its undiscounted expected future cash flows (recoverable amount). If the carrying value is determined to be non-recoverable, the impairment loss that must be recognized equals the difference between the asset's carrying amount and its fair value.

Under **IFRS** and **U.S. GAAP**, goodwill and identifiable intangible assets that are not amortized must be tested for impairment annually, or more frequently when there are indications that impairment may have occurred.

Analysis of Impairment

- An impairment charge in the current period may indicate that the historical depreciation charged on the asset did not accurately reflect the decline in the value of the asset. Therefore, historical earnings may have been inflated.
- Impairment charges are highly subjective in nature and offer management an avenue for earnings manipulation.
- A new management team may recognize a significant impairment charge in the current period so that future performance will present a favorable trend. Going forward, depreciation expense will be lower so reported profitability will improve. Further, ROA, ROE and asset turnover will also improve.
- Management may understate the impairment charge to meet earnings targets.
- Impairment charges on recent acquisitions can shed some light on management's ability to make successful acquisitions.
- Impairment charges are generally non-recurring so they are not considered in projecting future performance.

The Revaluation Model

IFRS allows companies to use the revaluation model or the cost model to report the carrying amounts of noncurrent assets on the balance sheet. Revaluation results in the carrying amount of an asset reflecting its fair value (as long as it can be measured reliably). Under **U.S. GAAP**, only use of the cost model is permitted.

A key difference between the revaluation and the cost model is that revaluation allows for the reported value of the asset to be higher than its historical cost. Under the cost model, the reported value of an asset can never exceed its historical cost.

IFRS allows the revaluation model to be used for certain classes of assets and for the cost model to be used for others as long as:

1. The company applies the same model to assets in a particular class (e.g. land and buildings, machinery, factory equipment etc.).
2. Whenever a revaluation is performed, all assets in the particular class must be revalued (to avoid selective revaluation).

The revaluation model may also be used to value intangible assets, but only if an active market for the asset exists, where its fair value can be determined.

The effects of an asset revaluation on the financial statements depend on whether a revaluation *initially* increases or decreases the asset's carrying value.

- If revaluation initially decreases an asset's carrying amount, it is recognized in the income statement as a revaluation loss (similar to an impairment loss). A subsequent increase in the asset's fair value will first offset the previously recognized revaluation loss recognized in the income statement, and any excess will be recognized in other comprehensive income (equity) as revaluation surplus.
- If revaluation initially increases an asset's carrying amount, it is recognized in other comprehensive income (equity) as revaluation surplus. A subsequent decrease in the asset's fair value will first offset the previously recognized revaluation surplus in other comprehensive income, and any remaining decline in value will be recognized on the income statement as a revaluation loss.

If an asset is sold or disposed of, any associated revaluation surplus recognized in other comprehensive income is transferred directly to retained earnings.

Considerations for Financial Statement Analysis

- An increase in the carrying value of depreciable long-lived assets increases total assets and shareholders' equity. Hence, revaluation of assets can be used to reduce reported **leverage**.
- Asset revaluations that decrease the value of an asset also decrease net income in the year of revaluation. In the year of revaluation, **return on assets** (Net profit /Assets) and **return on equity** (Net profit / Shareholders' equity) decline. In future years however, the lower values of assets and equity may result in higher ROE and ROA.
- If the carrying value of the asset is increased in a revaluation, assets and equity increase, and annual depreciation expense also increases. As a result, performance measures such as ROA and ROE may decline in the future.
- Analysts should also look into who performs asset value appraisals and how often revaluations are recognized. Regular appraisals can be good because the reported value of the asset is representative of its fair value. Appraisals performed by independent external sources are more reliable.

Analysis of Financial Statement Disclosures

$$\text{Estimated useful life} = \frac{\text{Gross investment in fixed Assets}}{\text{Annual depreciation expense}}$$

$$\text{Average life of asset} = \frac{\text{Annual depreciation}}{\text{Annual depreciation expense}}$$

$$\text{Remaining useful life} = \frac{\text{Net investment in fixed Assets}}{\text{Annual depreciation expense}}$$

The calculations of estimated useful life, average age, and remaining useful life are important because:
- They help identify older, obsolete assets that might make the firm's operations less efficient.
- They help forecast future cash flows from investing activities and identify major capital expenditures that the company might need to raise cash for in the future.

Another popular method for making comparisons across companies is calculating annual capital expenditure as a percentage of depreciation expense.

- A company for whom this ratio is significantly lower than 100% is currently replacing its fixed assets at a rate that is *slower* than the rate at which they are being depreciated. This might indicate the need for hefty capital expenditure in the future and that further examination of the company's capital expenditure policies is required.
- A company for whom this ratio is close to 100% is replacing its fixed assets at a rate similar to that of their use.

Leases

A lease is a contract between the owner of the asset (lessor) and another party that wants to use the asset (lessee). The lessee gains the right to use the asset for a period of time in return for periodic lease payments.

Leasing an asset holds the following advantages over purchasing the asset:
- Leases often have fixed interest rates.
- They require no down payment so they conserve cash.
- At the end of the lease the asset can be returned to the lessor so the lessee escapes the risk of obsolescence and is not burdened with having to find a buyer for the asset.
- Operating leases do not require recognition of an asset or a liability on the balance sheet so they improve reported performance and leverage ratios.
- In the U.S., leases can be structured as synthetic leases where the company can gain tax benefits of ownership, while not reflecting the asset on its financial statements.

U.S. GAAP requires classification as a finance (capital) lease if any of the following hold:
1. The lease transfers ownership of the asset to the lessee at the end of the term.
2. A bargain purchase option exists.
3. The lease term is greater than 75% of the asset's useful economic life.
4. The present value of the lease payments exceeds 90% of the fair value of the leased asset.

Under **IFRS**, classification of a lease depends on the economic substance of the transaction and managerial judgment.

LESSEE'S PERSPECTIVE

Operating Lease

The accounting treatment for an operating lease is similar to that of renting an asset for a period of time. The asset is not purchased; instead annual payments are made for using it. Under an operating lease, no lease-related entries are made on the balance sheet. The firm has not purchased the asset so there is no addition to fixed assets, and it has not borrowed any money to finance the purchase, so there is no related liability.

Accounting entries at inception
Balance sheet: None because no asset or liability is recognized.
Income statement: None because the asset has not been used yet.
Statement of cash flows: None because there has been no cash transaction.

Accounting entries every year during the lease term
Balance sheet: None because there are no lease-related assets and liabilities.
Income statement: Leasehold (rental) expense is charged every year.
Statement of cash flows: The lease-related expense is classified as a cash outflow from operating activities.

Capital or Finance Lease

A finance lease requires the company to recognize a lease-related asset and liability at inception. The accounting treatment for a finance lease is similar to that of purchasing an asset and financing the purchase with a long-term loan.

Accounting entries at inception
Balance sheet: The present value of lease payments is recognized as a long-lived asset. The same amount is also recognized as a long-term liability.
Income statement: None because the asset has not been used yet.
Statement of cash flows: None because no cash transaction has occurred. Disclosure of lease inception is reported as a "significant noncash financing and investing activity".

Accounting entries every year during the term of the lease
Balance sheet: The value of the asset falls every year as it is depreciated. Interest is charged on the liability (discount rate multiplied by the beginning-of-period liability). The excess of the lease payment over the year's interest expense reduces the liability.
Income statement: Depreciation expense (against the asset) and interest expense (on the liability) are charged every year.
Statement of cash flows: The portion of the lease payment attributable to interest expense is deducted from CFO, while the remainder that serves to reduce the liability is subtracted from CFF.

Finance versus Operating Lease: Lessee's Perspective

Income Statement Item	Finance Lease	Operating Lease
Operating expenses	Lower	Higher
Non-operating expenses	Higher	Lower
EBIT (operating income)	Higher	Lower
Total expenses- early years	Higher	Lower
Total expenses- later years	Lower	Higher
Net income- early years	Lower	Higher
Net income- later years	Higher	Lower

Balance Sheet Item	Capital Lease	Operating Lease
Assets	Higher	Lower
Current liabilities	Higher	Lower
Long term liabilities	Higher	Lower
Total cash	Same	Same

CF Item	Capital Lease	Operating Lease
CFO	Higher	Lower
CFF	Lower	Higher
Total cash flow	Same	Same

Ratio	Numerator under Finance Lease	Denominator under Finance Lease	Effect on Ratio	Ratio Better or Worse under Finance Lease
Asset turnover	Sales- same	Assets- higher	Lower	Worse
Return on assets*	Net income- lower	Assets- higher	Lower	Worse
Current ratio	Current assets- same	Current liabilities- higher	Lower	Worse
Leverage ratios (D/E and D/A**)	Debt- higher	Equity- same Assets- higher	Higher	Worse
Return on equity*	Net income- lower	Equity- same	Lower	Worse

*In early years of the lease agreement.

Note: Lower ROE under a finance lease is due to lower net income (numerator effect), while lower ROA is primarily due to higher assets (denominator effect).

LESSOR'S PERSPECTIVE

Lessors are required to recognize finance leases when any one of the four previously defined criteria for recognizing finance leases by lessees hold, and the following two criteria also hold:

1. Collectability of the lease payments is predictable.
2. There are no significant uncertainties regarding the amount of costs still to be incurred by the lessor under the provisions of the lease agreement.

Leases not meeting the above criteria must be classified as operating leases because the earnings process is not complete, or the risks and benefits of the leased assets have not been transferred.

- If the lessor classifies the lease as an operating lease, it records lease revenue when earned, continues to list the asset on its balance sheet, and depreciates it every year on its income statement. In this case, the lessee does not record a lease-related long-lived asset on its balance sheet.
- If the lessor classifies the lease as a finance lease, it records a receivable equal to the present value of lease payments on its balance sheet, and removes the asset from long-lived assets in its books. In this case, the lessee records a lease-related long-lived asset.

Direct Financing Leases

Financial institutions and leasing companies offer financial leases that generate interest income only. These are known as direct financing leases, where the present value of lease payments equals the carrying value of the asset. In direct financing leases, no gross profits are recognized.

Direct Financing versus Operating Leases: Lessor's Perspective

	Financing Lease	Operating Lease
Total net income	Same	Same
Taxes (early years)	Higher	Lower
Total CFO	Lower	Higher
Total CFI	Higher	Lower

Sales Type Leases

Some manufacturers offer their customers financing options to purchase their products. These sales-type leases include a gross profit (the normal selling price of the product minus the carrying value), which is recognized at inception of the lease, and interest income as payments are received over a period of time. In a sales-type lease, the present value of lease payments equals the selling price of the asset, which is higher than the cost or carrying value of asset.

Disclosures

Under **U.S. GAAP**, lease disclosures require a company to list the lease obligations of the firm for the next five years under all operating and finance leases. These disclosures allow analysts to evaluate the extent of off-balance sheet financing used by the company. They can also be used to determine the effects on the financial statements if all the operating leases were capitalized and brought "on to" the balance sheet.

Under **IFRS**, companies are required to:
- Present finance lease obligations as a part of debt on the balance sheet.
- Disclose the amount of total debt attributable to obligations under finance leases.
- Present information about all lease obligations (operating and finance leases).

Summary of Financial Statement Impact of Leases on the Lessee and Lessor

Lessee	Balance Sheet	Income Statement	Statement of Cash Flows
Operating Lease Finance Lease under IFRS (capital lease under U.S. GAAP)	No effect Recognizes leased asset and lease liability	Reports rent expense Reports depreciation expense on leased asset	Rent payment is an operating cash outflow Reduction of leased liability is a financing cash outflow
Lessor			
Operating Lease	Retains asset on balance sheet	Reports rent income	Rent payments received are an operating cash inflow
Finance Lease*			
When present value of lease payments equals the carrying amount of the leased asset (called a direct financing lease in U.S. GAAP)	Removes asset from balance sheet. Recognizes lease receivable.	Reports interest revenue on lease receivable	Interest position of lease payment received is either an operating or investing cash inflow under IFRS and an operating cash inflow under U.S. GAAP. Receipt of lease principal is an investing cash inflow**.
When present value of lease payments exceeds the carrying amount of the leased asset (called a sales-type lease in U.S. GAAP)	Removes asset. Recognizes lease receivable.	Reports profit on sale. Reports interest revenue on lease receivable.	Interest position of lease payment received is either an operating or investing cash inflow under IFRS and an operating cash inflow under U.S. GAAP. Receipt of lease principal is an investing cash inflow**.

* U.S GAAP distinguishes between a direct finance lease and a sales-type lease, but IFRS does not. The accounting is the same for IFRS and U.S. GAAP despite this additional classification under U.S. GAAP.

** If providing leases is part of a company's normal business activity, the cash flows related to the leases are classified as operating cash.

Study Session 6: Financial Reporting and Analysis—Intercorporate Investments, Post-Employment and Share-Based Compensation, and Multinational Operations

INTERCORPORATE INVESTMENTS
Cross-Reference to CFA Institute Assigned Reading #17

Table 1: Summary of Accounting Treatment for Investments

	In Financial Assets	In Associates	Business Combinations	In Joint Ventures
Influence	Not significant	Significant	Controlling	Shared Control
Typical percentage interest	Usually < 20%	Usually 20% – 50%	Usually > 50%	Varies
Current Financial Reporting Treatment (prior to IFRS 9 taking effect)	Classified as <ul><li>Held-to-maturity</li><li>Available-for-sale</li><li>Fair value through profit or loss (held for trading or designated as fair value).</li><li>Loans and receivables.</li></ul>	Equity method	Consolidation	IFRS: Equity method or proportionate consolidation.
New Financial Reporting Treatment (post IFRS 9 taking effect)	Classified as <ul><li>Fair value through profit or loss</li><li>Fair value through other comprehensive income.</li><li>Amortized cost</li></ul>	Equity method	Consolidation	IFRS: Equity method

INVESTMENTS IN FINANCIAL ASSETS: STANDARD IAS 39 (AS OF DEC 2012)

The accounting treatment of investments in financial assets is similar under IFRS and U.S. GAAP.

Under **IFRS**, financial assets may be classified as:
1. Held-to-maturity.
2. Available-for-sale.
3. Fair value through profit or loss; which includes
   - Held-for-trading, and
   - Designated as fair value through profit or loss.
4. Loans and receivables.

Held-to-Maturity (HTM) Investments

HTM investments are investments in financial assets with fixed or determinable payments and fixed maturities (debt securities) that the investor has a positive intent and ability to hold till maturity. HTM investments cannot be reclassified or sold prior to maturity except in unusual circumstances. Reclassification/sale of HTM investments can result in the investor being precluded from classifying investments under the HTM category going forward.

The initial and subsequent treatment of HTM securities is essentially the same under **IFRS** and **U.S. GAAP**. At each reporting date HTM securities are reported at **amortized cost** using the **effective interest method** (unless objective evidence of impairment exists).
- Interest income and realized gains/losses are recognized in the income statement.
- Unrealized gains/losses (due to changes in fair value) are ignored.

Fair Value through Profit or Loss (IFRS)

Under IFRS, investments classified as fair value through profit or loss include (1) held for trading (HFT) investments and (2) investments designated at fair value. U.S. GAAP is similar. The accounting treatment of both is similar:
- Investments are initially recognized at fair value.
- At each subsequent reporting date, investments are remeasured at fair value.
- Unrealized gains/losses, realized gains/losses, interest income and dividend income are all reported in profit or loss.

Available-for-Sale (AFS) Investments

AFS investments are debt and equity securities that are not classified as held-to-maturity or at fair value through profit or loss.

Under **IFRS**:
- AFS investments are initially recognized at fair value, and remeasured at each reporting date to reflect fair value.
- All unrealized gains/losses (except for gains/losses on AFS **debt** securities arising from exchange rate movements) are recognized (net of taxes) in equity under other comprehensive income. When they are sold, these (now realized) gains/losses are reversed out of other comprehensive income and reported in profit or loss as a reclassification adjustment.
- Unrealized gains/losses on AFS **debt** securities resulting from exchange rate movements are recognized on the income statement.
- Realized gains/losses, interest income and dividend income are also recognized on the income statement.

The accounting treatment of AFS securities is the same under **U.S. GAAP**, except that **all unrealized gains/losses** (including those on AFS debt securities caused by exchange rate movements) are reported in other comprehensive income.

Loans and Receivables

- IFRS has a **specific** definition for loans and receivables. Items that meet the definition are carried at amortized cost unless they are designated as (1) fair value through profit or loss or (2) available for sale.
- U.S. GAAP relies on **legal** form for the classification of debt securities. Loans and receivables that meet the definition of debt securities are classified as HFT, AFS or HTM, with HFT and AFS securities being measured at fair value.

Reclassification of Investments

Under **IFRS**:
- Reclassification of securities into and out of the "designated at fair value" category is generally prohibited.
- Reclassification out of the "held-for-trading" category is restricted.
- HTM (debt) securities can be reclassified as AFS securities if there is a change in intention or ability to hold the asset until maturity.
    - When HTM securities are reclassified as AFS securities, they are remeasured at fair value and any differences between fair value and carrying amount (amortized cost) are recognized in OCI.
    - Once a company has reclassified HTM securities, it may be prohibited from using the HTM classification for other existing debt securities and new purchases.
- Debt securities initially classified as AFS can be reclassified as HTM securities if there is a change in intention or ability to hold the asset until maturity.
    - When AFS debt securities are reclassified as HTM securities, their fair value at time of reclassification becomes their (new) amortized cost and any unrealized gains/losses previously recognized in OCI are amortized to profit or loss over the security's remaining life using the effective interest method.
    - Differences between the new amortized cost and par (maturity) value are also amortized over the remaining term of the securities using the effective interest method.
- Debt instruments may be reclassified from HFT or AFS to loans and receivables if (1) the definition is met; and (2) the company expects to hold them for the forseeable future.
- An investment classified as AFS may be measured at **cost** if there is no reliable measure of fair value and no evidence of impairment.
    - Note that once a reliable fair value estimate becomes available, the asset must be remeasured at fair value and any changes in value must be recognized in other comprehensive income.

U.S. GAAP generally allows reclassifications of securities between all categories when justified, with fair values being determined at the transfer date. However, if HTM securities are reclassified, the company may be precluded from using the HTM category for other investments.

The treatment of unrealized gains/losses on the transfer date depends on security's initial classification.
- For HFT securities that are being reclassified as AFS securities, any unrealized gains/ losses (differences between carrying value and current fair value) have already been recognized in profit and loss.

- When securities are reclassified as HFT securities, any unrealized gains/losses are recognized immediately in profit and loss.
    - When AFS securities are reclassified as HFT, the cumulative amount of unrealized gains/losses previously recognized in other comprehensive income is recognized in profit and loss on the date of transfer.
- When HTM securities are reclassified as AFS, unrealized gains/losses (differences between fair value and amortized cost) at the date of the transfer are reported in other comprehensive income.
- When AFS debt securities are reclassified as HTM, the cumulative amount of unrealized gains/losses that have been recognized in other comprehensive income are amortized over the security's remaining life as an adjustment of yield (interest income) in the same manner as a premium or discount.

Impairments

Under **IFRS**, at the end of each reporting period, all financial assets that are not carried at fair value must be assessed for impairment, and any current impairment must be recognized in profit or loss immediately. Securities classified as fair value through profit or loss are reported at fair value so any impairment losses have already been recognized in profit or loss.

A **debt** security is considered impaired if at least one loss event (which has an impact on its estimated future cash flows that can be reliably estimated) has occurred.

An **equity** security is considered impaired if:
- There has been a substantial and extended decline in the fair value of the security below its cost.
- There have been significant changes in the technology, market, and/or legal environment that have had an adverse impact on the investee, and indicate that the initial cost of the investment may not be recovered.

For (1) HTM (debt) securities; and (2) loans and receivables that have become impaired, the impairment loss is calculated as the difference between the security's carrying value and the present value of its expected future cash flows discounted at the initial effective interest rate.
- The carrying amount of the security is reduced either directly, or indirectly through an allowance account.
- The impairment loss is recognized in profit or loss.
- Reversals of previously-recognized impairment losses are allowed.
- A reversal of a previously-recognized impairment charge results in an increase in the carrying value of the asset and an increase in net income.

For AFS securities that have become impaired, the cumulative loss recognized in other comprehensive income (as the security is remeasured at fair value at each successive reporting date) is transferred from other comprehensive income to the income statement as a reclassification adjustment.
- Reversal of impairment losses is only allowed for AFS debt securities, not for AFS equity securities.
- The amount of reversal is recognized in profit or loss.

Under **U.S. GAAP**, AFS and HTM securities must be assessed for impairment at each balance sheet date. A security is considered impaired if the decline in its value is "other than temporary".

For debt securities classified as HTM, impairment means that the investor will be unable to collect all amounts owed according to contractual terms at acquisition.
- If the decline in fair value is deemed other than temporary, the cost basis of the securities is written down to their fair value, which then becomes the new cost basis.
- The impairment loss is treated as a realized loss on the income statement.

For AFS debt and equity securities:
- If the decline in fair value is deemed other than temporary, the cost basis of the securities is written down to their fair value, which then becomes the new cost basis.
- The impairment loss is treated as a realized loss on the income statement.
- However, the new cost basis cannot be increased if there is a subsequent increase in fair value i.e., reversals of impairment losses are not allowed.
- Subsequent increases in fair value (and decreases, of other than temporary) are treated as unrealized gains and included in other comprehensive income.

IAS 9 (AS OF DECEMBER 2012)

- The IASB has issued the first phase of their project dealing with classification and measurement of financial instruments by including relevant chapters in IFRS 9, which will take effect on 1 January 2015, but can be adopted early.
- When all phases of the project are complete this standard is expected to replace IAS 39.

Classification and Measurement of Financial Assets under IAS 9

All financial assets are measured at fair value when initially acquired. Subsequently, financial assets are measured at either fair value or amortized cost.

Debt instruments that meet the following two criteria are generally measured at amortized cost.
- The financial assets are being held to collect contractual cash flows (known as the business model test); and
- The contractual cash flows are solely payments of principal and interest on principal (known as the cash flow characteristic test).

Note that management may still choose to classify those debt instruments (that meet the above criteria) as fair value through profit or loss to avoid an "accounting mismatch". An accounting mismatch is an inconsistency resulting from different measurement bases for assets and liabilities.

Equity instruments are measured at fair value through profit or loss (FVPL) or at fair value through other comprehensive income (FVOCI).
- Equity investments **held-for-trading** must be measured at fair value through profit or loss (FVPL).
- Other equity investments can be measured at FVPL or FVOCI, but the choice is irrevocable.
- The terms available-for-sale and held-to-maturity no longer appear in IFRS 9.

Financial assets that are **derivatives** are measured at fair value through profit or loss (except for hedging instruments).

Reclassification of Investments

Under the new standards:

- Reclassification of **equity** instruments is not permitted (the initial classification as FVPL and FVOCI is irrevocable).
- Reclassification of **debt** instruments from FVPL to amortized cost (or vice versa) is only permitted if the objective for holding the assets (business model) has changed in a way that significantly affects operations.
  - When reclassification is deemed appropriate, there is no restatement of prior periods at the reclassification date.
  - If the financial asset is reclassified from amortized cost to FVPL, the asset is measured at fair value with gain or loss recognized in profit or loss.
  - If the financial asset is reclassified from FVPL to amortized cost, the fair value at the reclassification date becomes the carrying amount.

Analysis of Investments in Financial Assets

- Analysis of operating performance should exclude items related to investing activities (e.g. interest income, dividends, realized and unrealized gains/losses).
- Non-operating assets should be excluded from the calculation of return on operating assets.
- Use of market values of financial assets is encouraged when assessing performance ratios.

INVESTMENTS IN ASSOCIATES

Equity Method of Accounting

This method is used when the investor exercises significant influence, but not control over the investee.

- The investment is initially recognized on the investor's **balance sheet** at cost (within a single line item) under non-current assets.
  - The investor's proportionate share of investee earnings increases the carrying amount of the investment, while its proportionate share of losses and dividends decreases the carrying value of the investment.
- The investor's proportionate share of investee earnings is reported within a single line item on its **income statement**.
- If the value of the investment falls to zero (e.g. due to losses), use of the equity method to account for the investment is discontinued.
  - Use of the equity method may only be resumed if the investee subsequently reports profits and the investor's share of profits exceeds the losses not reported by it since abandonment of the equity method.

Excess of Purchase Price over Book Value and Amortization of Excess Purchase Price

- The excess amount is first allocated to specific assets whose fair value exceeds book value.
  - The excess related to inventory is expensed, while the excess related to PP&E is depreciated or amortized over an appropriate period of time.
  - Amounts allocated to land and other assets or liabilities that are not amortized continue to be reported at fair value as of the date of investment.
  - Since these expenses are not reflected in the investee's financials, the investor directly adjusts the carrying amount of the investment on its balance sheet by reducing its share of investee profits on the income statement.
- The remaining amount is treated as goodwill, which is not amortized but reviewed periodically for impairment.

Fair Value Option

Both U.S. GAAP and IFRS (with certain restrictions) now offer investors the option to account for their equity method investments using fair values. When the fair value method is applied:
- Unrealized gains/losses arising from changes in fair value, as well as interest and dividends received are included in the investor's income.
- The investment account on the investor's balance sheet does not reflect the investor's proportionate share in the investee's earnings, dividends, or other distributions.
- The excess of cost over the fair value of the investee's identifiable net assets is not amortized.
- Goodwill is not created.

Impairment

Under both IFRS and U.S. GAAP, equity method investments should be reviewed periodically for impairment. Since goodwill is included in the carrying amount of the investment (i.e. it is not separately recognized) under the equity method, it is not tested for impairment separately.
- Under IFRS, an impairment loss is recognized if there is objective evidence of a loss event and the recoverable amount of the investment is less than the carrying amount.
  - Recoverable amount is the higher of "value in use" and "net selling price".
- Under U.S. GAAP, an impairment loss is recognized if the fair value of the investment is less than the carrying amount and the decline is deemed to be permanent.
- Impairment results in a decrease in net income and reduces the investment's carrying amount on the balance sheet.
- Both IFRS and U.S.GAAP prohibit reversals of impairment losses.

Transactions with Associates

Profits from transactions between the investor and investee must be deferred until the profit is confirmed through use or sale to a third party.

Upstream sales (investee to investor): The profits on these sales are recognized on the investee's income statement, so a proportionate share of these profits is also included in the investor's income statement. Until these profits are confirmed, the investor must reduce its equity income by the amount of its **proportionate share** in profits from upstream sales. The investor may recognize these profits once they are confirmed.

Downstream sales (investor to investee): Associated profits are recognized on the investor's income statement. The investor's **proportionate share** in unconfirmed profits from sales made to the investee must be eliminated from the investor's equity income.

Analytical Issues

- Is use of the equity method of accounting appropriate given the ownership stake and degree of influence enjoyed by the investor over the investee?
- One-line consolidation results in significant assets and liabilities not being reported on the investor's balance sheet, which can distort debt ratios.
- Margin ratios may be overstated as a proportionate share of investee net income is included on the investor's income statement, but investee sales are not included.
- Earnings may be permanently reinvested. Earnings may not be available to the investor to the full extent of the investor's proportionate share in the investee's earnings.

JOINT VENTURES

A joint venture is a venture undertaken and controlled by two or more parties. IFRS identifies the following characteristics of joint ventures:

- A contractual agreement exists between two or more venturers; and
- The contractual arrangement establishes joint control.

Both **IFRS** and **U.S. GAAP** now require the use of the equity method to account for joint ventures.

BUSINESS COMBINATIONS

- IFRS does not differentiate between business combinations based on the structure of the surviving entity.
- U.S. GAAP categorizes business combinations into the following:
  - Mergers: The acquiring firm absorbs all the assets of the acquired company which ceases to exist. The acquiring firm is the only surviving entity.
  - Acquisitions: Both entities continue to exist, and are connected through a parent-subsidiary relationship.
  - Consolidation: A new entity is formed that absorbs both the companies.

Historically, companies could use the pooling-of-interests method or the purchase method to account for business combinations. However, IFRS and U.S. GAAP now prohibit use of the pooling-of-interests method and require the acquisition method (which has replaced the purchase method).

Pooling of Interests Method (U.S. GAAP) / Uniting of Interests Method (IFRS)

- The assets and liabilities of the two firms are combined using **book values**.
- Operating results for prior periods are combined and presented as if the companies were always combined.
- Fair values play no role in this method and the actual price paid for an acquisition is not evident on the financial statements.

Acquisition Method for Business Combinations

- All the assets, liabilities, revenues and expenses of the acquiree are combined with those of the parent.
    - All identifiable tangible and intangible assets and liabilities of the acquired entity are measured at fair value.
    - The acquirer must also recognize any assets and liabilities that the acquiree has not recognized on its financial statements.
- The acquirer must recognize any contingent liability assumed in the acquisition if (1) it is a present obligation that arises from past events, and (2) it can be measured reliably.
- The acquirer must recognize an indemnification asset if the acquiree contractually indemnifies the acquirer for (1) the outcome of a contingency, (2) an uncertainty related to a specific asset or liability of the acquiree, or (3) against losses above a specified amount on a liability arising from a particular contingency.
- If the purchase price is less than the fair value of the subsidiary's net assets, it is referred to as a bargain acquisition. Both IFRS and U.S. GAAP require the difference between the fair value of the acquired net assets and the purchase price to be recognized immediately as a gain in profit or loss.
- Transactions between the acquirer and acquiree are eliminated.
- The acquiree's shareholders' equity accounts are ignored.

Business Combinations with Less than 100 Percent Acquisition

If a parent controls a subsidiary, but owns less than a 100% equity interest in the company, it must also create a non-controlling interest account on the consolidated balance sheet and income statement to reflect the proportionate share in the net assets and net income of the subsidiary that belongs to minority shareholders.

Measuring Goodwill and Non-Controlling (Minority) Interests

U.S. GAAP requires the use of the full goodwill method, in which goodwill equals the excess of the **total fair value of the subsidiary** over the **fair value of its identifiable net assets**.

IFRS permits both the full goodwill method and the partial goodwill method. Under the partial goodwill method, goodwill equals the excess of the **purchase price** over the **fair value of the parent's proportionate share of the subsidiary's identifiable net assets**.

- If the full goodwill method is used, the non-controlling interest is measured based on its **proportionate share of the subsidiary's fair value**.
- If the partial goodwill method is used, the non-controlling interest is measured based on its **proportionate share of the fair value of the subsidiary's identifiable net assets**.
- The income statement is exactly the same under the full and partial goodwill methods.

Full versus Partial Goodwill Methods

Note that although net income is the same, return on assets and return on equity will be *lower* if the full goodwill method is used because it results in higher assets and higher equity than the partial goodwill method. Further, the value of the subsidiary will change over time due to (1) changes in equity or (2) net income. Therefore, the value of non-controlling interest on the consolidated balance sheet will also change.

Impairment of Goodwill

Since goodwill is an intangible asset with an **indefinite** life, it is not amortized. However, goodwill must be tested for impairment at least annually or more frequently if events and circumstances indicate that it may be impaired. Once an impairment charge has been made against goodwill, it cannot subsequently be reversed.

Under **IFRS**:
- At the time of acquisition, the total amount of goodwill recognized is allocated to each of the acquirer's **cash-generating units** that will benefit from the synergies expected from the business combination.
- There is a one-step approach: Goodwill is deemed impaired if the recoverable amount of the cash-generating unit is lower than its carrying amount (including goodwill).
- The impairment loss equals the difference between carrying value and recoverable amount of the unit.
- The impairment loss is first applied to the goodwill of the cash-generating unit. Once this has been reduced to zero, the remaining amount of the loss is allocated to all the other assets in the unit on a pro rata basis.

Under **U.S. GAAP**:
- At the time of acquisition, the total amount of goodwill recognized is allocated to each of the acquirer's **reporting units**.
- There is a two-step approach to goodwill impairment testing.
  - Test for impairment: If the carrying value of the reporting unit (including goodwill) exceeds its fair value, goodwill is deemed to be impaired.
  - Measurement of impairment loss: The impairment loss equals the difference between the implied fair value of the reporting unit's goodwill (implied goodwill) and its carrying amount.
    - Implied goodwill equals the fair value of the unit minus the fair value of the net assets of the unit.
- The impairment loss is applied to the goodwill allocated to the reporting unit. After the reporting unit's goodwill has been eliminated, no adjustments are made to the carrying amounts of the unit's other assets or liabilities.

Under both IFRS and U.S.GAAP, the impairment loss is recognized as a separate line item on the consolidated income statement.

Variable Interest Entities (U.S. GAAP) and Special Purpose Entities (IFRS)

Special purpose entities: Equity investors do not have a controlling financial interest. These entities are established for a particular purpose by the sponsoring company.

In the past, the structure of SPEs allowed sponsoring companies to:
- Avoid disclosures of significant guarantees to debt holders.
- Transfer assets and liabilities to the SPE and record revenues and gains related to these transactions.
- Avoid recognition of assets and liabilities of the SPE on their financial statements.

This resulted in improved asset turnover, higher profitability and lower levels of operating and financial leverage for sponsoring companies.

Now IFRS and U.S. GAAP require sponsoring companies to consolidate the SPE's financials with their own. Further, standards relating to measurement, reporting and disclosure of guarantees have been revised. For example, under U.S. GAAP, the primary beneficiary of a VIE must consolidate it as its subsidiary regardless of how much of an equity investment it has in the VIE.

- The primary beneficiary (which is often the sponsor) is defined as the entity that is (1) expected to absorb the majority of the VIE's expected losses, (2) receive the majority of the VIE's residual returns, (3) or both.
- If one entity will absorb a majority of the VIE's expected losses while another entity will receive a majority of the VIE's expected profits, the entity absorbing a majority of the losses must consolidate the VIE.
- If there are non-controlling interests in the VIE, these would also be shown in the consolidated balance sheet and consolidated income statement of the primary beneficiary.

Securitization of Assets

SPEs are often set up to securitize receivables held by the sponsor. The SPE issues debt to finance the purchase of these receivables from the sponsor, and interest and principal payments to debt holders are made from the cash flow generated from the pool of receivables.

The motivation for the sponsor to sell its accounts receivable to the SPE is to accelerate inflows of cash. However, an important aspect of the arrangement is whether the SPE's debt holders have recourse to the sponsor if sufficient cash is not generated from the pool of receivables. In this case, the transaction is basically just like taking a loan and collateralizing it with the receivables. If the receivables are not entirely realized, the loss is borne by the sponsor.

Adjusted Values Upon Reclassification of Sale of Receivables:

CFO	Lower
CFF	Higher
Total cash flow	Same
Current assets	Higher
Current liabilities	Higher
Current ratio	Lower

(Assuming it was greater than 1)

Table 2: Impact of Different Accounting Methods on Financial Ratios

	Equity Method	Acquisition Method
Leverage	Better (lower) as liabilities are lower and equity is the same	Worse (higher) as liabilities are higher and equity is the same
Net Profit Margin	Better (higher) as sales are lower and net income is the same	Worse (lower) as sales are higher and net income is the same
ROE	Better (higher) as equity is lower and net income is the same	Worse (lower) as equity is higher and net income is the same
ROA	Better (higher) as net income is the same and assets are lower	Worse (lower) as net income is the same and assets are higher

EMPLOYEE COMPENSATION: POST-EMPLOYMENT AND SHARE-BASED
Cross-Reference to CFA Institute Assigned Reading #18

Types of Post-Employment Benefits

Type of Benefit	Amount of Post-Employment Benefit to Employee	Obligation of Sponsoring Company	Sponsoring Company's Pre-funding of Its Future Obligation
Defined contribution pension plan	Amount of future benefit is not defined. Actual future benefit will depend on investment performance of plan assets. Investment risk is borne by employee.	Amount of the company's obligation (contribution) is defined in each period. The contribution, if any, is typically made on a periodic basis with no additional future obligation.	Not applicable.
Defined benefit pension plan	Amount of future benefit is defined, based on the plan's formula (often a function of length of service and final year's compensation). Investment risk is borne by company.	Amount of the future obligation, based on the plan's formula, must be estimated in the current period.	Companies typically pre-fund the DB plans by contributing funds to a pension trust. Regulatory requirements to pre-fund vary by country.
Other post-employment benefits (e.g., retirees' health care)	Amount of future benefit depends on plan specifications and type of benefit.	Eventual benefits are specified. The amount of the future obligation must be estimated in the current period.	Companies typically do not pre-fund other post-employment benefit obligations.

Measuring a Defined Benefit Pension Plan's Obligations

Under both IFRS and U.S. GAAP, a company's projected benefit obligation (PBO) is measured as the present value of all future benefits that its employees are entitled to (or have earned) for services provided to date.

Computing the pension obligation requires a company to make several estimates including:

- Future compensation increases and levels as they directly influence the dollar amount of the annual pension payment owed to an employee upon retirement.
- The discount rate, which is used to determine the present value of pension payments that must be paid in the future. The greater the discount rate, the lower the pension obligation (present value of promised future payments).

- The probability that some employees will not satisfy the company's vesting requirements.
  - If the employee leaves the company before satisfying these requirements, she would be entitled to none or only a portion of the benefits earned to date.
  - If the employee leaves the company after satisfying these requirements, she would be entitled to receive all the benefits earned to date.

Items that Directly Influence the Amount of a Company's Pension Obligation

- Current service costs refer to the increase in the present value of pension obligation as a result of an employee's service in the current period.
- Interest expense refers to accrued interest, or the increase in the value of the pension obligation (which represents the PV of promised payments) due to the passage of time.
- Past service costs (PSC)/ prior service costs refer to the increase in the pension obligation from retroactive benefits given to employees for years of service provided before the date of adoption or amendment of the plan.
- Changes in actuarial assumptions (e.g. discount rate, future compensation increases, life expectancy) result in changes in the value of pension obligation.
  - A change in actuarial assumptions that results in an increase in the pension obligation is an actuarial loss.
  - A change in actuarial assumptions that results in a decrease in the pension obligation is an actuarial gain.
- Benefits paid by the company decrease the pension obligation.

Items that Increase the Pension Obligation

- Current service costs.
- Interest costs accrued on the pension obligation.
- Prior service costs from plan amendments.
- Actuarial losses.

Items that Decrease the Pension Obligation

- Actuarial gains.
- Benefits paid.

Reconciling Beginning and Ending Pension Obligation

Pension obligation at the beginning of the period
+ Current service costs
+ Interest costs
+ Prior service costs
+ Actuarial losses
− Actuarial gains
− Benefits paid
Pension obligation at the end of the period

Measuring a Defined Benefit Pension Plan's Assets

The fair value of assets held in the plan will increase as a result of:
- A positive actual dollar return earned on plan assets; and
- Contributions made by the employer to the plan.

On the other hand, the fair value of plan assets will decrease when benefits are paid to employees.

Reconciling Beginning and Ending Balances of the Fair Value of Plan Assets

Fair value of plan assets at the beginning of the period
+ Actual return on plan assets
+ Contributions made by the employer to the plan
− Benefits paid to employees
Fair value of plan assets at the end of the period

Balance Sheet Presentation of Defined Benefit Pension Plans

Under **IFRS** and **U.S. GAAP**, the defined benefit liability (or asset) reported on the balance sheet equals the pension plan's **funded status (FS)**. The funded status equals the difference between the pension obligation (PO) and the fair value of plan assets (FVPA), so it represents a net amount.

- If the pension obligation is greater than the fair value of plan assets, the plan is said to be underfunded, and a **net pension liability** equal to the *positive difference* is recognized on the balance sheet.
- If the pension obligation is less than the fair value of plan assets, the plan is said to be overfunded, and a **net pension asset** equal to the *negative difference* is recognized on the balance sheet.
  - Note that the amount of net pension asset reported is subject to a **ceiling** equal to the present value of future economic benefits, such as refunds from the plan or reductions of future contributions.

It is very important that you understand that we compute the funded status as the PV of pension obligation minus the FV of plan assets. Therefore, a positive funded status represents a net pension liability (underfunded plan). This is why our formula for periodic pension cost is different from the curriculum's.

You can solve questions on this topic either way. Just remember that if you are using our formulas, you should treat a positive funded status as a liability, and that if you use the curriculum's formulas, you treat a positive funded status as a net asset.
- If Pension obligation > Fair value of plan assets:
    Plan is underfunded → Positive funded status → Net pension liability.
- If Pension obligation < Fair value of plan assets:
    Plan is overfunded → Negative funded status → Net pension asset.

Net Pension Liability (Asset)

The **net pension liability (asset)** is calculated as **pension obligation** minus the **fair value of plan assets**.

Periodic Pension Cost versus Periodic Pension Expense

- **Periodic pension cost** is the total cost related to a company's DB pension plan for a given period. Various components of this total cost can be recognized on the profit and loss (P&L) or in other comprehensive income (OCI) under IFRS and U.S. GAAP.
- **Periodic pension expense** refers to the components of periodic pension cost that are recognized on the P&L (not OCI).

PERIODIC PENSION COST

Calculating Periodic Pension Cost

There are two approaches to calculating periodic pension cost. Further, for a particular company over a given period, periodic pension cost would come to the same amount whether it subscribes to IFRS or to U.S. GAAP when preparing its financial statements.

Approach 1: Adjusting the Change in Net Pension Liability (Asset) for Employer Contributions

The periodic cost of a company's DB pension plan equals the change in the net pension liability/asset excluding the effects of employer contributions to the plan.

$$\text{Net periodic pension cost} = \text{Ending net pension liability} - \text{Beginning net pension liability} + \text{Employer contributions}$$

- An increase in net pension liability or a decrease in net pension asset over the reporting period entails a pension-related cost for the company.
- A decrease in net pension liability or an increase in net pension asset over the reporting period results in a pension-related benefit for the company.

Approach 2: Aggregating Periodic Components of Cost

The components of periodic pension cost are basically items that result in changes in the funded status (net pension liability or asset) other than employer contributions. Changes in the funded status come from (1) changes in the pension obligation and/or (2) changes in the fair value of plan assets.

Changes in the pension obligation are caused by:
- Economic expenses for the period. These include:
  - Current service costs
  - Interest costs
  - Past service costs
  - Actuarial losses (gains)
- Benefits paid to employees.

Changes in the fair value of plan assets are caused by:
- The actual return on plan assets.
- Benefits paid to employees.
- Employer contributions.

Benefits paid to employees reduce the pension obligation and the fair value of plan assets so they have no impact on the overall funded status. Therefore, the periodic pension cost of a company's DB pension plan equals the increase in the pension obligation (excluding the impact of benefits paid to employees) minus actual earnings on plan assets.

$$\text{Periodic pension cost} = \text{Current service costs} + \text{Interest costs} + \text{Past service costs}$$
$$+ \text{Actuarial losses} - \text{Actuarial gains} - \text{Actual return on plan assets}$$

Periodic Pension Cost Under IFRS and U.S. GAAP

While total periodic pension cost is the same under IFRS and U.S. GAAP, the manner in which total pension cost is divided between the P&L and OCI is different under the two sets of standards.

Under **IFRS**, periodic pension cost is divided into three components. Two of them are recognized in P&L, while one is recognized in OCI.

1. Service costs: Both current and past service costs are recognized as an expense on the P&L under IFRS.
2. Net interest expense/income: Net interest expense/income is also recognized on the P&L under IFRS.

$$\text{Net interest expense (income)} = \text{Net pension liability (asset)} \times \text{Discount rate}$$
$$= (\text{Pension obligation} - \text{Fair value of plan assets}) \times r$$
$$= \text{Pension obligation} \times r - \text{Fair value of plan assets} \times r$$

3. Remeasurement: This component of periodic pension cost is recognized in OCI under IFRS. Further, remeasurement amounts are **not subsequently amortized** into P&L. Remeasurement of the net pension liability/asset includes:
   - Actuarial gains and losses.
   - The difference between the actual return on plan assets and the return on plan assets (based on the discount rate, r) that has already been accounted for in the calculation of net interest expense/income.
     - Actual return on plan assets − (Fair value of plan assets × r)

Contrasting U.S. GAAP Treatment of Periodic Pension Cost with IFRS Treatment

Under U.S. GAAP:
- Service costs are recognized in P&L. However, past service costs are reported in OCI in the period during which the change that gave rise to the costs occurred. In subsequent years, these past service costs are amortized to P&L over the average service lives of affected employees. Under IFRS, past service costs are also recognized on the P&L as *pension expense* for the period.
- Periodic pension cost includes interest expense on pension obligations (which increases pension cost) and returns on plan assets (which decrease pension cost). However, unlike IFRS:
  - These two components are not presented in a single net amount. The second component of pension cost under IFRS i.e., net interest expense/income, represents a single net amount.
  - The return on plan assets is calculated based on an assumed expected return on plan assets. The difference between the actual return and the expected return on plan assets is *another* source (in addition to changes in assumptions that determine the value of the pension obligation e.g. discount rate and life expectancy) of actuarial gains and losses under U.S. GAAP.

Note that generally speaking, actuarial gains and losses have an impact on the pension obligation and the funded status. However, this **additional** source of actuarial gains and losses under U.S. GAAP (from differences between actual and expected returns on plan assets) does **not** have an impact on the plan's funded status.

- All actuarial gains and losses can be reported either in P&L or in OCI. Typically, companies report actuarial gains and losses in OCI and recognize gains and losses in P&L by applying the corridor method. Under IFRS, actuarial gains and losses are a part of the remeasurement component, which is never amortized into P&L from OCI.

Under the **corridor method**, if the net cumulative amount of unrecognized actuarial gains and losses at the beginning of the reporting period exceeds 10% of the greater of (1) the defined benefit obligation or (2) the fair value of plan assets, then the *excess* is amortized over the expected average remaining working lives of the employees participating in the plan and included as a component of periodic *pension expense* on the P&L.

Table 1: Components of a Company's Defined Benefit Pension Periodic Costs

IFRS Component	IFRS Recognition	U.S. GAAP Component	U.S. GAAP Recognition
Service costs	Recognized in P&L.	Current service costs Past service costs	Recognized in P&L. Recognized in OCI and subsequently amortized to P&L over the service life of employees.
Net interest income/ expense	Recognized in P&L as the following amount: Net pension liability or asset × interest rate[a]	Interest expense on pension obligation Expected return on plan assets	Recognized in P&L. Recognized in P&L as the following amount: Plan assets × expected return.
Remeasurements: Net return on plan assets and actuarial gains and losses	Recognized in OCI and <u>not</u> subsequently amortized to P&L. - Net return on plan **assets** = Actual return – (Plan assets × Interest rate). - Actuarial gains and losses = Changes in a company's pension obligation arising from changes in actuarial assumptions.	Actuarial gains and losses including differences between the actual and expected returns on plan assets	Recognized immediately in P&L or, more commonly, recognized in OCI and subsequently amortized to P&L using the corridor or faster recognition method.[b] - Difference between expected and actual return on assets = Actual return – (Plan assets × Expected return). - Actuarial gains and losses = Changes in a company's pension obligation arising from changes in actuarial assumptions.

(a) The interest rate used is equal to the discount rate used to measure the pension liability (the yield on high-quality corporate bonds.)

(b) If the cumulative amount of unrecognized actuarial gains and losses exceeds 10 percent of the greater of the value of the plan assets or of the present value of the DB obligation (under U.S. GAAP, the projected benefit obligation), the difference must be amortized over the service lives of the employees.

Reporting the Periodic Pension Cost

For pension costs that are not capitalized (e.g. certain costs recorded in inventory as mentioned earlier):

- **IFRS** only differentiates between components included in P&L and in OCI. It does not specify where exactly the various components of pension cost must be presented.
- **U.S. GAAP** also differentiates between components included in P&L and in OCI. Further, it requires all components of pension expense recognized in P&L to be aggregated and presented within one net line item on the income statement.

Note that both IFRS and U.S. GAAP require total periodic pension cost to be disclosed in the notes to the financial statements.

Effects of Changes in Key Assumptions

The Discount Rate

An increase in the assumed discount rate:
- Decreases the opening pension obligation (as the PV of promised payments decreases).
- Typically decreases total periodic pension cost.
- Typically decreases the closing pension obligation.

Compensation Growth Rate

If the pension formula is based on the final year's salary, an increase in the assumed rate of growth in compensation:
- Increases the pension obligation.
- Increases periodic pension cost.

Expected Return on Plan Assets

Under U.S. GAAP, the expected return on plan assets reduces the periodic *pension expense*. An increase in the assumed expected return on plan assets:
- Has no impact on a company's net pension liability (funded status) reported on the balance sheet.
- Decreases the company's *pension expense* (under U.S. GAAP). Note that total periodic pension cost is not affected by a change in the expected return on plan assets.

Expected Life Expectancy

If, under the terms of the plan, the sponsoring company must make pension payments to employees until their death, an increase in assumed life expectancy will result in an increase in the annual unit credit and the pension obligation. Further, service costs and interest costs will also increase so periodic pension cost will rise.

Table 2: Impact of Key Assumptions on Net Pension Liability and Periodic Pension Cost

Assumption	Impact of Assumption on Net Pension Liability (Asset)	Impact of Assumption on Periodic Pension Cost and Pension Expense
Higher discount rate	Lower obligation	Pension cost and pension expense will both typically be lower because of lower opening obligation and lower service costs
Higher rate of compensation increase	Higher obligation	Higher service and interest costs will increase periodic pension cost and pension expense
Higher expected return on plan assets	No effect, because fair value of plan assets are used on balance sheet	Not applicable for IFRS No effect on periodic pension cost under U.S. GAAP Lower periodic pension expense under U.S. GAAP

Disclosures of Pension and Other Post-Employment Benefits

When comparing financial results of different companies using ratios, analysts should consider the impact of pensions and other post-employment benefits on the financial statements. Comparisons across companies can be affected by:

- Differences in key assumptions.
- Amounts reported on the balance sheet at net amounts (net pension liability or asset). Adjustments to incorporate gross amounts would impact financial ratios.
- Non-comparability of periodic pension *expense*. Pension expense may not be comparable as IFRS and U.S. GAAP differ with regards to how periodic pension costs can be recognized on the P&L vs. OCI.
- Differences across IFRS and U.S. GAAP regarding the reporting of components of pension expense on the income statement.
- Differences across IFRS and U.S. GAAP regarding the classification of pension contributions on the cash flow statement. Under IFRS, a portion of contributions may be treated as financing cash flows rather than operating cash flows. Under U.S. GAAP, all contributions are treated as operating cash flows.

Assumptions

Companies disclose their assumptions about discount rates, expected compensation increases, medical expense inflation rates and (for U.S. GAAP companies) expected return on plan assets. Analysts should examine these assumptions over time and across companies to assess whether a company is becoming increasingly conservative or aggressive in accounting for its DB obligations. A company could employ aggressive pension-related assumptions to improve reported financial performance by assuming:
- A higher discount rate.
- A lower compensation growth rate.
- A higher expected rate of return on plan assets.

Accounting for other post-employment benefits also requires companies to make several assumptions. All other things constant, each of the following assumptions will lead to an increase in the company's medical obligation and associated periodic cost:

- A higher health care inflation rate.
- A longer life expectancy.
- A higher ultimate health care trend rate.
- A longer time to reach the ultimate health care trend rate.

Periodic Pension Costs Recognized in P&L vs. OCI

Total periodic pension cost recognized under IFRS and U.S. GAAP is the same. However, the two sets of standards differ in their provisions regarding which components are recognized in P&L and which ones are recognized in OCI. These differences are important for analysts when evaluating companies that use different sets of standards.

- Under IFRS, current and past service costs are recognized in P&L. Under U.S. GAAP, the P&L only reflects current service costs (and amortization of any past service costs).
- Under IFRS, pension expense on the P&L incorporates a return on plan assets equal to the discount rate (used for measuring the pension obligation) times the value of plan assets. Under U.S. GAAP, pension expense on the P&L incorporates a return on plan assets equal to an estimated rate of return on plan assets times the value of plan assets.
- Under IFRS, the P&L would never show amortization of pension-related amounts previously recognized in OCI. Under U.S. GAAP, the P&L would reflect amortization of any past service costs, and may reflect amortization of actuarial gains and losses if they were initially recorded in OCI and if the "corridor" has been exceeded.

An analyst comparing the financial statements of a company that follows IFRS to one that follows U.S. GAAP would have to make adjustments to reported amounts to achieve comparability. To make a U.S. GAAP-following company's P&L comparable to the P&L of a company following IFRS, she would:

- Include past service costs on the P&L as pension expense.
- Exclude the effects of amortization of past service costs arising in previous periods.
- Exclude the effects of amortization of unrecognized actuarial gains and losses arising in previous periods.
- Incorporate the effects of the expected return on plan assets based on the discount rate (rather than the expected rate).

Alternatively, she could use total periodic pension cost as the basis for comparison by focusing on comprehensive income (which includes net income and other comprehensive income).

Classification of Periodic Pension Costs Recognized in P&L

Analysts should make the following adjustments to reflect a company's operating performance more accurately on the income statement:

1. Add back the entire amount of pension costs recognized on the P&L (pension expense) to operating income.
2. Subtract service costs before determining operating profit.
3. Add the interest component of pension expense to the company's interest expense.
4. Add the return on plan assets to non-operating income.

Further, analysts may also make adjustments to reflect the actual return on plan assets. Recall that:

- Under IFRS, net interest expense/income on the P&L incorporates a return on plan assets based on the discount rate. The difference between this return and the actual return is a part of remeasurement, which is included in OCI.
- Under U.S. GAAP, pension expense incorporates a return on plan assets based on an expected rate of return assumption. The difference between the actual and expected return is a source of actuarial gains (losses), which are typically initially reported in OCI.

Note that adjusting the P&L to incorporate the actual return on plan assets introduces an element of volatility in net income. However, reclassification of interest expense has no impact on net income.

Cash Flow Information

For a funded plan, the impact of the plan on the sponsoring company's cash flows is the amount of contributions the company makes to fund the plan. For an unfunded plan, the impact of the plan on the sponsoring company's cash flows is the amount of benefits paid. Note that in both cases, these cash flows are usually classified as operating cash flows. From an economic perspective however, classification of employer contributions to DB pension plans depends on how they relate to total pension costs for the period.

- If a company's contribution to the plan over the period is greater than total pension cost for the period, the excess may be viewed as a reduction in the overall pension obligation.
- If a company's contribution to the plan over the period is lower than total pension cost for the period, the shortfall results in an increase in the overall pension obligation.

If the amount of pension obligation is material, analysts may choose to reclassify the excess (shortfall) in contributions as a use (source) of cash from financing activities rather than operating activities.

Share-Based Compensation

Advantages
- Aligns interests of management along with those of shareholders.
- Requires no cash outlays.

Disadvantages
- The employee may have limited influence on the company's market value.
- Increased ownership may make management more risk averse.
- The option-like payoff may make management take excessive risks.
- Ownership dilution.

Accounting for Share-Based Compensation

- Both IFRS and U.S. GAAP require companies to **measure** share-based compensation expense based on the **fair value** of the compensation granted.
- Both IFRS and U.S. GAAP require companies to **disclose** the following:
  - The nature and extent of share-based compensation for the period.

- The basis for determining the fair value of share-based compensation over the period.
    - The effects of share-based compensation on the company's net income for the period and its financial position.
- As far as **accounting** for share-based compensation is concerned, the specifics depend on the type of compensation.

Stock Grants

Stock grants include outright stock grants, restricted stock grants and performance shares. Compensation expense equals the fair value (typically market value) of the shares issued and is allocated over the employee's service period.

Stock Options

Compensation expense for stock options issued is also measured at fair value (as opposed to intrinsic value, which would result in lower reported compensation expense). Fair value of employee stock options must be estimated because they contain features that make them different from traded options.

- Assumptions of higher volatility, longer estimated life, lower dividend yield and higher risk-free rate increase the estimated fair value of employee stock options.
- If the number of shares and option price are known, compensation expense is measured at the grant date.
- If the fair value of options depends on events after the grant date, compensation expense is measured at the exercise date.

Accounting for Compensation Expense Related to Stock Options

- If stock options vest immediately, the entire cost (fair value) of options awarded is recognized on the grant date (in the current period).
- If stock options vest after a specified service period, compensation expense is allocated over the service period.
- If vesting of stock options is conditional (e.g. upon a target share price being reached), compensation expense is recognized over the estimated service period.

Stock Appreciation Rights (SARs)

SARs compensate employees based on the changes in the value of the company's shares without requiring employees to actually hold the shares.

- The potential for risk aversion is limited as SARs holders have asymmetrical upside and downside potential.
- Share ownership is not diluted.
- They require a current period cash outflow
- Compensation expense is measured at fair value and allocated over the service life of the employee.

Phantom Shares

Compensation expense is based on the performance of hypothetical stock rather than the company's actual stock. They can be used by private companies and highly illiquid companies.

MULTINATIONAL OPERATIONS
Cross-Reference to CFA Institute Assigned Reading #19

Definitions

- The presentation currency (PC) is the currency in which the parent company reports its financial statements. It is typically the currency of the country where the parent is located.
- The functional currency (FC) is the currency of the primary business environment in which an entity operates. It is usually the currency in which the entity primarily generates and expends cash.
- The local currency (LC) is the currency of the country where the subsidiary operates.

Foreign Currency Transaction Exposure to Foreign Exchange Risk

- For an import purchase, foreign exchange transaction exposure for the importing company arises when it defers a payment that must be made in foreign currency. The importer faces the risk that the value of the foreign currency will increase between the purchase date and the settlement date. Appreciation of the foreign currency would mean that the importer will have to spend more units of domestic currency to purchase the required amount of foreign currency to settle the obligation.

- For an export sale, foreign exchange transaction exposure for the exporting company arises when it allows the purchaser to make the payment sometime after the purchase date and agrees to be paid in foreign currency. The exporter faces the risk that the value of the foreign currency will decrease between the date of sale and the settlement date. Depreciation of the foreign currency would mean that the exporter will receive a lower number of units of domestic currency upon converting the foreign currency amount when it is received.

Note that foreign currency transaction risk only arises when the payment and settlement dates are different.

Both, U.S. GAAP and IFRS require that changes in the value of a foreign currency asset/liability resulting from a foreign currency transaction be recognized as gains/losses on the income statement. The exact amount of gains/losses recognized depends on:
- Whether the company has an asset or a liability that is exposed to foreign exchange risk.
- Whether the foreign currency increases or decreases in value versus the domestic currency.

Transaction	Type of Exposure	Foreign Currency	
		Strengthens	Weakens
Export sale	Asset (account receivable)	Gain	Loss
Import purchase	Liability (account payable)	Loss	Gain

If the balance sheet date occurs between the transaction date and settlement date, foreign exchange gains/losses are still recognized (based on the difference between the spot rate at transaction date and the exchange rate on the balance sheet date). Once the transaction is settled, additional gains/losses are recognized (based on the difference between the exchange rate at balance sheet date and the exchange rate at settlement date).

Analytical Issues

- The calculation of operating profit margin is affected by where translation gains/losses are recorded on the income statement.
- The eventual translation gain/loss can be different from the amount recognized initially if the balance sheet date lies between the transaction and settlement dates.

Translation of Foreign Currency Financial Statements

- The current rate method (also known as the all-current method) is used to translate financial statements presented in the functional currency (FC) into amounts expressed in the parent's presentation currency (PC).
- The temporal method (also known as remeasurement) is used to translate financial statements presented in local currency (LC) into amounts expressed in the functional currency (FC).

The translation method that applies to a particular situation depends on the entity's functional currency.

- If the local currency is deemed to be the functional currency (LC = FC ≠ PC), the current rate method is used to translate foreign currency financial statements into the parent's presentation currency.
  - Such instances usually arise when the subsidiary is independent and its operating, investing, and financing activities are decentralized from the parent.
- If the presentation currency is deemed to be the functional currency (LC ≠ FC = PC), the temporal method is used to translate foreign currency financial statements into the parent's presentation currency.
  - Such instances usually arise when the subsidiary and parent are well-integrated.
- If local currency, functional currency, and presentation currency are different (LC ≠ FC ≠ PC), then:
  - The temporal method is used to convert local currency amounts into functional currency; and then
  - The current rate method is used to convert functional currency amounts into presentation currency.

Methods for Translating Foreign Currency Financial Statements of Subsidiaries

Current Rate/ Temporal Method	Local Currency	T	Functional Currency	CR	Presentation Currency
Temporal Method	Local Currency	T	Functional Currency	=	Presentation Currency
Current Rate Method	Local Currency	=	Functional Currency	CR	Presentation Currency

The Current Rate Method

- The income statement and statement of retained earnings is translated first, and then the balance sheet is translated.
- All income statement accounts are translated at the historical rate (which for practical purposes is assumed to equal the average rate).
- All balance sheet accounts (except common equity) are translated at the current rate.
- Common equity is translated at the historical rate.
- Dividends are translated at the rate that applied when they were declared.
- The translation gain/loss for the period is included in shareholders' equity under the cumulative translation adjustment (CTA).

The Temporal Method

- The balance sheet is translated first, followed by the income statement and statement of retained earnings.
- Monetary assets and monetary liabilities are translated at the current rate.
  - Monetary assets include cash and receivables.
  - Monetary liabilities include accounts payable, accrued expenses, long-term debt and deferred income taxes. Most liabilities are monetary liabilities.
- Nonmonetary assets and liabilities measured at historical cost are translated at historical rates.
  - Nonmonetary assets measured at historical cost include inventory measured at **cost** under the lower of cost or market rule, PP&E, and intangible assets.
  - Nonmonetary liabilities measured at historical cost include deferred revenue.
- Nonmonetary assets and liabilities measured at current value are translated at the exchange rate that existed when current value was determined.
  - Nonmonetary assets measured at current cost include marketable securities and inventory measured at **market** under the lower of cost or market rule.
- Shareholders' equity accounts are translated at historical rates.
- Revenues and expenses (other than expenses related to nonmonetary assets) are translated at the average rate.
- Expenses related to nonmonetary assets (e.g. COGS, depreciation, and amortization) are translated at historical rates prevailing at time of purchase of the related nonmonetary assets.
- The translation gain/loss is reported on the income statement.

Note that the historical exchange rate used to translate inventory and COGS under the temporal method will differ according to the cost flow assumption (FIFO, LIFO, AVCO) used.
- If FIFO is used:
  - Ending inventory is composed of recent purchases so inventory will be translated at relatively recent exchange rates.
  - Units sold are from the older purchases so COGS will be translated at relatively old exchange rates.
- If LIFO is used:
  - Ending inventory is composed of older purchases so inventory will be translated at relatively old exchange rates.
  - Units sold are from the more recent purchases so COGS will be translated at relatively recent exchange rates.

Differences in the Results of the Temporal and Current Rate Method

- Income before translation gain/loss is different under the two methods.
  - The current rate method uses the average rate for depreciation and COGS.
  - The temporal method uses historical rates.
- The translation gain/loss is different between the two methods.
  - Exposure under the current rate method equals the subsidiaries' net assets.
  - Exposure under the temporal method equals the subsidiaries' net monetary assets.
- Net income is different between the two methods.
  - COGS and depreciation are converted at different rates under the two methods.
  - Under the current rate method, the translation gain/loss is reported in shareholders' equity. Under the temporal method, it is reported on the income statement.
- Total assets are different between the two methods.
  - Inventory and fixed assets are translated at current rates under the current rate method, but at historical rates under the temporal method.

Rules for Foreign Currency Translation

Income Statement Component	Current Rate Method FC = LC	Temporal Method FC = PC
	Exchange Rate Used	
Sales	Average rate	Average rate
Cost of goods sold	Average rate	Historical rate
Selling expenses	Average rate	Average rate
Depreciation expense	Average rate	Historical rate
Amortization expense	Average rate	Historical rate
Interest expense	Average rate	Average rate
Income tax	Average rate	Average rate
Net income before translation gain (loss)		Computed as Rev – Exp
Translation gain (loss)	N/A	Plug in Number
Net income	Computed as Rev – Exp	Computed as ΔRE + Dividends
Less: Dividends	Historical rate	Historical rate
Change in retained earnings	Computed as NI – Dividends Used as input for translated B/S	From B/S

Balance Sheet Component	Current Rate Method FC = LC	Temporal Method FC = PC
	Exchange Rate Used	
Cash	Current rate	Current rate
Accounts receivable	Current rate	Current rate
Monetary assets	Current rate	Current rate
Inventory	Current rate	Historical rate
Nonmonetary assets measured at current value	Current rate	Current rate
Property, plant and equipment	Current rate	Historical rate
Less: Accumulated depreciation	Current rate	Historical rate
Nonmonetary assets measured at historical cost	Current rate	Historical rate
Accounts payable	Current rate	Current rate
Long-term notes payable	Current rate	Current rate
Monetary liabilities	Current rate	Current rate
Nonmonetary liabilities:		
Measured at current value	Current rate	Current rate
Measured at historical cost	Current rate	Historical rate
Capital stock	Historical rate	Historical rate
Retained earnings	From I/S	To balance Used as input for translated I/S
Cumulative translation adjustment	Plug in Number	N/A

Balance Sheet Exposure under the Current Rate and Temporal Methods

Exposure to translation adjustment is referred to as balance sheet translation, or accounting exposure.

- A foreign operation will have a net asset balance sheet exposure when the value of assets translated at the current exchange rate is greater than the value of liabilities translated at the current exchange rate.
- A foreign operation will have a net liability balance sheet exposure when the value of liabilities translated at the current exchange rate is greater than the value of assets translated at the current exchange rate.

Whether the current period's translation adjustment results in a gain or loss depends on (1) the nature of the balance sheet exposure (net asset versus net liability) and (2) the direction of change in the value of the foreign currency (appreciating or depreciating).

	Foreign Currency (FC)	
Balance Sheet Exposure	Strengthens	Weakens
Net asset	Positive translation adjustment	Negative translation adjustment
Net liability	Negative translation adjustment	Positive translation adjustment

Under the current rate method:

- The parent's foreign currency exposure equals its **net asset position** in the subsidiary.
- If the subsidiary has a net asset (liability) exposure, an appreciating foreign currency will result in a translation gain (loss), which will be reflected in an increasing (decreasing) cumulative translation adjustment on the balance sheet.
- The current rate method usually results in a net asset balance sheet exposure (unless the entity has negative shareholders' equity, which is very rare).
- Elimination of balance sheet exposure under the current rate method is rather difficult as it would require total assets to equal total liabilities (or zero shareholders' equity in the foreign subsidiary).

Items Translated at Current Exchange Rate
Total assets > Total Liabilities → Net asset balance sheet exposure

Under the temporal method:

- The parent's exposure is limited to the subsidiary's **net monetary assets (liabilities)**.
- If the subsidiary has a net monetary asset (liability) exposure, an appreciating foreign currency will result in a translation gain (loss) on the income statement.
- Most liabilities are monetary liabilities (which are translated at the current exchange rate and entail exposure to translation adjustment), while most assets are nonmonetary assets (which are translated at historical exchange rates and do not entail exposure to translation adjustment). Therefore, liabilities translated at the current exchange rate usually exceed assets translated at the current exchange rate, which results in a net monetary liability exposure under the temporal method.
- Elimination of balance sheet exposure under the temporal method is relatively easy as the parent simply has to ensure that the monetary assets of the foreign subsidiary equal its monetary liabilities.

Items Translated at Current Exchange Rate
Exposed assets > Exposed liabilities → Net asset balance sheet exposure
Exposed assets < Exposed liabilities → Net liability balance sheet exposure

Financial Statement Ratios (Originally in Local Currency versus Current Rate Method)

- Pure income statement and balance sheet ratio remain unaffected by the method used.
- If the foreign currency is appreciating (depreciating) mixed ratios (based on end-of-year balance sheet values) will be smaller (larger) after translation.

Effects of Direction of Change in the Exchange Rate on Translated Amounts

Current Rate Method

Compared to a scenario where the exchange rate remains stable:
- If the foreign currency appreciates against the parent's presentation currency, revenues, assets, liabilities and total equity reported on the parent's consolidated financial statements will be higher.
- If the foreign currency depreciates against the parent's presentation currency, revenues, assets, liabilities and total equity reported on the parent's consolidated financial statements will be lower.

Temporal Method

Compared to a scenario where the exchange rate remains stable:

- If the foreign currency appreciates against the parent's presentation currency, revenues, assets and liabilities reported on the parent's consolidated financial statements will be higher. However, net income and shareholders' equity will translate into lower amounts (assuming that the subsidiary has a net monetary liability exposure) because of the translation loss.
- If the foreign currency depreciates against the parent's presentation currency, revenues, assets and liabilities reported on the parent's consolidated financial statements will be lower. However, net income and shareholders' equity will translate into higher amounts (assuming that the subsidiary has a net monetary liability exposure) because of the translation gain.

Effects of Exchange Rate Movements on Financial Statements

	Temporal Method, Net Monetary Liability Exposure	**Temporal Method, Net Monetary Asset Exposure**	**Current Rate Method**
Foreign currency strengthens relative to parent's presentation currency	↑ Revenues ↑ Assets ↑ Liabilities ↓ Net income ↓ Shareholders' equity Translation loss	↑ Revenues ↑ Assets ↑ Liabilities ↑ Net income ↑ Shareholders' equity Translation gain	↑ Revenues ↑ Assets ↑ Liabilities ↑ Net income ↑ Shareholders' equity Positive translation adjustment
Foreign currency weakens relative to parent's presentation currency	↓ Revenues ↓ Assets ↓ Liabilities ↑ Net income ↑ Shareholders' equity Translation gain	↓ Revenues ↓ Assets ↓ Liabilities ↓ Net income ↓ Shareholders' equity Translation loss	↓ Revenues ↓ Assets ↓ Liabilities ↓ Net income ↓ Shareholders' equity Negative translation adjustment

Hyperinflationary Economies

- U.S. GAAP defines a high inflationary economy as one where the cumulative three-year inflation rate exceeds 100%, which equates to an average of approximately 26% per year.
- IFRS provides no specific definition of high inflation, but does indicate that a cumulative three-year inflation rate approaching or exceeding 100% indicates high inflation.

Under **U.S. GAAP**, the functional currency is assumed to be the parent's presentation currency and the temporal method is used to translate the subsidiary's financial statements. The translation gain/loss is included in net income.

Under **IFRS**, the subsidiary's foreign currency accounts are restated for inflation (using the procedures described below) and then translated into the parent's presentation currency using the current exchange rate.

- Nonmonetary assets and liabilities are restated for changes in the general purchasing power of the local currency.
  - ○ Nonmonetary items carried at historical cost are restated for inflation by multiplying their values by the change in the general price index from the date of acquisition to the balance sheet date.
  - ○ Nonmonetary items carried at revalued amounts are restated for inflation by multiplying their revised values by the change in the general price index from the date of revaluation to the balance sheet date.
- Monetary assets and liabilities (e.g. cash, receivables and payables) are not restated for inflation.
- Shareholders' equity accounts are restated for inflation by multiplying their values by the change in the general price index from the beginning of the period, or from the date of contribution (if later), till the balance sheet date.
- Income statement items are restated for inflation by multiplying their values by the change in the general price index from the dates when the items were originally recorded to the balance sheet date.
- All items are then translated into the parent's presentation currency using the current exchange rate.
- The gain/loss in purchasing power is recorded on the income statement.

Under this method, a company's net monetary asset (liability) position is exposed to inflation risk as monetary assets and liabilities are not restated for inflation. In an inflationary environment, borrowers (who have payables) gain while lenders (who hold receivables) lose out. Therefore, a company will recognize a purchasing power gain (loss) if it holds more monetary liabilities (assets) than monetary assets (liabilities).

Translation Disclosures and Analysis

Under both IFRS and U.S.GAAP, companies are required to disclose:

- The total amount of exchange differences (foreign currency transaction and translation gains and losses) recognized in net income.
- The total amount of cumulative translation adjustment classified as a separate component of shareholders' equity, as well as a reconciliation of the amount of cumulative translation adjustment at the beginning and end of the period.

Further, note that:

- Disclosures relating to foreign currency translation are typically found in the MD&A section and the notes to the financial statements in the annual report.
- Multinational companies typically have several subsidiaries in different regions so the translation gain/loss on the income statement and cumulative translation adjustment on the balance sheet include the effects of translation of foreign currency accounts of all the parent's subsidiaries.
- In order to facilitate comparisons across companies, analysts may add the change in CTA over the year to net income for the year. This adjustment where gains/losses that are reported directly in equity, are instead reported in net income, is known as clean surplus accounting.

> Under dirty surplus accounting certain gains/losses are included in shareholders' equity directly under comprehensive income. Examples of dirty surplus items include unrealized gains and losses on available-for-sale securities.

Multinational Operations And A Company's Effective Tax Rate

Entities with operations in multiple countries with different tax rates have an incentive to set transfer prices (i.e., the prices at which divisions within the company transact with each other) such that a higher portion of profits is allocated to lower tax rate jurisdictions. This has prompted countries to establish various laws and practices to prevent aggressive transfer pricing practices.

Accounting standards require companies to explain the relationship between tax expense and accounting profit in a detailed reconciliation between the average effective tax rate (tax expense divided by pretax accounting profits) and the relevant statutory tax rate. Changes in impact of foreign taxes on the parent's effective tax rate can be caused by (1) changes in applicable tax rates and/or (2) changes in the mix of profits earned in different countries (with different tax rates).

Additional Disclosures on the Effects of Foreign Currency

Disclosures Related to Sales Growth

Companies often include disclosures related to the impact of exchange rate movements on sales growth in (1) the MD&A and sometimes in (2) other financial reports such as company presentations to investors and earnings announcements. For multinationals, sales growth can be attributed to changes in price, volumes, and/or exchange rates. Analysts should consider organic sales growth (excluding foreign currency effects on sales growth) when forecasting future performance or evaluating management performance.

Disclosures Related to Major Sources of Foreign Exchange Risk

In order to assist users of financial statements, a multinational may:
- Describe the source(s) of its currency risks and approach to measuring and managing those risks (usually in MD&A); and
- Present a sensitivity analysis on the effects of currency fluctuations (usually in the additional disclosures sections of the notes).

STUDY SESSION 7: FINANCIAL REPORTING AND ANALYSIS—QUALITY OF FINANCIAL REPORTS AND FINANCIAL STATEMENT ANALYSIS

QUALITY OF FINANCIAL REPORTS
Cross-Reference to CFA Institute Assigned Reading #20

Conceptual Framework for Assessing the Quality of Financial Reports

- Financial reporting quality refers to the usefulness of information contained in the financial reports, including disclosures in the notes.
    - High-quality reporting provides information that is useful in investment decision-making in that it is relevant and faithfully represents the company's performance and position.
- Earnings quality (or results quality) pertains to the earnings and cash generated by the company's core economic activities and its resulting financial condition.
    - High-quality earnings (1) come from activities that the company will be able to sustain in the future, and (2) provide an adequate return on the company's investment.
    - Note that the term, **earnings** quality, encompasses quality of earnings, cash flow, and balance sheet items.

Relationship between Financial Reporting Quality and Earnings Quality

		Financial Reporting Quality	
		Low	High
Earnings (Results) Quality	High	LOW financial reporting quality impedes assessment of earnings quality and impedes valuation.	HIGH financial reporting quality enables assessment. HIGH earnings quality increases company value.
	Low		HIGH financial reporting quality enables assessment. LOW earnings quality decreases company value.

Quality Spectrum of Financial Reports

GAAP, Decision-Useful, Sustainable, and Adequate Returns: These are high-quality reports that provide useful information about high-quality earnings.

GAAP, Decision-Useful, but Sustainable? This level refers to a situation where high-quality reporting provides useful information, but the economic reality being depicted is not of high quality (i.e., earnings do not provide an adequate rate of return or they are not expected to recur).

Within GAAP, but Biased Accounting Choices: This level refers to a situation where high-quality reporting provides useful information, but biased choices result in financial reports that do not faithfully represent the company's true economic situation.

- Management can make aggressive or conservative accounting choices, both of which go against the concept of neutrality as *unbiased* financial reporting is the ideal.

- Aside from biases in determining reported amounts, biases can also creep into the way information is *presented*. A company may choose to present information in a manner that obscures unfavorable information and/or highlights favorable information.

Within GAAP, but "Earnings Management": This level refers to a situation where high-quality reporting provides useful information, but where earnings are "managed." Earnings can be managed by taking real actions or through accounting choices.

Departures from GAAP Non-Compliant Accounting: This level reflects financial information that deviates from GAAP. Such financial information cannot be used to assess earnings quality, as comparisons with other entities or earlier periods cannot be made.

Departures from GAAP Fictitious Transactions: The level reflects the lowest quality of financial reports, where actual transactions are omitted and/or fictitious transactions are reported.

POTENTIAL PROBLEMS THAT AFFECT THE QUALITY OF FINANCIAL REPORTS

Reported Amounts and Timing of Recognition

While the choice regarding the reported amount and timing of recognition may focus on a single financial statement element (assets, liabilities, owners' equity, revenues and gains, or expenses and losses), it can affect other elements as well.

- Aggressive, premature, and fictitious revenue recognition results in overstated income and, consequently, overstated equity. Further, assets (typically accounts receivable) are also overstated.
- Conservative revenue recognition, such as deferred recognition of revenue, results in understated net income, understated equity, and understated assets.
- Omission and delayed recognition of expenses result in understated expenses and overstated income, overstated equity, overstated assets, and/or understated liabilities.
  - An understatement of bad debt expense results in overstated accounts receivable.
  - Understated depreciation or amortization results in overstated long-lived assets.
  - Understated interest, taxes, or other expenses result in understated related liabilities (accrued interest payable, taxes payable, or other payables).
- Understatement of contingent liabilities comes with overstated equity resulting from understated expenses and overstated income or overstated other comprehensive income.
- For financial assets and liabilities that must be reported at fair value, overstatement of financial assets and understatement of financial liabilities are associated with overstated equity resulting from overstated unrealized gains or understated unrealized losses.
- Cash flow from operations may be increased by deferring payments on payables, accelerating payments from customers, deferring purchases of inventory, and deferring other expenditures (e.g., maintenance and research).

Classification

While choices relating to reported amounts and timing of recognition usually affect more than one financial statement element, classification choices typically relate to how an item is classified within a particular financial statement.

Accounting Warning Signs[1]

Potential Issues	Possible Actions/Choices	Warning Signs
• Overstatement or non-sustainability of operating income and/or net income ○ Overstated or accelerated revenue recognition ○ Understated expenses ○ Misclassification of revenue, gains, expenses, or losses	• Contingent sales with right of return, "channel stuffing" (the practice of inducing customers to order products they would otherwise not order or order at a later date through generous terms), "bill and hold" sales (encouraging customers to order goods and retain them on seller's premises) • Lessor use of finance (capital) leases • Fictitious (fraudulent) revenue • Capitalizing expenditures as assets • Lessee use of operating leases • Classifying non-operating income or gains as part of operations • Classifying ordinary expenses as non-recurring or non-operating • Reporting gains through net income and losses through other comprehensive income	• Growth in revenue higher than that of industry or peers • Increases in discounts to and returns from customers • Higher growth rate in receivables than revenue • Large proportion of revenue in final quarter of year for a non-seasonal business • Cash flow from operations is much lower than operating income • Inconsistency over time in the items included in operating revenues and operating expenses • Increases in operating margin • Aggressive accounting assumptions, such as long, depreciable lives • Losses in non-operating income or other comprehensive income and gains in operating income or net income • Compensation largely tied to financial results

1 - 2015 CFA Program Curriculum Volume 2, Exhibit 4.

Potential Issues	Possible Actions/Choices	Warning Signs

• Misstatement of balance sheet items (may affect income statement)
  ○ Over- or understatement of assets
  ○ Over- or understatement of liabilities
  ○ Misclassification of assets and/or liabilities
	• Choice of models and model inputs to measure fair value
	• Classification from current to non-current
	• Over- or understating reserves and allowances
	• Understating identifiable assets and overstating goodwill
		• Models and model inputs that bias fair value measures
		• Inconsistency in model inputs when measuring fair value of assets compared with that of liabilities
		• Typical current assets, such as accounts receivable and inventory, included in non-current assets
		• Allowances and reserves that fluctuate over time or are not comparable with peers
		• High goodwill value relative to total assets
		• Use of special purpose vehicles
		• Large changes in deferred tax assets and liabilities
		• Significant off-balance-sheet liabilities

• Overstatement of cash flow from operations	• Managing activities to affect cash flow from operations • Misclassifying cash flows to positively affect cash flow from Operations	• Increase in accounts payable and decrease in accounts receivable and inventory • Capitalized expenditures in investing activities • Sales and leaseback • Increases in bank overdrafts

Quality Issues and Mergers and Acquisitions

- Companies that are finding it difficult to generate cash may acquire other companies to increase cash flow from operations.
- A potential acquisition may create an incentive for management to use aggressive choices or even misreport.
- Misreporting can also be an incentive to make an acquisition.
- Acquisitions also provide opportunities to make choices that affect (1) the initial consolidated balance sheet and (2) consolidated income statements in the future.

GAAP Compliant Financial Reporting that Diverges from Economic Reality

- Recognition of asset impairments and restructuring charges in a single accounting period is consistent with most GAAP, even though they are both likely the results of past activities over an extended period.
- Other items that are commonly encountered by analysts include the following:
  - ○ Revisions to estimates, such as the remaining economic lives of assets
  - ○ Sudden increases in allowances and reserves
  - ○ Large accruals for losses (e.g., environmental or litigation-related liabilities)
- Some economic assets and liabilities may not be reflected on the financial statements (e.g., leases classified as operating leases, research and development (R&D) expenses, sales order backlogs).
- Certain items presented in other comprehensive income should be included in an analysis of net income.

Quantitative Tools to Assess the Likelihood of Misreporting

Beneish Model

$$M\text{-score} = -4.84 + 0.920\,(\text{DSR}) + 0.528\,(\text{GMI}) + 0.404\,(\text{AQI}) + 0.892\,(\text{SGI})$$
$$+ 0.115\,(\text{DEPI}) - 0.172\,(\text{SGAI}) + 4.670\,(\text{Accruals}) - 0.327\,(\text{LEVI})$$

M-score = Score indicating probability of earnings manipulation.

- The higher the M-score (i.e., the less negative the number) the higher the probability of earnings manipulation.
- Generally speaking, a probability of earnings manipulation greater than 3.75% (corresponding to an M-score greater than –1.78) is considered a higher-than-acceptable probability of manipulation.

INDICATORS OF EARNINGS QUALITY

Recurring Earnings

- Generally speaking, reported earnings that contain a high proportion of non-recurring items (e.g., discontinued operations, one-off asset sales, one-off litigation settlements, one-off tax settlements) are less likely to be sustainable and are therefore, considered low-quality.
  - ○ For the purpose of analysis, it is important to include non-recurring items when making historical comparisons and in developing input estimates for valuation. However, analysts should always keep an eye out for classification shifting when estimating recurring or core earnings.
- Companies also understand that investors focus on recurring or core earnings. Therefore, in addition to reporting net income (on the face of the income statement), many companies voluntarily disclose pro forma income (also known as adjusted income or as non-GAAP measures) that excludes non-recurring items.
  - ○ Analysts must recognize that some companies may be motivated to classify an item non-recurring if it improves a performance metric that is important to investors.

Earnings Persistence and Related Measures of Accruals

The higher the persistence of a company's earnings, the higher its intrinsic value.

$$\text{Earnings}_{t+1} = \alpha + \beta_1 \text{Cash flow}_t + \beta_2 \text{Accruals}_t + \varepsilon$$

- The cash component of earnings is more persistent than the accruals component so β_1 tends to be greater than β_2. The larger the accruals component of earnings, the lower the level of persistence and therefore, the lower the quality of earnings.

Discretionary versus Non-Discretionary Accruals

- Discretionary accruals arise from transactions or accounting choices outside the normal, which are possibly made with the intent to manage earnings.
- Non-discretionary accruals arise from normal transactions.

Identifying Abnormal Discretionary Accruals

- Model the company's normal accruals and then identify outliers.
- Compare the magnitude of total accruals across companies.

Other Important Points

- A relatively strong signal that earnings are being manipulated is when a company reports positive net income, but with negative operating cash flows.
- However, note that although significant accruals can suggest earnings manipulation, it is not necessary for all fraudulent companies to have sizeable accruals.
- Research has shown that extreme levels of earnings, both high and low, are mean reverting, i.e., they tend to revert to normal levels over time. Therefore, extremely high/low earnings should not simply be extrapolated into the future when constructing forecasts. If earnings have a significant accruals component, they will be expected to revert towards the mean more quickly.
- Analysts should be wary of companies that consistently report earnings that exactly meet or only narrowly beat forecasts as they may be managing reported earnings.
- Two external indicators of poor-quality earnings are (1) enforcement actions by regulatory authorities and (2) restatements of previously-issued financial statements.

Looking for Quality in Revenues[2]

Start with the Basics

- The first step should be to fully understand the revenue recognition policies as stated in the most recent annual report. Without context for the way revenue is recognized, an analyst will not understand the risks involved in the proper reporting of revenue. For instance, analysts should determine the following:
    - What are the shipping terms?
    - What rights of return does a customer have: limited or extensive?
    - Do rebates affect revenues, and if so, how are they accounted for? What estimates are involved?

---

2 - 2015 CFA Program Curriculum Volume 2, pages 332–333.

- Are there multiple deliverables to customers for one arrangement? If so, is revenue deferred until some elements are delivered late in the contract? If there are multiple deliverables, do deferred revenues appear on the balance sheet?

Age Matters

- A study of DSO can reveal much about their quality. Receivables do not improve with age. Analysts should seek reasons for exceptions appearing when they
  - Compare the trend in DSOs or receivables turnover over a relevant time frame.
  - Compare the DSO of one company with the DSOs of similar competitors over similar time frames.

Is It Cash or Accrual?

- A high percentage of accounts receivable to revenues might mean nothing, but it might also mean that channel-stuffing has taken place, portending high future returns of inventory or decreased demand for product in the future. Analysts should
  - Compare the percentage of accounts receivable to revenues over a relevant time frame.
  - Compare the company's percentage of accounts receivable to revenues with that of competitors or industry measures over similar time frames.

Compare with the Real World When Possible

- If a company reports non-financial data on a routine basis, try relating revenues to those data to determine whether trends in the revenue make sense. Examples include
  - Airlines reporting extensive information about miles flown and capacity, enabling an analyst to relate increases in revenues to an increase in miles flown or capacity.
  - Retailers reporting square footage used and number of stores open.
  - Companies across all industries reporting employee head counts.
- As always, analysts should compare any relevant revenue-per-unit measure with that of relevant competitors or industry measures.

Revenue Trends and Composition

- Trend analysis, over time and in comparison with competitors, can prompt analysts to ask questions of managers, or it can simply evoke discomfort with the overall revenue quality. Some relationships to examine include
  - The relationships between the kinds of revenue recognized. For example, how much is attributable to product sales or licenses, and how much is attributable to services? Have the relationships changed over time, and if so, why?
  - The relationship between overall revenue and accounts receivable. Do changes in overall revenues make sense when compared with changes in accounts receivable?

Relationships

- Does the company transact business with entities owned by senior officers or shareholders? This is a particularly sensitive area if the manager/shareholder-owned entities are private and there are revenues recognized from the private entity by a publicly owned company; it could be a dumping ground for obsolete or damaged inventory while inflating revenues.

Looking for Quality in Expense Recognition[3]

Start with the Basics

- The first step should be to fully understand the cost capitalization policies as stated in the most recent annual report. Without context for the costs stored on the balance sheet, analysts will not be able to comprehend practice exceptions they may encounter. Examples of policies that should be understood include the following:
  - What costs are capitalized in inventory? How is obsolescence accounted for? Are there reserves established for obsolescence that might be artificially raised or lowered?
  - What are the depreciation policies, including depreciable lives? How do they compare with competitors' policies? Have they changed from prior years?

Trend Analysis

- Trend analysis, over time and in comparison with competitors, can lead to questions the analyst can ask managers, or it can simply evoke discomfort with overall earnings quality because of issues with expenses. Some relationships to examine include the following:
  - Each quarter, non-current asset accounts should be examined for quarter-to-quarter and year-to-year changes to see whether there are any unusual increases in costs. If present, they might indicate that improper capitalization of costs has occurred.
  - Profit margins—gross and operating—are often observed by analysts in the examination of quarterly earnings. They are not often related to changes in the balance sheet, but they should be. If unusual buildups of non-current assets have occurred and the profit margins are improving or staying constant, it could mean that improper cost capitalization is taking place. Recall WorldCom and its improper capitalization of "line costs": Profitability was maintained by capitalizing costs that should have been expensed. Also, the overall industry environment should be considered: Are margins stable while balance sheet accounts are growing and the industry is slumping?
  - Turnover ratio for total assets; property, plant, and equipment; and other assets should be computed (with revenues divided by the asset classification). Does a trend in the ratios indicate a slowing in turnover? Decreasing revenues might mean that the assets are used to make a product with declining demand and portend future asset write-downs. Steady or rising revenues and decreasing turnover might indicate improper cost capitalization.
  - Compute the depreciation (or amortization) expense compared to the relevant asset base. Is it decreasing or increasing over time without a good reason? How does it compare with that of competitors?

---

3 - 2015 CFA Program Curriculum Volume 2, page 332–333.

○ Compare the relationship of capital expenditures with gross property, plant, and equipment over time. Is the proportion of capital expenditures relative to total property, plant, and equipment increasing significantly over time? If so, it may indicate that the company is capitalizing costs more aggressively to prevent their recognition as current expenses.

Relationships

- Does the company transact business with entities owned by senior officers or shareholders? This is a particularly sensitive area if the manager/shareholder-owned entities are private. Dealings between a public company and the manager-owned entity might take place at prices that are unfavorable for the public company in order to transfer wealth from the public company to the manager-owned entity. Such inappropriate transfers of wealth can also occur through excessive compensation, direct loans, or guarantees. These practices are often referred to as "tunneling."
- In some cases, sham dealings between the manager-owned entity and the public company might be falsely reported to improve reported profits of the public company and thus enrich the managers whose compensation is performance based. In a different type of transaction, the manager-owned entity could transfer resources to the public company to ensure its economic viability and thus preserve the option to misappropriate or to participate in profits in the future. These practices are often referred to as "propping."

Bankruptcy Protection Models

Altman Model

$$Z\text{-score} = 1.2 \text{ (Net working capital/Total assets)} + 1.4 \text{ (Retained earnings/Total assets)}$$
$$+ 3.3 \text{ (EBIT/Total assets)} + 0.6 \text{ (Market value of equity/Book value of liabilities)}$$
$$+ 1.0 \text{ (Sales/Total assets)}$$

- A higher Z-score is better.

CASH FLOW QUALITY

Indicators of Cash Flow Quality

For more established companies high-quality cash flow has the following characteristics:

- Positive OCF
- OCF derived from sustainable sources
- OCF adequate to cover capital expenditures, dividends, and debt repayment
- OCF with relatively low volatility (relative to industry participants)

Generally speaking, OCF is viewed as being less easily manipulated than operating income and net income. However, the importance of OCF to investors creates a strong incentive for managers to manipulate amounts reported. Examples of issues relating to cash flow reporting quality are:

- Boosting OCF by selling receivables to a third-party.
  - A decrease in a company's days of sales outstanding may suggest this is happening.
- Boosting OCF by delaying repayment of payables.
  - An increase in a company's days of payables may suggest this is happening.
- Misclassifying cash flows. Management may try to shift inflows of cash from investing or financing activities into the operating section of the cash flow statement to inflate reported OCF.

BALANCE SHEET QUALITY

When it comes to the balance sheet, high financial *results* quality (i.e., a strong balance sheet) is indicated by an optimal amount of leverage, adequate liquidity, and optimal asset allocation. High financial *reporting* quality is indicated by (1) completeness, (2) unbiased measurement, and (3) clear presentation.

SOURCES OF INFORMATION ABOUT RISK

- The company's financial statements
- Auditor's opinion
- Notes to the financial statements
- Management commentary (management discussion and analysis, or MD&A)
- Other required disclosures
- Financial press as a source of information about risk

INTEGRATION OF FINANCIAL STATEMENT ANALYSIS TECHNIQUES
Cross-Reference to CFA Institute Assigned Reading #21

A Financial Statement Analysis Framework:[1]

Phase	Sources of Information	Examples of Output
1. Define the purpose and context of the analysis.	• The nature of the analyst's function, such as evaluating an equity or debt investment or issuing a credit rating. • Communication with client or supervisor on needs and concerns. • Institutional guidelines related to developing specific work product.	• Statement of the purpose or objective of analysis. • A list (written or unwritten) of specific questions to be answered by the analysis. • Nature and content of report to be provided. • Timetable and budgeted resources for completion.
2. Collect input data.	• Financial statements, other financial data, questionnaires, and industry/economic data. • Discussions with management, suppliers, customers, and competitors. • Company site visits (e.g., to production facilities or retail stores)	• Organized financial statements. • Financial data tables. • Completed questionnaires, if applicable.
3. Process input data, as required, into analytically useful data.	• Data from the previous phase.	• Adjusted financial statements. • Common-size statements. • Forecasts.
4. Analyze/interpret the data.	• Input data and processed data	• Analytical results
5. Develop and communicate conclusions and recommendations (e.g., with an analysis report).	• Analytical results and previous reports • Institutional guidelines for published reports	• Analytical report answering questions posed in Phase 1 • Recommendations regarding the purpose of the analysis, such as whether to make an investment or grant credit.
6. Follow-up.	• Information gathered by periodically repeating above steps as necessary to determine whether changes to holdings or recommendations are necessary	• Update reports and recommendations

Integrated Financial Statement Analysis

- The extended Dupont decomposition is used to identify the company's key performance drivers. Equity income from associates should be removed from net income to evaluate the company's performance on a stand-alone basis.

- The company's asset base is analyzed to look for changes in the composition of the balance sheet.

- The capital structure is evaluated to determine if the company can support its strategic objectives and fulfill payment obligations.

- Segment disclosures are examined to attribute the company's overall performance to different components of the business.

- Earnings should be broken down into their cash flow and accruals components to assess their persistence and sustainability.

- The company's market value should be adjusted for the market value of the company's ownership interests in associates. The implied value of the company on a stand-alone basis should be evaluated in light of peer company valuation ratios.

- The effects of sources of off balance sheet financing on the company's operating and leverage ratios should be measured.

- The impact of proposed changes in accounting standards should be assessed as these may have a significant impact on the company's valuation.

CAPITAL BUDGETING
Cross-Reference to CFA Institute Assigned Reading #22

Capital Budgeting Analysis

Initial investment

Initial investment for a new investment = FCInv + NWCInv
- NWCInv = ΔNon-cash current assets − ΔNon-debt current liabilities

Initial investment for a replacement project = FCInv + NWCInv − Sal_0 + T (Sal_0 − B_0)

Annual after-tax operating cash flows

For a new investment: CF = (S − C − D) (1 − T) + D or CF = (S − C) (1 − T) + TD

For a replacement project: ΔCF = (ΔS − ΔC) (1 − t) + tΔD

Terminal year after-tax non-operating cash flows

TNOCF = Sal_T + NWCInv − T (Sal_T − B_T)

When calculating terminal year after-tax non-operating cash flow for replacement project only consider the changes in cash flows that result from the replacement.

Important:
- Accelerated depreciation methods result in greater tax savings in the early years of a capital project compared to the straight-line method. Therefore, all other factors remaining the same, accelerated depreciation methods result in a greater net present value (NPV) for a project compared to straight-line depreciation.
- Spreadsheets are commonly used to evaluate capital budgeting proposals as they provide an effective way of building complex models that allow analysts to examine the effects of changes in assumptions on valuations.

Inflation and Capital Budgeting Analysis

Analysts should use a nominal discount rate to discount nominal cash flows and a real discount rate to discount real cash flows.

(1 + Nominal rate) = (1 + Real rate) × (1 + Inflation rate)

- Inflation reduces the value of depreciation tax savings.
- If inflation is higher (lower) than expected, then the profitability of the project will be lower (higher) than expected.
- If inflation is higher (lower) than expected, real payments to bondholders are lower (higher) than expected.
- Inflation does not affect all revenues and costs uniformly.

Mutually Exclusive Projects with Unequal Lives

Least Common Multiple of Lives Approach

The lives of both the projects are extended by replicating them until both the project chains extend over the same time horizon. Given equal time horizons, the two projects are compared based on the NPVs of all the cash flows in the chain and the chain with higher NPV is chosen.

Equivalent Annual Annuity Approach

This approach calculates the annuity payment over the project's life that is equivalent in value to the project's NPV. The investment project with the higher EAA is chosen.

Capital Rationing

In an ideal situation, companies would want to invest in all available projects that generate a positive NPV. Typically however, a company will have to choose its investments in a manner that will maximize shareholder wealth given the budget constraint. This is known as capital rationing.
- Under hard capital rationing, the budget is fixed. In such situations, managers should use the NPV or PI valuation methods.
- Under soft capital rationing, the managers may be allowed to exceed their budgets if they can invest the additional funds in a profitable manner.

Risk Analysis of Capital Investments

Stand-Alone Methods

Sensitivity analysis determines the effect of a change in one input variable at a time on the NPV of the project.

Scenario analysis calculates the NPV of a project in a number of different scenarios.

Simulation (Monte Carlo) analysis estimates the probability distribution of outcomes for the NPV of a project.

Market Risk Methods

The discount rate used to calculate a project's NPV should reflect the risk associated with the project. Analysts typically use the capital asset pricing model (CAPM) to calculate this discount rate.

Required return for a project = Risk-free rate of return + Beta of the project (Market risk premium)

The required rate of return can be used in two ways. It can either be used to calculate the:

- NPV of the project and positive NPV projects are accepted; or
- IRR of the project and projects whose IRR exceeds the required rate of return are accepted.

Real Options

Real options are just like financial options and give their holders the right, but not the obligation, to make a capital budgeting decision in the future. Real options are contingent upon future events and provide managers with greater flexibility, which enhances the NPV of projects. There are several types of real options:

- Timing options give the company an option to delay investment.
- Sizing options give the company an option to either abandon a project if market conditions deteriorate, or to expand it if market conditions improve.
- Flexibility options give the company an option to either set a different price, or change the number of units produced depending on market conditions.
- Fundamental options are projects that behave as options as their payoffs are contingent on the price of an underlying asset.

Evaluating Capital Budgeting Projects with Real Options

- Use DCF analysis without considering real options.
- Use DCF analysis and add an estimated value of the real option.
- Use decision trees.
- Use option pricing models.

Common Capital Budgeting Pitfalls

- Not incorporating economic responses into the investment analysis.
- Misusing capital budgeting templates.
- Undertaking pet projects of senior managers.
- Basing investment decisions on EPS, net income, or return on equity instead of incremental cash flows.
- Using IRR instead of NPV to make investment decisions.
- Accounting for cash flows inaccurately.
- Over- or under-estimating of overhead costs.
- Not using the appropriate risk-adjusted discount rate.
- Spending the entire investment budget just because it was available.
- Failing to consider investment alternatives.
- Handling sunk costs and opportunity costs incorrectly.

Other Income Measures

Economic Income

Economic income is measured as an investment's after-tax cash flows plus the change in the investment's market value.

Economic income = After-tax cash flows + Increase in market value

Economic income = After-tax cash flows – Economic depreciation

Economic income does not explicitly deduct interest expense when calculating cash flows; interest expense is reflected in the discount rate.

Accounting Income

Accounting income refers to a company's reported net income. It differs from economic income in the following two ways:

- Accounting income subtracts interest expenses to arrive at net income.
- Unlike economic depreciation, which is based on the market value of the investment, accounting depreciation is based on the original cost of the investment.

Valuation Models

Economic Profit

Economic profit = [EBIT (1 – Tax rate)] – \$WACC = NOPAT – \$WACC

Future economic profit should be discounted at the weighted average cost of capital to calculate NPV.

Residual Income

Residual income = Net income for the period – Equity charge for the period

Equity charge for the period = Required return on equity × Beginning-of-period book value of equity

Future residual income should be discounted at the required return on equity to calculate NPV.

Claims Valuation

This approach values a firm based on the values of claims of debt and equity holders against the firm's assets. Cash flows available to debt and equity holders are separated and the cash flows available to debt holders are discounted at the cost of debt, while cash flows available to equity holders are discounted at the cost of equity. The present values of the two are added to calculate the NPV.

CAPITAL STRUCTURE
Cross-Reference to CFA Institute Assigned Reading #23

The Capital Structure Decision

A company's capital structure refers to the combination of debt and equity capital it uses to finance its business. The goal is to determine the capital structure that results in the minimum weighted average cost of capital and consequently, in the maximum value of the company.

$$r_{WACC} = \left(\frac{D}{V}\right)r_D(1-t) + \left(\frac{E}{V}\right)r_E$$

MM Assumptions

- Investors have homogeneous expectations.
- Capital markets are perfect.
- Investors can borrow and lend at the risk-free rate.
- There are no agency costs.
- The financing decision and the investment decision are independent of each other.

MM Proposition I without Taxes: Capital Structure Irrelevance

Given the assumptions listed above and no taxes, changes in capital structure do not affect company value.

$$V_L = V_U$$

MM Proposition II without Taxes: Higher Financial Leverage Raises the Cost of Equity

Debt finance is cheaper than equity finance. However, increased use of debt leads to an increase in the required rate of return on equity. The higher required return on equity is exactly offset by the cheaper cost of debt and therefore, there is no change in the company's weighted average cost of capital. Basically, the company's cost of capital is not determined by its capital structure but by business risk.

$$r_E = r_0 + (r_0 - r_D)\frac{D}{E}$$

$$V = \frac{\text{Interest}}{r_D} + \frac{\text{EBIT} - \text{Interest}}{r_E}$$

Relaxing the Assumption of no Taxes

MM Proposition I with Taxes

Use of debt would actually increase the value of a company. Interest paid is tax deductible in most countries, so the use of debt results in tax savings for the company. Therefore, the value of a levered company is greater than that of an unlevered company by an amount equal to the marginal tax rate multiplied by the value of debt:

$$V_L = V_U + tD$$

In this scenario (with no costs of financial distress), the value of a company would be maximized if its capital structure comprised of 100% debt.

MM Proposition II with Taxes

The cost of equity would still increase with increased debt financing, but not fast enough to exactly offset the use of (cheaper) debt, thereby decreasing the company's weighted average cost of capital. Under this scenario, a company's weighted average cost of capital is minimized at 100% debt.

$$r_{WACC} = \left(\frac{D}{V}\right) r_D (1-t) + \left(\frac{E}{V}\right) r_E$$

$$r_E = r_0 + (r_0 - r_D)(1-t)\left(\frac{D}{E}\right)$$

$$V_L = \frac{Interest}{r_D} + \frac{EBIT - Interest}{r_E}$$

MM Propositions

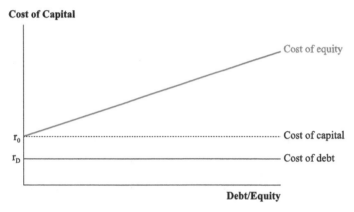

Cost of Capital

r_0

r_D

Cost of equity

Cost of capital

Cost of debt

Debt/Equity

Figure 1a:
Cost of Capital with No Taxes

MM Proposition II (without taxes) states that the use of cheaper debt increases the cost of equity. The increase in the cost of equity exactly offsets the benefit of adding cheaper debt to the capital structure, resulting in a constant WACC (cost of capital).

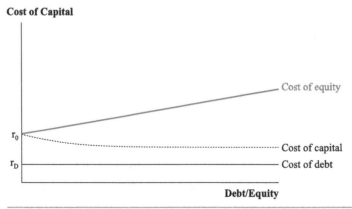

Cost of Capital

r_0

r_D

Cost of equity

Cost of capital

Cost of debt

Debt/Equity

Figure 1b:
Cost of Capital with Taxes

Under MM Proposition II (with taxes) the cost of equity still increases, but not fast enough to completely undo the benefit of using cheaper debt (since debt also results in an interest tax shield), resulting in a decrease in the company's weighted average cost of capital.

Costs of Financial Distress

The expected cost of financial distress equals the actual cost of financial distress times the probability that the company will face financial distress. Leverage increases the costs of financial distress and the probability of financial distress.

Agency Costs

The conflicts of interest between owners and managers in all public and large private companies give rise to agency costs, which include:

- Monitoring costs
- Bonding costs
- Residual loss

Using more debt in the capital structure reduces net agency costs of equity.

Costs of Asymmetric Information

Information asymmetry arises from the fact that a company's managers generally have more information about its performance than outsiders. Managers prefer internal financing and debt over equity as sources of raising capital (pecking order theory). Costs of asymmetric information decrease as more debt is issued.

The Optimal Capital Structure - Static Trade-Off Theory

Managers must balance the use of debt in a way that its tax shield benefits are exactly offset by its associated costs of financial distress.

$$V_L = V_U + tD - PV \text{ (Costs of financial distress)}$$

The capital structure at which company value is maximized is the same as the capital structure at which the cost of capital (WACC) is minimized. Further, note that the WACC curve is U-shaped:

- Initially as more debt is added to the capital structure, the WACC falls due to the lower cost of debt (compared to equity).
- Eventually, WACC increases as the cost of equity and the cost of debt both rise to compensate for the higher risk associated with high debt levels.

Trade-Off Theory with Taxes and Costs of Financial Distress

Value of Company and the D/E Ratio

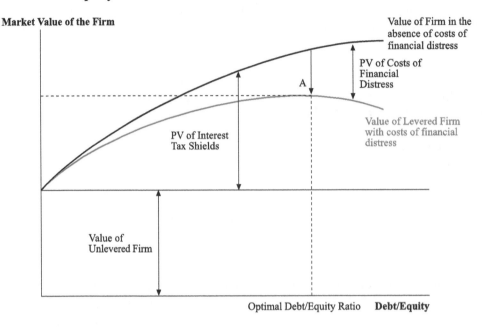

Cost of Capital and the D/E Ratio

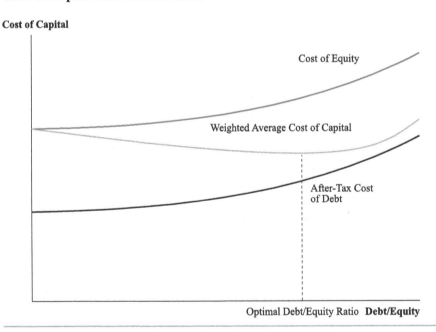

The weight of debt in an optimal capital structure is less than 100%. Companies usually adopt their optimal capital structure as their target capital structure with periods during which they temporarily deviate from their target capital structure due to the following reasons:

- It may make sense to exploit short-term opportunities in another source of financing.
- Changes in market values of debt and equity result in a change in the company's capital structure.
- It might be impractical or expensive to maintain the target capital structure.

Practical Issues in Capital Structure Policy

Debt Ratings

Higher financial leverage lowers a company's debt ratings, which results in higher costs of raising additional debt. Companies therefore strive to maintain a level of debt which would not result in a downgrade in their credit rating.

Capital Structure Policy

When evaluating a company's capital structure policy an analyst should consider:

- Changes in the company's capital structure over time.
- The capital structure of competitors that have similar business risks.
- Company specific factors that may affect agency costs (e.g. corporate governance).

Leverage in an International Setting

Differences in capital structures across countries may be explained by:

- Institutional and legal environment.
- Financial markets and banking sector.
- Macroeconomic environment.

The impact of these factors is summarized in the following table:[1]

Country-Specific Factor	D/E Ratio	Maturity of Debt
Institutional Framework		
Efficient legal system	Lower	Longer
Common law as opposed to civil law	Lower	Longer
Lower information asymmetry	Lower	Longer
Favorable taxes on equity	Lower	N/A
Financial Markets and Banking System		
Active bond and stock market	N/A	Longer
Bank-based financial system	Higher	N/A
Large institutional investors	Lower	Longer
Macroeconomic Environment		
High inflation	Lower	Shorter
High GDP growth	Lower	Longer

DIVIDENDS AND SHARE REPURCHASES: ANALYSIS
Cross-Reference to CFA Institute Assigned Reading #24

Dividend Policy Does Not Matter

Miller and Modigliani proposed that under the assumptions of perfect capital markets a company's dividend policy should have no impact on its cost of capital or on shareholders' wealth because:

- A company's dividend policy is independent of its investment and financing decisions.
- If shareholders needed investment income, they could construct their own cash flow stream by selling a sufficient number of shares without incurring any costs (homemade dividends).

Note that under the MM assumptions, there is no distinction between dividends and share repurchases.

Market imperfections make it difficult to apply this theory in the real world.

- Companies and individuals incur transactions costs.
- Stock price volatility creates difficulties in creating homemade dividends.

Dividend Policy Matters: The Bird in Hand Argument

- Even under perfect capital markets, shareholders prefer current dividends over uncertain capital gains in the future.
- Shareholders require a lower return from companies that pay dividends, which lowers the cost of capital for those companies and increases their share prices.

MM counter: Paying dividends does not affect the risk of future cash flows; it only lowers the ex-dividend price of the stock with no impact on shareholder wealth.

Dividend Policy Matters: The Tax Argument

- Many countries impose a higher tax on dividends than on capital gains.
- Taxable investors therefore prefer companies that pay lower cash dividends and reinvest their earnings in profitable growth opportunities.
- In cases where companies do not have profitable growth opportunities, those investors would prefer share repurchases over cash dividends.

Other Theoretical Issues

Clientele Effect

- Different groups of investors prefer different dividend policies and are attracted to companies that match their desired policies.
- Investors' marginal tax rates also have an effect on their preference for dividends.
- Some institutional investors prefer to invest only in companies that pay dividends.

The clientele effect does not lead to the conclusion that dividend policy affects shareholder wealth; it only asserts that dividend policy attracts investors who prefer that particular policy. Therefore, a change in a company's dividend policy would have no effect on shareholders' wealth and would only result in a switch in its clientele.

More on tax considerations:

The expected decrease in share price when a stock goes ex-dividend can be calculated using the following expression:

$$P_w - P_x = \frac{1 - T_D}{1 - T_{CG}} \times D$$

- If the investor's marginal tax rate on dividends is equal to that on capital gains, the decrease in share price when it goes ex-dividend should be equal to the amount of the dividend.
- If the investor's marginal tax rate on dividends is higher (lower) than that on capital gains, the decrease in share price when it goes ex-dividend should be less (more) than the amount of the dividend.

Signalling Effect

Dividends are seen by investors as signals regarding management's outlook on the company.
- Studies have shown that dividend initiations or increases in dividends are usually taken as positive signals and lead to an increase in a company's share price.
- Many researchers argue that managers may initiate or increase the amount of dividends if they believe the company's share to be undervalued.
- Dividend cuts or omissions are usually taken as negative signals and lead to a decrease in a company's share price.
- Companies may sometimes attempt to send a positive signal alongside dividend cuts by stating that the additional funds would be used in profitable growth opportunities which in turn would lead to future gains.

Controlling Agency Costs

- Shareholders are often concerned about management investing in projects that may increase the size of the company, but reduce shareholder wealth. In such cases, payment of cash dividends constrains management's ability to overinvest.
- Excessive dividends reduce the amount of cash available to the company to make payments to its bondholders. Bondholders often restrict the amount of dividends that can be paid by a company during the term of their bonds through covenants.

Factors Affecting Dividend Policy

- Investment opportunities: All else being equal, companies that have greater profitable investment opportunities tend to pay lower dividends.
- Expected volatility of future earnings: All else being equal, companies with high expected volatility of future earnings tend to be more cautious in the size and frequency of dividend increases.
- Financial flexibility: A company's management may omit or cut dividends to keep substantial cash in hand to deal with any unforeseen circumstances.
- Tax considerations: The lower an investor's marginal tax rate on dividends relative to her marginal tax rate on capital gains, the stronger her preference for dividends. However, an important factor that works in favour of income from capital gains is that capital gains taxes do not have to be paid until shares are sold, while taxes on dividends must be paid when dividends are received.

- Flotation costs: Internally generated funds are the cheapest source of finance for a company. Companies with profitable investment opportunities tend to pay lower dividends and reinvest cash as opposed to issuing equity (with high associated flotation costs) when cash needs arise.
- Contractual and legal restrictions: Companies may be contractually or legally obligated to pay out dividends or to restrict the amount of dividends paid. This may be due to government regulations or bond covenants.

Taxation Methods

- Double taxation: A company's earnings are first taxed at the corporate level and then again at the shareholder level when distributed as dividends.

$$ETR = CTR + [(1 - CTR) \times MTR_D]$$

- Split-rate: A company's earnings that are distributed as dividends are taxed at a lower rate than earnings that are retained by the company. Dividends are then taxed again at the shareholder level as ordinary income.

- Imputation: A company's earnings that are distributed as dividends are taxed only once, at the shareholder's marginal tax rate.

$$ETR = CTR_D + [(1 - CTR_D) \times MTR_D]$$

Payout Policies

Stable Dividend Policy

Companies attempt to pay a regular stream of dividends (unaffected by short-term earnings volatility) and increase dividends only when forecasts suggest that the increase will be sustainable. Companies following this policy usually set a target payout ratio based on long-term sustainable earnings and make dividend increases accordingly.

Expected increase in dividends = Increase in earnings × Target payout ratio × Adjustment factor

Constant Dividend Payout Ratio Policy

This policy is followed by companies that want to reflect the cyclical nature of their business in the payment of dividends. They aim to pay out a constant percentage of net income as dividends.

Residual Dividend Policy

Companies following this policy pay out dividends only if there is sufficient cash after accounting for investment opportunities in positive NPV projects.
- This policy results in significant fluctuations in the amount of dividends paid.
- To smooth their dividend payments, companies usually forecast earnings and capital expenditure requirements for a number of years in the future. This helps them determine residual dividends, which are then paid evenly over the forecast period.

Cash Dividends versus Share Repurchases

All else being equal, the impact of share repurchases on shareholders' wealth is the same as that of cash dividends. Managers often prefer share repurchases over cash dividends because of the following reasons:

- Potential tax advantages.
- Share price support / signalling that the company considers its shares a good investment.
- Added managerial flexibility.
- Offset dilution from employee stock options.
- Increasing financial leverage.

Share repurchases can signal that:
- Management thinks that the company's shares are undervalued.
- The company has few positive NPV investment opportunities.

Analysis of Dividend Safety

All else being equal, a *higher* dividend payout ratio or a *lower* dividend coverage ratio *increases* the risk of a dividend cut or omission. Generally speaking:
- Large, mature companies typically target a payout ratio of 40-60%.
- To evaluate a company's payout and coverage ratios, analysts usually compare them to industry averages.
    - Companies in growth industries have lower payout ratios than those in mature and highly-regulated industries.
- Dividends of companies that have a record of stable or increasing dividends are considered safer than dividends of companies that have cut their dividend in the past.

A more comprehensive measure of dividend safety is the FCFE-coverage ratio:

FCFE coverage ratio = FCFE / [Dividends + Share repurchases]

- If the ratio equals 1, the company is distributing all available cash to shareholders.
- If the ratio is greater than 1, the company is retaining some earnings to enhance liquidity.
- If the ratio is less than 1, the company is borrowing cash to pay dividends.

Past financial data is not always an accurate determinant of future dividend safety. Unforeseen circumstances may force dividend-paying companies to cut or even omit their dividends altogether.

STAKEHOLDERS AND CORPORATE PERFORMANCE
Cross-Reference to CFA Institute Assigned Reading #25

A company's stakeholders are individuals or groups with an interest, claim, or stake in the company. Internal stakeholders include stockholders and employees (including managers, executives, and board members), while external stakeholders include customers, suppliers, creditors, governments, unions, local communities, and the general public.

Stakeholder Impact Analysis

In making choices between stakeholder groups, the company should prioritize the interests of its most important stakeholders. In order to identify its most important stakeholders, companies perform stakeholder impact analysis (SIA). This exercise has typically led companies to the conclusion that their three most important stakeholder groups are customers, employees, and stockholders.

Improving a company's profitability and profit growth rate goes a long way in satisfying stockholders as well as the claims of several stakeholder groups (other than just stockholders). However, not all stakeholder groups want the company to maximize its long-run profitability and profit growth (e.g., suppliers and customers)

Agency Theory

Agency theory seeks to explain why managers might engage in behavior that is either illegal or, at the very least, not in the interests of the company's stockholders.

Information asymmetry arises because stockholders delegate decision-making authority to the CEO, who by virtue of his or her position inside the company is likely to know far more than stockholders do about the company's operations. While stockholders are aware of this information asymmetry, they have no choice but to trust that the agent will serve their interests. Principals try to deal with these challenges through a series of governance mechanisms that:

- Shape the behavior of agents so that they act in line with the goals set by principals.
- Reduce the information asymmetry between agents and principals.
- Remove agents who do not prioritize the goals of principals and mislead them.

Ethical Issues in Strategy

Those who take the stakeholder view of business ethics often argue that managers should behave in an ethical manner because doing so will ensure the support of stakeholders and thus ultimately benefit the firm and its managers (i.e, managers who behave ethically only do so in "enlightened self-interest"). Others go a step further and argue that businesses need to recognize their noblesse oblige and give something back to the society that made their success possible.

The Roots of Unethical Behavior

- An agent who lacks a strong sense of personal ethics is more likely to behave in an unethical manner in a business setting.
- An agent may not realize that she is behaving unethically, probably because the decision-making process used does not incorporate ethical considerations.
- An organizational culture that encourages making all decisions purely on economic grounds.
- Pressure from senior management to meet unrealistic performance goals.
- Unethical leadership that sets a precedent within the company that leads to violations.

Behaving Ethically

Managers should:

- Favor hiring and promoting people with a well-grounded sense of personal ethics.
- Build an organizational culture that places a high value on ethical behavior.
- Establish systematic decision-making processes that provide managers with a moral compass.
- Appoint ethics officers who (1) train employees to always be ethically aware, (2) review decisions to make sure that are ethically responsible, and (3) handle confidential inquiries/complaints from employees.
- Establish strong corporate governance procedures to ensure that managers adhere to ethical norms.
- Strengthen the moral courage of employees by supporting employees who exercise moral courage, say no to superiors, or otherwise complain about unethical actions.

Philosophical Approaches to Ethics

The Friedman Doctrine

- The only social responsibility of business is to increase profits, as long as the company stays within the **rules of law**.
- Businesses have no responsibility to make social investments. If stockholders wish to undertake social expenditures, they can do it with their own money.
- Businesses should behave in an ethical manner, and not engage in deceit or fraud.
- Businesses should remain "within the rules of the game." Unfortunately, rules of the game are not always well-established, and tend to be different across cultures.

Utilitarian Ethics

- The best decisions are those that produce the greatest good for the greatest number of people.
- While it is theoretically appealing, this philosophy has its drawbacks.
  - First, measuring the benefits, costs, and risks of an action is not always straightforward.
  - Second, the philosophy does not consider justice.

Kantian Ethics

- People should be treated as ends and never purely as means to the ends of others.
- While the argument here is widely accepted, it is still an incomplete ethical framework.

Rights Theories

- People have certain fundamental rights that take precedence over a collective good. These rights form the basis for the moral compass that managers should apply in evaluating the ethical component of business decisions.
- The obligation to ensure that the rights of others are secured falls on more than one moral agent (a person or institution that is capable of moral action, including the government and corporations).

Justice Theories

- There should be a just (i.e., fair and equitable) distribution of economic goods and services.
- In a system where everyone is under the veil of ignorance (i.e., if everyone is ignorant of his or her particular characteristics, e.g., race, sex, intelligence, nationality, family background, etc.), people would unanimously agree on two fundamental principles of justice.
  - First, that each person should be permitted the maximum amount of basic liberty.
  - Second, that once equal basic liberty is ensured, inequality in basic social goods (income, wealth, and opportunities) is acceptable only if it benefits the least advantaged person (differencing principle).

CORPORATE GOVERNANCE
Cross-Reference to CFA Institute Assigned Reading #26

Objectives of Corporate Governance

- Eliminate or reduce conflicts of interest, especially those between managers and shareholders, and
- Ensure that the company's assets are used in the best interests of its investors and other stakeholders.

An Effective Corporate Governance System

- Describes the rights of shareholders and other important stakeholders.
- Defines to stakeholders the responsibilities of managers and directors.
- Identifies measurable accountabilities for the performance of responsibilities.
- Ensures fairness and equitable treatment in all dealings between managers, directors, and shareholders.
- Ensures complete transparency and accuracy in disclosures regarding operations, performance, risk, and financial position.

The system of corporate governance is affected by the way a business is structured. Three main forms of businesses are discussed below:

Conflicts of Interest in Agency Relationships

- **Manager-shareholder conflicts:** Managers are entrusted with the capital provided by shareholders. Conflicts arise when, instead of using those funds for the benefit of shareholders, managers may use them for their own welfare. Managers may only invest in projects that increase the size of the firm or the firm's revenue, but are not in the best interests of shareholders in the long-term.
- **Director-shareholder conflicts:** The board of directors of a company serves as an intermediary between the managers and owners. Directors act as agents of shareholders, entrusted with the responsibility of keeping a check on management. Conflicts arise when directors identify with the interests of management and prioritize those interests ahead of those of shareholders.

Responsibilities of the Board of Directors

- Establish corporate values and governance structures in the company to ensure that the business is conducted in an ethical, competent, fair and professional manner.
- Ensure that all legal and regulatory requirements are met and complied with fully in a timely manner.
- Establish long-term strategic objectives for the company with the goal of ensuring that the interests of shareholders come first and that the company's obligations to others are met in a timely and complete manner.
- Establish clear lines of responsibility and a strong system of accountability and performance measurement in all areas of the company's operations.
- Hire the chief executive officer, determine the compensation package, and periodically evaluate the officer's performance.

- Ensure that management has supplied the board with sufficient information for it to be fully-informed and prepared to make the decisions that are its responsibility, and to be able to adequately monitor and oversee the company's management.
- Meet frequently enough to adequately perform its duties, and meet in extraordinary sessions as required by events.
- Acquire adequate training so that members are able to perform their duties properly.

Desirable Characteristics of an Effective Board of Directors

An effective board of directors should have the following characteristics:

- 75% of the board should consist of independent members.
- The CEO and the Chairman of the Board should be separate.
- Directors should possess the appropriate skills and experience to fulfil their fiduciary responsibilities to stakeholders.
- The whole board should either be elected annually or only a portion of directors should be up for re-election each year (staggered board).
- The board of directors should conduct a self-evaluation at least annually.
- The directors should meet at least annually without management being present.
- There should be an audit committee consisting of independent board members responsible for complete oversight of the company's audit practices.
- There should be a nominations committee consisting of independent board members responsible for identifying and evaluating candidates for the board of directors and senior management.
- There should be a compensation committee consisting of independent board members responsible for setting directors' and managers' compensation.
- The board should have access to independent or expert legal counsel.
- There should be a statement of governance policies.

Environmental, Social and Governmental Risk Exposures

- Legislative and regulatory risk
- Legal risk
- Reputational risk
- Operating risk
- Financial risk

Valuation Implications of Corporate Governance

Studies show that the quality of the corporate governance system of a company is directly related to shareholder wealth. Weak corporate governance systems pose the following risks to investors:

- Accounting risk
- Asset risk
- Liability risk
- Strategic policy risk

An acquisition refers to the purchase of some portion of one company by another.

A merger occurs when a company purchases an entire company.

- In a statutory merger, all the assets and liabilities of the acquired company become part of the purchasing company and the acquired company ceases to exist as an identifiable entity.
- In a subsidiary merger, the acquired company becomes a subsidiary of the purchasing company.
- In a consolidation, both companies terminate their previous legal existence and form a new company.

Types of Mergers

- A horizontal merger occurs when two companies operating in the same kind of business merge.
- A vertical merger occurs when a company merges with another company in the same chain of production.
- A conglomerate merger occurs when a company merges with another company operating in a completely different line of business.

Motives for Mergers

- Synergy
- Growth
- Increasing market power
- Acquiring unique capabilities
- Diversification
- Bootstrapping earnings
- Managers' personal incentives
- Tax considerations
- Unlocking hidden value
- Cross-border motivations
  - To exploit market imperfections, e.g. lower cost of labor.
  - To overcome adverse government policies, such as protective tariffs, quotas, or other barriers to free trade.
  - To transfer superior technology to new markets.
  - To differentiate products from those of competitors as well as to acquire a good reputation.
  - To follow clients globally.

Mergers and Industry Life Cycles

Industry Life Cycle Stage	Industry Description	Motives for Merger	Types of Merger
Pioneering development	• Low but slowly increasing sales growth. • Substantial development costs.	• Younger, smaller companies may sell themselves to larger firms in mature or declining industries to enter into a new growth industry. • Young companies may merge with firms that allow them to pool management and capital resources.	• Conglomerate • Horizontal
Rapid accelerating growth	• High profit margins. • Low competition.	• To meet substantial capital requirements for expansion.	• Conglomerate • Horizontal
Mature growth	• Decrease in the entry of new competitors. • Growth potential remains.	• To achieve economies of scale, savings, and operational efficiencies.	• Horizontal • Vertical
Stabilization and market maturity	• Increasing capacity constraints. • Increasing competition.	• To achieve economies of scale in research, production, and marketing to match low costs and prices of competitors. • Large companies may buy smaller companies to improve management and provide a broader financial base.	• Horizontal
Deceleration of growth and decline	• Overcapacity. • Eroding profit margins.	• Horizontal mergers to ensure survival. • Vertical mergers to increase efficiency and profit margins. • Conglomerate mergers to exploit synergy. • Companies in the industry may acquire companies in young industries.	• Horizontal • Vertical • Conglomerate

Transaction Characteristics

Forms of Acquisition

- **Stock purchase:** This occurs when the acquirer purchases the target company's stock from its shareholders.
- **Asset purchase:** This occurs when the acquirer purchases the target company's assets by making a direct payment to the target company.

Major Differences of Stock versus Asset Purchases

	Stock Purchase	Asset Purchase
Payment	Target shareholders receive compensation in exchange for their shares.	Payment is made to the selling company rather than directly to shareholders.
Approval	Shareholder approval required.	Shareholder approval might not be required.
Tax: Corporate	No corporate-level taxes.	Target company pays taxes on any capital gains.
Tax: Shareholder	Target company's shareholders are taxed on their capital gain.	No direct tax consequence for target company's shareholders.
Liabilities	Acquirer assumes the target's liabilities.	Acquirer generally avoids the assumption of liabilities.

Methods of Payment

An acquirer may pay for the merger either with cash, by offering its own securities, or through a mixed offering.

- A stock offering transfers a portion of the risks and rewards of the acquisition to target company's shareholders. Therefore, if the acquirer is highly confident about the benefits of the merger, it would prefer to pay cash (in order to enjoy all the benefits of acquisition). Further, the more strongly target shareholders believe that the merger will create value, the more they will push for a stock offering.

- If the acquirer's shares are considered overvalued by the market relative to the target company's shares, the acquirer would prefer to pay in stock.

- The method of payment also depends on the acquirer's preference regarding the capital structure. Cash payment requires the issuance of debt which increases financial leverage. On the other hand, issuance of new shares for a stock offering dilutes the ownership interests of existing shareholders.

Mind-Set of Target Management

Friendly Mergers

Before reaching a formal deal, both parties conduct due diligence in which they both examine the others' books and records to confirm the accuracy of their statements in negotiations. After the completion of due diligence and successful negotiations, the parties enter into a definitive merger agreement, which contains the details of the transaction. This is the stage at which the parties publicly announce their intention to merge and the merger is now subject to shareholder approval.

Hostile Mergers

A hostile merger is one that is opposed by the target company's management. In this case, the acquirer may bypass management to make the offer directly to the target company's board of directors in a tactic known as a bear hug. If the company's directors consider the offer to be high enough, they may appoint a special committee to negotiate the sale.

In some situations, the acquirer may directly approach the shareholders of the target company through a tender offer. A tender offer can be made with cash, shares of the acquirer's own stock, other securities, or some combination of securities and cash.

An acquirer may also try to take control of the target company through a proxy fight. Shareholders are asked to vote for the acquirer's proposed list of directors. If elected, the new board of directors may change the target company's management and the takeover may turn friendly.

Takeovers

Pre-Offer Takeover Defense Mechanisms

- Poison pills
- Poison puts
- Incorporation in a state with restrictive laws
- Staggered board of directors
- Restricted voting rights
- Supermajority voting provisions
- Fair price amendments
- Golden parachutes

Post-Offer Takeover Defense Mechanisms

- "Just say no" defense
- Litigation
- Greenmail
- Share repurchase
- Leveraged recapitalization
- "Crown Jewel" defense
- "Pac-man" defense
- White knight defense
- White squire defense

Regulation

Antitrust Laws

These laws ensure that markets remain competitive. A common measure of market power is the Herfindahl-Hirschman Index (HHI). It measures market concentration by summing the squares of the market shares for each company in an industry.

$$HHI = \sum_{i}^{n} \left(\frac{\text{Sales or output of firm } i}{\text{Total sales or output of market}} \times 100 \right)^2$$

A higher HHI means that the industry is highly concentrated and there is little competition. Regulatory authorities are not only concerned with the HHI before the merger, but also with the change in HHI due to the merger.

HHI concentration level

Post-Merger HHI	Concentration	Change in HHI	Government Action
Less than 1,000	Not concentrated	Any amount	No action
Between 1,000 and 1,800	Moderately concentrated	100 or more	Possible challenge
More than 1,800	Highly concentrated	50 or more	Challenge

Additional considerations used in evaluating market power:

- Responsiveness of consumers to price changes.
- Efficiency of companies in the industry.
- Financial viability of merger candidates.
- Ability of U.S. companies to compete in foreign markets.

Securities Laws

These laws aim to maintain both fairness in merger activities and confidence in financial markets. The most important securities law is the Williams Act.

Merger Analysis

Target Company Valuation

Discounted Cash Flow Analysis

In discounted cash flow (DCF) models, analysts estimate the future cash flows expected to be generated by a company and discount these cash flows to the present in order to estimate the value of the company. These models require careful estimation of the growth rate in cash flows and the required rate of return.

Calculating FCFF:

	Net income
+	Net interest after tax
=	Unlevered income
+	Changes in deferred taxes
=	NOPLAT (net operating profit less adjusted taxes)
+	Net noncash charges
−	Change in net working capital
−	Capital expenditures (capex)
	Free cash flow to the firm (FCFF)

Net interest after tax = (Interest expense − Interest income) (1 − tax rate)
Working capital = Current assets (excl. cash and equivalents) − Current liabilities (excl. short-term debt)

Calculating terminal value:

The terminal value may either be calculated using the constant growth formula or by applying a multiple for which the analyst expects the average company to sell at the end of the forecasting horizon.

$$\text{Terminal value}_T = \frac{FCFF_T(1+g)}{(WACC-g)}$$

Advantages of DCF analysis:
- It is easy to model expected changes in the target company's cash flows.
- The estimated intrinsic value is based on forecasted fundamentals.
- It is easy to change assumptions and estimates.

Disadvantages of DCF analysis:
- It is difficult to apply when free cash flows do not align with profitability.
- Estimates of earnings entail a great deal of uncertainty.
- Changes in discount rates due to capital market developments can have a significant impact on valuation.
- Terminal value estimates may vary across calculation methods.

Comparable Company Analysis

Under this approach, relative valuation measures are used to estimate the market value of the target company, and then a takeover premium is added to determine a fair acquisition price.

The following steps are followed in comparable company analysis:
- Identify a set of comparable companies.
- Calculate different relative value measures based on current market prices of comparable companies.
- Calculate specific relative value metrics and apply these to the target firm.
- Estimate the takeover premium.
  - $$TP = \frac{(DP-SP)}{SP}$$

Advantages:
- The target company's value is estimated using similar companies in the market.
- Most of the required data is readily available.
- Value estimates are derived directly from the market.

Disadvantages:
- A mispricing in one of the companies will cause the estimated value to be incorrect as well.
- The takeover premium needs to be estimated separately.
- It is difficult to incorporate any specific plans for the target company into the analysis.
- The data available for past premiums may not be suitable for the target company.

Comparable Transaction Analysis

This approach utilizes recent merger transactions involving comparable companies to determine a fair acquisition price (directly) for the target company. It requires the following steps:

- Identification of relevant merger transactions.
- Based on completed deals and transaction prices, relative valuation metrics are calculated for the companies in sample.
- Apply multiples to the target company.

Advantages of comparable transaction analysis:

- There is no need to estimate the takeover premium separately as it is built into the transaction prices used to calculate valuation multiples.
- Actual (and recent) transaction values are used in deriving the target's value, as opposed to the subjective estimates and assumptions used in DCF analysis.
- Challenges to valuation (litigation risk for target board members or management) are less likely given that recent comparable transaction prices are used.

Disadvantages of comparable transaction analysis:

- Recent transaction prices can be influenced by market conditions. In such instances, these inaccuracies flow through to the estimates of target company value.
- A lack of recent and relevant transaction data for companies in the same industry may force the use of data from related sectors. As a result, the value derived for the target may not be accurate.
- It is difficult to incorporate any anticipated target capital structure changes and merger synergies into the analysis.

Bid Evaluation

Target shareholders' gain = Premium = Price paid for the target company − Pre-merger value of the target company

Acquirers' gain = Synergies − Premium

The post-merger value of the combined company can be calculated as:

$$V_A^* = V_A + V_T + S - C$$

V_A^* = Post-merger value of the combined company
V_A = Pre-merger value of the acquirer
V_T = Pre-merger value of the target company
S = Synergies created by the business combination
C = Cash paid to target shareholders

When evaluating a merger offer, the minimum bid that target shareholders would accept is the pre-merger market value of the target company, while the maximum amount that any acquirer would be willing to pay is the pre-merger value of the target plus the value of potential synergies.

Bidding prices therefore generally lie between these two amounts. This also implies that analysis of a merger not only depends on the assessment of pre-merger target value, but also assessments of estimated synergies.

Factors Affecting Choice of Payment

- The more confident the counterparties are that estimated synergies will be realized from the merger, the more the acquiring company would want to pay in cash, and the more the target shareholders would prefer receiving stock.
    - The greater the proportion of the acquisition price represented by stock, the more that the risk and rewards of the merger will be passed on to target shareholders.
- The more confident the acquiring company is in its estimates of the target's value, the more it would prefer to pay in cash and the more the target would prefer to receive stock.

Who Benefits from Mergers?

- Empirical studies show that over the short-term, merger transactions benefit target company shareholders, while acquiring company shareholders suffer.
- In the long-term, acquiring companies tend to underperform comparable companies.

Based on empirical results, the characteristics of mergers and acquisitions that create value are:

- The buyer is strong.
- The transaction premiums are relatively low.
- The number of bidders is low.
- The initial market reaction is favorable.

Corporate Restructuring

Corporate restructuring typically refers to when a company gets smaller by selling, splitting off, or shedding operating assets. When a company sells a division or a subsidiary, it is referred to as a divestiture. Common reasons for restructuring are:

- Change in strategic focus.
- Poor fit.
- Reverse synergy.
- Financial or cash flow needs.

CORPORATE FINANCE

Forms of Restructuring

- Equity carve-out: A company separates one of its divisions to create a new legal entity offering its equity to outsiders.

- Spin-off: A company separates one of its divisions to create a new legal entity offering its current shareholders a proportional number of shares in the new entity. A spin-off does not result in a cash inflow to the parent.

- Split-off: A company separates one of its divisions to create a new legal entity offering its current shareholders shares in the newly formed entity in exchange for their shares of the parent.

- Liquidation: A company is broken and sold in parts.

168

© 2015 Wiley

Study Session 10: Equity Valuation—Valuation Concepts

EQUITY VALUATION: APPLICATIONS AND PROCESSES
Cross-Reference to CFA Institute Assigned Reading #28

Intrinsic Value

Intrinsic value is the actual or "true" value of an asset based on its underlying investment characteristics. Estimates of intrinsic value depend on an analyst's forecasts as well as the valuation model used.

Efficient market hypothesis assumes that market price is the best available estimate of a security's intrinsic value. Active management is based on the notion that various factors can cause market price to diverge from intrinsic value. Active investment managers expect to earn abnormal risk-adjusted returns by trading on perceived mispricings (differences between a security's market price and intrinsic value).

There are two possible sources of mispricing:
- The difference between the unobservable true intrinsic value and the observed market price.
- The difference between the intrinsic value estimate and the unobservable true intrinsic value.

Perceived mispricing = True mispricing + Error in the estimate of intrinsic value.

$$V_E - P = (V - P) + (V_E - V)$$

V_E = Estimate of intrinsic value
P = Market price
V = True (unobservable) intrinsic value

Going-Concern Value and Liquidation Value

- The going-concern value of a company is based on the going-concern assumption i.e., the company will continue to exist for the foreseeable future.
- The liquidation value is based on the assumption that the company will immediately be dissolved and its assets sold individually.

The difference between the going-concern and liquidation values for a company depends on:
- The amount of value created by the application of human capital to the assets' productive capacity.
- The time frame available for liquidating assets.

Fair Market Value and Investment Value

- Fair market value is the price at which an asset or a liability can be exchanged between knowledgeable, willing parties in an arm's length transaction. Market prices should in the long-run generally reflect fair market values.
- There might be instances when investors are willing to pay more than the fair market value for an asset (e.g. due to potential synergies). This unique value to the particular buyer based on its requirements and expectations is known as investment value.

Applications of Equity Valuation

- Selecting stocks.
- Inferring market expectations regarding company fundamentals (profitability, risk, etc.).
- Evaluating corporate events (mergers, acquisitions, divestures, etc.).
- Rendering fairness opinions from third parties (e.g. on the terms of a merger).
- Evaluating business strategies and models.
- Communicating with analysts and shareholders.
- Appraising private businesses for transactional and tax reporting purposes.
- Estimating value of share-based payments (compensation).

Steps in the Valuation Process

1. Understanding the business.
2. Forecasting company performance.
3. Selecting the appropriate valuation model.
4. Converting forecasts to a valuation.
5. Applying the valuation conclusions.

Industry and Competitive Analysis

How attractive are the industries in which the company operates?
- Intra-industry rivalry: Low rivalry among the industry participants enhances overall industry profitability.
- New entrants: High barriers to entry result in higher industry profitability.
- Substitutes: A few potential substitutes and high switching costs increase industry profitability.
- Supplier power: A large number of suppliers for inputs benefit the industry.
- Buyer power: A large number of customers for an industry's product is generally better for the industry.

What is the company's corporate strategy?
- Cost leadership: A company following this strategy aims to become the lowest cost producer of a specific product.
- Differentiation: A company following this strategy charges premium prices in return for its unique products and services that are valued by customers.
- Focus: A company following this strategy aims to seek competitive advantage in a particular target segment or segments either based on cost leadership or differentiation.

How well has the company executed its strategy and what are its prospects for future execution?
- Evaluate qualitative factors (e.g. ownership structure, economic value of intangible assets, etc.).
- Do not assume that past performance will be replicated going forward.

How persistent are the company's earnings?
- Identify those aspects of reported performance that are not likely to recur.
- Decompose income into its cash and accrual components. Accrual components are less persistent and result in lower ROA in the future.

Forecasting Company Performance

The top-down forecasting approach starts with international and national macroeconomic forecasts followed by industry forecasts and finally, individual company and asset forecasts. The bottom-up forecasting approach aggregates individual company forecasts into industry forecasts, which in turn are aggregated to macroeconomic forecasts.

Valuation Models

Absolute valuation models look to estimate an asset's intrinsic value which can then be compared with its market price (e.g. dividend discount models and asset-based valuation models). Relative valuation models are based on the assumption that similar assets should be priced similarly and estimate an asset's value relative to that of another asset. Relative valuation is typically implemented using price multiples, the most common of which is the price-to-earnings ratio (P/E).

Instead of valuing a company as a single entity, analysts may estimate the values of its various businesses individually as going-concerns and then add them up to arrive at a value for the company. This method is known as sum-of-the-parts valuation. Conglomerate discounts may need to be applied when using this approach.

Criteria for Model Selection

The model must be:
* Consistent with the characteristics of the company being valued.
* Appropriate, given the availability and quality of data.
* Consistent with the purpose of valuation, including the analyst's perspective.

Converting Forecasts to a Valuation

* Sensitivity analysis aims to determine how changes in an assumed input would alter the outcome of the analysis.
* Situational adjustments include:
  * **Control premiums:** An investor willing to acquire a controlling interest in a company will need to pay a premium for control.
  * **Lack of marketability discount:** An investor requires a greater return from securities that are not traded publicly to compensate her for the lack of marketability.
  * **Illiquidity discount:** Securities that are not traded very frequently often reflect an illiquidity discount.

Analysts

* Sell-side analysts issue research reports that are widely distributed to current and prospective retail and institutional brokerage clients.
* Buy-side analysts work at investment management firms, trust, and bank trust departments where they issue reports that are used by the portfolio manager or investment committee as inputs in investment decision-making.

Analysts' Role and Responsibilities

In performing valuations, analysts should hold themselves accountable to (1) standards of competence and (2) standards of conduct.

- Analysts help clients achieve their investment objectives.
- Analysts contribute to the efficient functioning of capital markets.
- Analysts benefit the suppliers of capital by effectively monitoring management performance.

Characteristics of an Effective Research Report

- Contains timely information.
- Is written in clear, incisive language.
- Is objective and well researched, with key assumptions clearly identified.
- Distinguishes clearly between facts and opinions.
- Contains analysis, forecasts, valuation, and a recommendation that are internally consistent.
- Presents sufficient information to allow a reader to critique the valuation.
- States the key risk factors involved in an investment in the company.
- Discloses any potential conflicts of interests faced by the analyst.

RETURN CONCEPTS
Cross-Reference to CFA Institute Assigned Reading #29

Holding Period Return (HPR)

HPR is the return earned on an investment over the entire investment horizon and consists of two components- investment income and price return. It is calculated as:

$$\text{Holding period return} = \frac{P_1 - P_0 + D_1}{P_0}$$

- Holding period returns based on past information (in which the selling price and dividends are known) are referred to as realized holding period returns.
- Holding period returns in a forward-looking context (in which the selling price and dividends are not known) are referred to as expected holding period returns.

Required Return

The required return is the minimum level of return required by an investor to invest in a particular asset (given the level of risk) over a specified period of time.

- If the expected return is equal to the investor's required return, the asset is fairly valued.
- If the expected return exceeds the investor's required return, the asset is undervalued.
- If the expected return is lower than the investor's required return, the asset is overvalued.

The difference between an asset's expected return and required return is called the asset's expected alpha or expected abnormal return. The difference between actual holding period return and the required return for the same period is called realized alpha.

- If an asset's current price *equals* its intrinsic value, the expected return is the same as the required return and the expected alpha is zero.
- If an asset's current price *exceeds* its intrinsic value, the expected return is less than the required return and the expected alpha is negative.
- If an asset's current price is *lower* than its intrinsic value, the expected return is greater than the required return and the expected alpha is positive.

When an asset's current price is lower than its intrinsic value, an investor would expect the market price to converge to intrinsic value over time. In such a situation, the investor's expected return has two components; the required return and a return from convergence of price to intrinsic value. However, the convergence component of expected return can be risky because:

- The analyst's estimates may not be accurate.
- The price may not converge to its intrinsic value over the investor's time horizon.

Discount Rate

The discount rate is used by investors to calculate the present value of a future stream of cash flows. It is based on the characteristics of the investment.

Internal Rate of Return (IRR)

The internal rate of return on an investment is the discount rate that equates the present value of all expected inflows from the investment to its current price. If an asset is assumed to be efficiently priced (i.e., market price equals its intrinsic value), the IRR can be calculated using the dividend discount model as follows:

$$\text{Required return}(\text{IRR}) = \frac{\text{Next year's dividend}}{\text{Market price}} + \text{Expected dividend growth rate}$$

The Equity Risk Premium (ERP)

ERP refers to the additional return (premium) required by investors to invest in equities rather than a risk-free asset.

The required rate of return on a particular stock can be computed using either of the following two approaches. Both these approaches require the equity risk premium to be estimated first.

1. Required return on share i = Current expected risk-free return + β_i (Equity risk premium)
   - A beta greater (lower) than 1 indicates that the security has greater-than-average (lower-than-average) systematic risk.
2. Required return on share i = Current expected risk-free return + Equity risk premium $\pm$ Other risk premia/discounts appropriate for i
   - This method of estimating the required return is known as the build-up method. It is discussed later in the reading and is primarily used for valuations of private businesses.

The equity risk premium may be estimated based on:
- Historical estimates of the difference between broad-based equity market-index returns and government debt returns over the same time period.
  - Use of the geometric mean is preferred over use of the arithmetic mean.
  - Use of the long-term government bond rate is preferred to use of a short-term rate as a proxy for the risk-free rate.
  - Estimates may be adjusted for survivorship bias, and to bring them in line with independent forward-looking estimates.
- Forward-looking estimates, which can be drawn from:
  - The Gordon growth model.
  - Macroeconomic models.
  - Surveys.

Estimating the Required Return on Equity

The required return on equity may be estimated using anyone of the following models:

1. The Capital Asset Pricing Model (CAPM)

    Required return on a stock = Expected risk-free rate + Beta × Equity risk premium

    The CAPM uses only one factor and is therefore very simple. However, choosing the appropriate factor can be problematic and the model may have low explanatory power in some cases.

2. Multifactor Models

    Required return = Risk-free rate + (Risk premium)$_1$ + (Risk premium)$_2$ + ... + (Risk premium)$_k$

*   Fama-French Model
    * $r_i = RF + \beta_i^{mkt}RMRF + \beta_i^{size}SMB + \beta_i^{value}HML$
*   The Pastor-Stambaugh model adds a liquidity factor to the Fama-French model.

*   Macroeconomic multifactor models use economic variables that affect the value of companies as factors.

*   Statistical factor models use statistical methods to determine a portfolio of securities (serving as factors) that explain historical returns.

    Multifactor models generally have higher explanatory power but are more complex and costly.

3. Build-Up Method

    The build-up method starts with the risk-free rate and adds premiums for different risks, but does not use betas to adjust factor risk premiums.

    r_i = Risk-free rate + Equity risk premium + Size premium + Specific-company premium

    Another example of this method is the bond-yield plus risk premium approach.

    BYPRP cost of equity = YTM on the company's long-term debt + Risk premium

    Build-up models tend to be very simple and can be applied to closely-held companies. However, they use historical estimates that may no longer be relevant.

Methods of Estimating Beta

*   Through a regression of the return of a stock on the return of the market. The value obtained is called "raw" or unadjusted beta and needs to be adjusted for beta drift.

    Adjusted beta = (2/3) (Unadjusted beta) + (1/3) (1.0)

- For thinly-traded stocks or non-public companies, beta may be estimated using the pure-play method:
  - ○ Identify a comparable public company.
  - ○ Estimate the beta of the comparable public company.
  - ○ Un-lever the beta of the public company to estimate the beta of its assets.
  - ○ Re-lever the asset beta of the public company based on the financial leverage of the subject company.

Issues in Estimating the Required Return on Equity in an International Context

- Analysts should incorporate exchange rate forecasts into their expectations of the local currency performance of the equity market and the risk-free asset.
- It is difficult to estimate the required return and risk premium in emerging markets.
  - ○ The country spread and country risk rating models can be used to estimate the equity risk premium.

The Weighted Average Cost of Capital (WACC)

$$WACC = \frac{MVD}{MVD + MVCE} r_d (1 - Tax\ rate) + \frac{MVCE}{MVD + MVCE} r$$

- The cost of debt is adjusted downwards by a factor of $(1 - t)$ to reflect the tax deductibility of corporate interest payments.
- Use of the marginal tax rate is preferred over use of the effective tax rate in adjusting the cost of debt.
- Analysts often use target weights instead of current market value-weights of equity and debt in the capital structure when calculating the WACC.

Discount Rate Selection in Relation to Cash Flows

- When a cash flow to equity is discounted, the nominal required return on equity is the appropriate discount rate.
- When a cash flow to the firm is discounted, the nominal after-tax WACC is the appropriate discount rate.

THE FIVE COMPETITIVE FORCES THAT SHAPE STRATEGY
Cross-Reference to CFA Institute Assigned Reading #30

Forces that Shape Competition

Threat of Entry- What are the chances of new firms entering the industry?

- Significant economies of scale make it difficult for new companies to enter the market.
- Large demand-side benefits of scale deter new companies from entering the market.
- High product switching costs make it difficult for existing customers to move to a competitor's product.
- High capital requirements are a hindrance for new entrants.
- Incumbent firms may have cost or quality advantages.
- It may be difficult for new firms to secure or bypass existing distribution channels.
- Government policies (e.g. patents and licenses) may act as a hindrance for new firms.
- New firms may not be inclined to enter the industry fearing retaliation from existing firms.

The Power of Suppliers - How strong is the negotiating position of suppliers of production inputs to the industry? The relative power of suppliers depends on whether:

- The supplier group is more concentrated than the industry it caters to.
- The supplier group is heavily dependent on the industry for its revenues.
- The supplier group offers differentiated products.
- Substitutes for suppliers' products are easily available.
- It is relatively easy for suppliers to integrate forward into the industry.
- Switching costs for the industry participants are high.

The Power of Buyers - How strong is the negotiating position of buyers of industry output? The relative power of customers depends on whether:

- There are only a few buyers that purchase industry output in large volumes.
- The industry offers standardized or differentiated products.
- Buyers face low costs in switching to other vendors.
- It is relatively easy for them to integrate backwards.

The Threat of Substitutes - To what extent can substitute products limit the profit potential of an industry? The threat of substitutes is high if:

- Potential substitutes offer a better price-performance trade-off.
- Buyers face low switching costs.

Rivalry among Existing Competitors - To what extent does the rivalry among existing firms in the industry limits their profit potential? The intensity of rivalry is high if:

- There are a large number of competitors of similar size and power.
- Industry growth is slow.
- There are high exit barriers.
- Firms are highly committed to the business.
- Firms are not familiar with each other's competitive strategies and goals.

Price competition usually reduces overall industry profitability. However, competition based on other aspects (e.g. product features, brand image, etc.) enhances value for customers and could potentially increase profitability through premium prices.

A study of the five competitive forces helps management understand the overall structure of an industry. This in turn helps the company devise strategies relating to positioning the company to cope with the competitive forces, anticipating and exploiting shifts in the forces, and shaping the balance of forces to create a new industry structure that is more favorable to the company.

Fleeting Factors

The following factors affect an industry's prospects over the short term (as opposed to Porter's five forces that affect industry profitability and structure over the long term).

Industry Growth Rate

A high industry growth rate may not always be a positive sign for an industry:
- It can increase the relative power of suppliers.
- It can draw in new entrants.

Technology and Innovation

It is not necessary that a high-technology industry will be relatively more profitable. A low-tech industry may be profitable if it has high barriers to entry, buyers are not price sensitive, or if switching costs for customers are high.

Government

- Licensing requirements raise barriers to entry in an industry.
- Government policies in favour of labor unions increase the power of suppliers, limiting an industry's profitability.
- Bankruptcy rules that allow companies to reorganize can lead to excess capacity and intense competition.

Complementary Products and Services

Complements can have a negative or positive effect on an industry. They can raise or lower barriers to entry, can affect the threat of substitutes, and can also influence industry rivalry.

Industry Structure

Eliminating rivals is a risky strategy because removing existing competitors to increase profits might attract new firms to the industry, and may also sometimes result in a backlash from customers or suppliers.

Achieving a Competitive Advantage

Based on their understanding of competitive forces, managers may improve company prospects by:

- Positioning the company in a manner that allows it to effectively cope with the current environment;
- Anticipating and exploiting shifts in the forces; and/or
- Shaping industry structure so that it is more favorable for the company.

Typical Steps in Industry Analysis

1. Define the relevant industry:
   - What products are in it? Which ones are part of another distinct industry?
   - What is the geographic scope of competition?

2. Identify the participants and segment them into groups, if appropriate:
   Who are:
   - the buyers and buyer groups?
   - the suppliers and supplier groups?
   - the competitors?
   - the substitutes?
   - the potential entrants?

3. Assess the underlying drivers of each competitive force to determine which forces are strong and which are weak and why.

4. Determine overall industry structure, and test the analysis for consistency:
   - Why is the level of profitability what it is?
   - Which are the controlling forces for profitability?
   - Is the industry analysis consistent with actual long-run profitability?
   - Are more-profitable players better positioned in relation to the five forces?

5. Analyze recent and likely future changes in each force, both positive and negative.

6. Identify aspects of industry structure that might be influenced by competitors, by new entrants, or by your company.

Common Pitfalls

- Defining the industry too broadly or too narrowly.
- Making lists instead of engaging in rigorous analysis.
- Paying equal attention to all of the forces rather than digging deeply into the most important ones.
- Confusing effect (price sensitivity) with cause (buyer economics).
- Using static analysis that ignores industry trends.
- Confusing cyclical or transient changes with true structural changes.
- Using the framework to declare an industry attractive or unattractive rather than using it to guide strategic choices.

YOUR STRATEGY NEEDS A STRATEGY
Cross-Reference to CFA Institute Assigned Reading #31

Finding the Right Strategic Style

Typically, an analysis of (1) predictability and (2) malleability can go a long way in determining the type of strategy a company should employ.

Predictability refers to how far into the future and how accurately the company can forecast the following:
- Industry demand.
- Corporate performance.
- Competitive dynamics.
- Market expectations.

Malleability (or **mutability**) refers to the extent to which industry firms can influence these factors.

Table 1: Strategic Styles

	Less Predictable	More predictable
Less malleable	Adaptive	Classical
More malleable	Shaping	Visionary

SALIENT FEATURES OF VARIOUS STRATEGIC STYLES

Classical

- The central goal of the classical style is typically to optimize efficiency.
- Once strategic plans are set, they tend to stay in place for several years.
- Since specialized analytical and quantitative skills are required, the strategic planning function can operate as a stand-alone function.

Adaptive

- The focus here is not as much on optimizing efficiency, as it is on engineering flexibility.
- The company strives to attain the ability to shift, acquire, or divest resources smoothly and promptly.
- Planning cycles are much shorter (typically less than a year or even continuous).
- Strategy is closely linked to operations so that the company is able to efficiently respond to any changes signaled by the market.

Shaping

- Short or continual planning cycles with a strategy that is more like a portfolio of experiments.
- The company focuses beyond its own boundaries, and tries to develop an ecosystem of customers and suppliers by developing new markets, technology platforms and business practices.

- Extensive use of marketing, lobbying, and partnership-building to develop this ecosystem.

Visionary

- Companies devote the necessary resources, and focus on executing carefully-laid plans to back their (big) bets. There is unwavering confidence in a particular strategic direction.
- The attitude is that of a pioneer: "build-it-and-they-will-come".

Survival

- The company thinks and behaves defensively, focusing on trimming costs and preserving capital.
- At the same time it keeps an eye out for any favorable changes in the environment, ready to adopt a more growth-oriented strategy when the crisis is over.

TRAPS THAT EXECUTIVES TEND TO FALL INTO IN STRATEGY FORMULATION

Misplaced Confidence

There tends to be a tendency on part of executives to overestimate both (1) how predictable their industry is, and (2) the extent to which they can mold it.

Unexamined Habits

While most executives recognize the importance of being able to adapt to an ever-changing business environment, most are not sufficiently competent in building those capabilities.

Culture Mismatches

If a company has been successful by following a particular strategy style for an extended period, it may be difficult to change over to another style (even though changes in industry predictability and/or malleability may demand it) if the style has become ingrained in the company culture.

INDUSTRY AND COMPANY ANALYSIS
Cross-Reference to CFA Institute Assigned Reading #32

APPROACHES TO PROJECTING FUTURE REVENUE

- Under a **top-down approach**, the analyst begins with the overall economy and then moves to more narrowly defined levels (sector, industry or specific product) before eventually arriving at a revenue forecast for a particular company. There are two common top-down approaches to modeling revenue:
  - In the growth relative to GDP growth approach, the analyst considers how a company's growth rate will compare with growth in nominal GDP.
  - In the market growth and market share approach, the analyst first forecasts growth for a particular market, and then considers how the company's current market share is likely to grow over time.

- Under a **bottom-up approach**, an analyst begins at the individual company level or the individual unit level (product line, segment or location) within the company, and then aggregates those forecasts to project total revenue for the company. Subsequently, revenue projections for individual companies are aggregated to develop forecasts for the sector, industry or overall economy. Bottom-up approaches to forecasting revenue include:
  - Time series, where forecasts are based on historical growth rates or time series analysis.
  - Return on capital, where forecasts are based on balance sheet accounts.
  - Capacity-based measures, e.g. same store sales growth or sales related to new stores in the retail industry.

Under a **hybrid approach**, elements of both the top-down and bottom-up approach are combined. Hybrid approaches are the most commonly-used approaches as they are useful (1) in uncovering implicit assumptions made, and (2) in identifying any errors made when using a single approach.

Income Statement Modeling

When forecasting costs, analysts must carefully consider fixed and variable costs.
- **Variable costs** are usually directly linked to revenue growth and are often modeled as (1) a percentage of revenue or (2) projected unit volumes multiplied by variable costs per unit.
- **Fixed costs** are not related to revenue; instead they are typically linked to (1) future investment in PP&E and (2) total capacity growth.

Economies of scale occur when average cost per unit declines as total output increases. Factors that can lead to economies of scale include:
- Greater bargaining power with suppliers.
- Lower cost of capital.
- Lower per-unit marketing costs.

If a company/industry is benefiting from economies of scale, its gross and/or operating margins would be positively correlated with sales levels. An analysis of common-size income statements would show that larger companies in the industry would have lower COGS and/or SG&A as a percentage of sales compared to smaller companies.

Cost of Goods Sold (COGS)

Generally speaking, COGS tends to be the largest component of total cost for manufacturing and merchandising companies.

Future COGS = (Historical COGS / Revenue) × Projected sales

Future COGS = (1 − Historical GP margin) × Projected sales

- Given that COGS comprises the bulk of operating costs, analysts may find it useful to break down these costs (e.g. by segment, by product category, or by volume and price components) to improve forecasting accuracy.
- Analysts should also consider the company's general strategy regarding hedging various input costs.
- Finally, analysts should also check their gross margin assumptions against those of the company's competitors.

Selling, General and Administrative Expenses (SG&A)

Generally speaking, SG&A have less of a correlation with revenue than COGS. While some components may be forecasted as a percentage of sales (e.g. wages and salaries), others tend to be less variable in nature (e.g. R&D expense and employee overheads).

Financing Expenses

- Interest income depends on (1) the amount of cash and cash equivalents held by the company, and (2) the rate of return earned on investments.
- Interest expense depends on (1) the amount of debt in the company capital structure, and (2) the interest rate associated with the debt.

Corporate Income Tax

- The statutory tax rate, which is the legally applicable rate charged in the country where the company is located.
- The effective tax rate, which is calculated as the reported tax amount (income tax expense) on the income statement divided by pre-tax income.
- The cash tax rate, which is calculated as tax actually paid divided by pre-tax income.

Differences between cash taxes and reported taxes result from (temporary) timing differences in the recognition of certain items between the tax return and the financial statements of a company. These differences are reflected in deferred tax assets and liabilities. On the other hand, differences between the statutory tax rate and the effective tax rate arise from permanent differences. Examples include tax credits, withholding taxes on dividends, adjustments to prior years, and expenses not deductible for tax purposes. A reconciliation of these two is typically contained in the notes to the financial statements.

- Effective tax rates can differ if a company operates in multiple jurisdictions with different statutory tax rates.
- In order to minimize taxes, some companies create special purpose entities to minimize profits reported in high-tax rate countries.

- Analysts should adjust the effective tax rate for one-time events. Further, if income from investments in subsidiaries accounted for using the equity method forms a substantial and volatile part of pre-tax income, analysts should exclude this item in estimating the future tax expense.
- Generally speaking, analysts project future tax expense using a tax rate based on normalized operating income (i.e., income before special items and income from associates).
- While the effective tax rate is used for forecasting earnings, it is the cash tax rate that is used for forecasting cash flows. Any differences between the tax amount on the P&L (income tax expense) and the amount on the cash flow statement (cash taxes) should be reconciled through a change in deferred tax assets/liabilities.

Other Items

- A company's stated dividend policy can be used to project future dividends. Typically, analysts assume that dividends grow each year (1) by a particular dollar amount, or (2) as a proportion of net income.
- If a company owns more than 50% of an affiliate, it will generally consolidate the affiliate's results with its own and report the portion of income that does not belong to it as minority interest.
- If a company owns less than 50% of an affiliate, it will report its share of income from the affiliate using the equity method.
- Share count (shares issued and outstanding) is a key input in the calculation of an intrinsic value estimate and earnings per share. Changes in a company's share count may come from (1) dilution related to exercise of stock options, convertible bonds, and similar securities, (2) issuance of new shares, and (3) share repurchases.
- Analysts usually exclude unusual charges from their forecasts as they are very difficult to predict. However, if a company has a history of classifying certain recurring costs as "unusual", analysts may want to include a "normalized" level of unusual charges in their forecasts.

Balance Sheet and Cash Flow Statement Modeling

Working capital accounts are typically forecast using efficiency ratios.

Long term assets such as net PP&E are not strongly linked to the income statement. Net PP&E changes are linked to capital expenditures and depreciation (which are both important components of the cash flow statement).

- Depreciation forecasts are based on historical depreciation and disclosures relating to depreciation schedules.
- Capital expenditure forecasts depend on estimated future need for new PP&E. Capital expenditure includes:
  - Maintenance capital expenditures, which are required to sustain current business.
  - Growth capital expenditures, which are required to expand the business.

In order to project future debt and equity levels, analysts must make assumptions regarding leverage ratios (e.g. debt-capital, debt-equity and debt-EBITDA). Analysts must also consider the company's historical practices, current financial strategy and capital requirements when projecting future capital structure.

Return on Invested Capital

Return on invested capital (ROIC) measures the profitability of capital invested by the company.

ROIC = NOPLAT / Invested capital

- NOPLAT = Net operating profit less adjusted taxes.
- Invested capital = Operating assets − Operating liabilities.

ROIC is a better measure of profitability than return on equity (ROE) as it is not affected by the company's financial leverage/capital structure. Generally speaking, a sustainably high ROIC indicates a competitive advantage.

Return on Capital Employed (ROCE)

Return on capital employed (ROCE) is similar to ROIC, but focuses on pretax operating profit.

ROCE = Operating profit / Capital employed

- Operating profit is a pretax measure of profitability.
- Capital employed = Debt capital + Equity capital.

Since it is a pretax measure, ROCE is useful in performing comparisons across companies in different countries with different tax structures.

INFLATION AND DEFLATION

Industry Sales and Inflation or Deflation

The relationship between increases in input costs and increases in the price of final products depends on the following factors:
- Industry structure.
- Price elasticity of demand.
- Reaction of competitors and availability of substitutes.

Company Sales and Inflation or Deflation

In order to forecast revenue for a company that faces rising input costs, analysts must consider the following:
- Price elasticity of demand for its products.
- The different rates of cost inflation in countries where the company operates.
- Likely inflations in costs for individual product categories.
- Pricing strategy and market position.

Industry Costs and Inflation or Deflation

In order to forecast industry costs, analysts must consider the following:
- Specific purchasing characteristics.
- Underlying drivers of input prices.
- The competitive environment.

Company Costs and Inflation or Deflation

In order to forecast company costs, analysts should:
- Break down costs by category and geography, and evaluate the impact of inflation or deflation on each individual item.
- Consider whether the company can find cheaper substitutes or increase efficiency to offset the impact of higher input prices.

Technological Developments

Since the impact of technological innovation can be so unpredictable and significant, analysts typically employ a variety of assumptions and use scenario and/or sensitivity analysis to project future earnings.

- If a new innovation threatens to cannibalize sales of an existing product, a unit sales forecast for the new product must be combined with an expected cannibalization factor to project demand for the existing product.
- Technological developments can affect demand, supply or both.

Longer-Term Forecasting

In determining the appropriate forecasting horizon, analysts must consider the following:

- Investment strategy for which the stock is being considered.
- Industry cyclicality.
- Company-specific factors.
- Valuation methods mandated by supervisor.

Longer term projections typically provide a better reflection of normalized earnings than short term forecasts. Normalized earnings reflect mid-cycle earnings for a company after excluding any unusual or temporary factors that (favorably or unfavorably) affect profitability.

Considerations in Deriving a Terminal Value Estimate

- If historical multiples are used to estimate terminal value, the implicit assumption is that the past is a good reflection of future expectations regarding growth and required returns. If the future growth and/or profitability of the company is likely to be significantly different from the historical average, a premium/discount should be applied to the historical multiple to reflect those differences.

- If the discounted cash flow (DCF) approach is used to estimate terminal value, the analyst should first determine whether the terminal year free cash flow forecast actually reflects normalized (mid-cycle) cash flows. If it does not, then an adjustment to reflect the normalized amount must be performed.

  Further, the analyst should also consider how the future long-term growth rate may be different from the historical growth rate.

- A final challenge for analysts in long term forecasting is anticipating inflection points, where the future will significantly differ from the recent past. Such abrupt changes can come from:
  - Economic disruption (e.g. the 2008 financial crisis).
  - Changes in business cycle stage.
  - Government regulation.
  - Technological advances.

Building a Model

1. Collect industry information.

2. Collect company information including segment-wise financial information.

3. Construct the pro forma financial income statement.
   a. Forecast revenues for each individual segment using a top-down, bottom-up or hybrid approach.
      - Under the top-down approach, any of the market growth plus market share, trend growth rate, or growth relative to GDP growth approaches can be used.
      - In the bottom-up approach, sales revenues are forecast based on assumptions of future prices, volumes, and exchange rates.
   b. Estimate COGS. COGS can be estimated based on a percentage of sales, or on a more detailed method which examines the company's business strategy, and competitive environment.
   c. Estimate SG&A. SG&A can be assumed to be fixed, or be related to sales.
   d. Estimate financing costs. Financing costs require making assumptions regarding future interest rates, debt levels, capital structure, and capital expenditure requirements.
   e. Estimate income tax expense. This is based on the historical effective tax rate (with adjustments if necessary).
   f. Estimate cash taxes. This requires consideration of changes in deferred tax items.

4. Construct the pro forma balance sheet.
   a. Most balance sheet accounts (retained earnings, accounts receivable, accounts payable and inventory) are related to the income statement.
   b. Net PP&E is estimated based on depreciation estimates and capital expenditures (for maintenance and growth) which are typically estimated based on sales.
   c. Liability and capital accounts are influenced by the target capital structure, dividend payments, share repurchases and debt redemptions/issues.

5. Construct the pro forma cash flow statement. Most of the inputs for the pro forma cash flow statement (e.g. operating profit, capital expenditures, working capital estimates, and capital structure changes) are estimated while constructing the pro forma income statement and balance sheet.

Analysts must use sensitivity analysis or scenario analysis to come up with a range of potential outcomes and assign probabilities to each outcome when appropriate.

DISCOUNTED DIVIDEND VALUATION
Cross-Reference to CFA Institute Assigned Reading #33

Present Value Models

Dividend Discount Models

The advantage of using dividends as a measure of cash flow is that dividends are less volatile than earnings and other return measures. The use of dividends as a measure of cash flow is appropriate when:

- The firm has a history of paying dividends.
- The company has an established dividend policy where dividends are related to the firm's earnings.
- The investor takes a non-control perspective.

Discounting Free Cash Flow

- Free cash flow to the firm (FCFF): The cash flow generated from a firm's operations less capital expenditure (investments in new assets and working capital).
- Free cash flow to equity (FCFE): The cash flow generated from a firm's operations less capital expenditures and net payments to debt holders.

The advantage of using DCF approaches is that they can be used for most companies, even those that do not currently pay dividends. However, free cash flows may sometimes be negative, which makes the application of the model difficult. The use of discounted free cash flow models is appropriate when:

- The firm does not have a history of paying dividends.
- The firm does pay dividends, but dividends significantly deviate from FCFE.
- The firm's free cash flow is related to its profitability.
- The investor takes a control perspective.

Residual Income Models

Residual income is calculated as the firm's earnings over a given period minus the investors' required rate of return on the beginning-of-period investment. The model asserts that the value of a company equals its book value plus the present value of expected future residual earnings. Use of the residual income is appropriate when:

- The firm does not have a history of paying dividends.
- The firm's expected free cash flows are negative for the foreseeable future.
- The firm's quality of accounting disclosures is good.

The Dividend Discount Model

One-Period DDM

$$V_0 = \frac{D_1}{(1+r)^1} + \frac{P_1}{(1+r)^1} = \frac{D_1 + P_1}{(1+r)^1}$$

Multiple-Year Holding Period DDM

$$V_0 = \frac{D_0(1+g)}{(r-g)}, \text{ or } V_0 = \frac{D_1}{(r-g)}$$

Infinite Period DDM (Gordon Growth Model)

$$V_0 = \frac{D_0(1+g)}{(r-g)}, \text{ or } V_0 = \frac{D_1}{(r-g)}$$

The relation between r and g is critical:
- As the difference between r and g increases, the intrinsic value of the stock falls.
- As the difference narrows, the intrinsic value of the stock rises.
- Small changes in either r or g can cause large changes in the value of the stock.

For the infinite-period DDM model to work, the following assumptions must hold:

- Dividends grow at a rate, g, which is not expected to change.
- r must be greater than g; otherwise, the model breaks down because of the denominator being negative.

The long-term constant growth rate can be calculated as earnings retention rate times return on equity.

$$g = \text{Retention rate} \times \text{Net profit margin} \times \text{Asset turnover} \times \text{Financial leverage}$$

The Gordon growth formula can be rearranged to calculate either the implied required rate of return on equity or the implied growth rate, given the other variables.

$$r = D_1/P_0 + g$$

$$g = r - D_1/P_0$$

DDM models can also be used to value companies that repurchase stock as long as the effect of expected repurchases on the dividend growth rate is taken into account.

If the firm distributes all of its earnings to shareholders in the form of dividends, the growth rate would equal zero. In this case, the value of the firm would equal current dividend divided by the required rate of return.

$$V_0 = \frac{D_0}{r}$$

Present value of Growth Opportunities

The value of a stock can be broken down into two components:
- The value of the company without the earnings reinvestment (E_1/r) – known as no-growth value per share.
- The present value of growth opportunities (PVGO).

$$V_0 = \frac{E_1}{r} + PVGO$$

PVGO is determined by:
- The company's options or opportunities to invest.
- The company's available real options and managerial flexibility.

Explaining Negative PVGO

- There may be an expectation that management's current competitive and investment strategy will destroy value.
- The stock may be severely undervalued (possibly as a result of a significant recent market crash).
- The estimate of the no-growth value may be too high (i.e., the earnings estimate is too high and/or required return estimate is too low).

Gordon Growth Model and the Price-to-Earnings Ratio

The P/E ratio derived from the Gordon growth model is referred to as the justified P/E ratio as it is "justified" on the basis of fundamentals.

The P/E ratio based on forecasted next year's earnings is called leading P/E.

$$\text{Justified leading P/E ratio} = \frac{P_0}{E_1} = \frac{D_1/E_1}{r-g} = \frac{(1-b)}{r-g}$$

The P/E ratio based on earnings over the last four quarters is called trailing P/E.

$$\text{Justified trailing P/E} = \frac{P_0}{E_0} = \frac{D_1/E_0}{r-g} = \frac{D_0(1+g)/E_0}{r-g} = \frac{(1-b)(1+g)}{r-g}$$

Strengths and Limitations of the Gordon Growth Model

Strengths
- The model is applicable to stable, mature, and dividend-paying companies.
- It is applicable to broadly developed market equity indices.
- It is very simple and easy to implement.
- It can be used to determine the growth rate, cost of equity, and the present value of growth opportunities implied by a security's current market price.
- As you will see in the next section of this reading, it is used in multistage DDMs to compute company value in the mature phase.

Weaknesses
- Valuations are very sensitive to estimates of the required return on equity and the growth rate.
- The model cannot be applied to non-dividend-paying stocks.
- It cannot be applied to companies whose growth patterns are not expected to remain constant indefinitely.

Value of Non-Callable Fixed-Rate Perpetual Preferred Stock

$$V_0 = \frac{D_0}{r}$$

Terminal Value

The value estimated at the end of the high-growth stages, based on the assumption of a constant future growth rate, is referred to as the terminal value of the stock (also known as continuing value).

The terminal value of a stock may be calculated by either:
- Using the Gordon growth model; or
- Applying a multiple (e.g. P/E) to a forecasted value of a fundamental (e.g. earnings).

Multistage Dividend Discount Models

Companies usually go through the following phases:

- Growth phase: High growth in earnings, low or zero dividend payout ratios, and heavy reinvestments.
- Transition phase: Relatively lower earnings growth rate, declining capital requirements, and increasing dividend payout ratios.
- Mature phase: Earnings growth rates, dividend payout ratios, and return on equity stabilize at their long-run levels.

Two-Stage DDM

This model assumes that a company experiences a relatively high growth rate in the short-run (the first stage) and then growth stabilizes in the long run (the second stage).

$$V_0 = \sum_{t=1}^{n} \frac{D_0(1+g_s)^t}{(1+r)^t} + \frac{D_0(1+g_s)^n(1+g_L)}{(1+r)^n(r-g_L)}$$

g_S = Short-term supernormal growth rate
g_L = Long-term sustainable growth rate
r = required return
n = Length of the supernormal growth period

H-Model

The H-Model employs a more realistic assumption (relative to the 2-stage DMM) that the growth rate declines linearly from a temporary short-run extraordinarily high rate to a long-run constant sustainable growth rate.

$$V_0 = \frac{D_0(1+g_L)}{r-g_L} + \frac{D_0 H(g_s-g_L)}{r-g_L}$$

g_S = Short-term high growth rate
g_L = Long-term sustainable growth rate
r = required return
H = Half-life = 0.5 times the length of the high growth period

The above equation can also be rearranged to calculate the required rate of return as follows:

$$r = \left(\frac{D_0}{P_0}\right)[(1+g_L)+H(g_s-g_L)]+g_L$$

Three-Stage Dividend Discount Models

There are two versions of the three-stage DDM. The difference between the two lies in the modeling of the second stage.

In the first version, the company is assumed to have three stages of growth, where the growth rate during each stage is different but constant. For example, Stage 1 may have 25% growth for 3 years, Stage 2 may have 15% growth for 5 years, and Stage 3 could have 5% growth thereafter. Valuing the company under this DDM model requires the following steps:

- Estimate dividends for each year during the first 2 stages of growth and then discount them to the present.

- Estimate the dividend for the first year of the 3rd (constant growth into perpetuity) stage.
- Compute the terminal value at the beginning of the 3rd stage.
- Compute the present value of the terminal value.
- Add up the present values of the dividends over the first 2 stages and the present value of the terminal value.

In the second version of the three-stage DDM, the middle stage is similar to the first stage of the H-model. For example, Stage 1 may have 25% growth for 3 years, Stage 2 may see a linear decline in the growth rate to 5% over 5 years, and Stage 3 could have 5% growth into perpetuity. Valuing the company under this DDM model requires the following steps:

- Estimate dividends for each year during the first stage of growth and then discount them to the present.
- Apply the H-model to the second and third stages to obtain an estimate of value as of the beginning of the second stage. Then discount this estimated value to the present.
- Add up the present values of the dividends over the first stage, and the present value of value obtained from applying the H-model to the second and third stages.

The Sustainable Growth Rate

The sustainable growth rate (SGR) is defined as the growth rate of dividends (and earnings) that the company can sustain for a given return on equity, assuming that the capital structure remains unchanged over time, and no new equity is issued. The long-term sustainable growth rate can be calculated as earnings retention rate times return on equity:

$$g = b \times ROE$$
$$b = \text{Earnings retention rate, calculated as } 1 - \text{Dividend payout ratio}$$

- The higher the return on equity, the higher the sustainable dividend (earnings) growth rate.
- The higher the earnings retention rate, the higher the sustainable dividend (earnings) growth rate. This relationship is referred to as dividend displacement of earnings.

STUDY SESSION 12: EQUITY INVESTMENTS—VALUATION MODELS

FREE CASH FLOW VALUATION
Cross-Reference to CFA Institute Assigned Reading #34

The use of free cash flow as the definition of return is appropriate when:

- The company does not pay dividends.
- The company does pay dividends, but dividends paid deviate significantly from the ability of the firm to pay dividends.
- The company's free cash flows are in line with profitability over the forecasting horizon.
- The perspective is that of an investor with a controlling interest in the company.
- There is a high probability of the company being acquired.

Definition of Free Cash Flow

- Free Cash Flow to the Firm (FCFF): This is the cash flow generated from a firm's operations after operating expenses (and taxes) have been paid, and investments in fixed and working capital have been made. In other words, it is the cash flow available to be distributed to a firm's bondholders and stockholders. In order to calculate the value of the firm, FCFF must be discounted at the weighted average cost of capital.

$$\text{Firm Value} = \sum_{t=1}^{\infty} \frac{FCFF_t}{(1+WACC)^t}$$

- Free Cash Flow to Equity (FCFE): This is the cash flow available to holders of common equity after all operating expenses, interest, and principal payments have been paid, and necessary investment in fixed and working capital have been made. In order to calculate the value of a firm's equity, FCFE is discounted at the required rate of return on equity.

$$\text{Equity Value} = \sum_{t=1}^{\infty} \frac{FCFE_t}{(1+r)^t}$$

Analysts prefer the use of FCFF and FCFE over other cash-flow concepts as they can be used directly in a DCF framework without any adjustments. Other measures, such as CFO, net income, EBIT and EBITDA require a few adjustments before they can be used as proxies for free cash flow.

FCFE versus FCFF

- If the company's capital structure is relatively stable, using FCFE is more direct and simple than using FCFF.
- FCFE may sometimes be negative. In such cases, the value of the firm's equity can be calculated as the difference between the value of the firm (estimated using FCFF) and the market value of the firm's debt.
- The growth in FCFF may reflect a company's fundamentals more accurately than FCFE, which is affected by fluctuating amounts of net borrowings.

Computing FCFF

Computing FCFF from Net Income

$$FCFF = NI + NCC + Int\ (1 - Tax\ rate) - FCInv - WCInc$$

- Non-cash charges are subtracted from revenue to arrive at a firm's net income. These need to be added back as they do not result in any cash outflows.
  - Depreciation, amortization, and losses on sale of assets must be added back to net income. Similarly, gains on sales of investments must be subtracted from net income.
  - Restructuring charges must be added back to net income, while any income from reversals of restructuring charges must be subtracted from net income.
  - Amortization of bond discounts must be added back to net income, while accretion of bond premiums must be subtracted from net income.
  - Increases in deferred tax liabilities that are not expected to reverse must be added back to net income, while increases in deferred tax assets that are not expected to reverse must be subtracted from net income.
- Interest expense is subtracted from a firm's earnings in order to arrive at net income. Interest expense is a financing cash outflow and therefore, must be added back to net income in order to arrive at FCFF. However, only the after-tax portion of interest expense is added back. Similarly, any dividends on preferred stock must be added back to net income to arrive at FCFF.
- Investment in fixed assets is a non-operating cash outflow and therefore, must be subtracted from net income to arrive at FCFF.
  - FCInv = Capital expenditures – Proceeds from sales of long-term assets
- Investments in working capital can be estimated as the increase in working capital from year to year excluding cash, cash equivalents, notes payable, and the current portion of long-term debt.

Computing FCFF from CFO

$$FCFF = CFO + Int\ (1 - Tax\ rate) - FCInv$$

When computing FCFF from CFO, do not make any adjustments related to non-cash charges and investments in working capital as they have already been made in the calculation of CFO.

Computing FCFF from EBIT

$$FCFF = EBIT\ (1 - Tax\ rate) + Depreciation - FCInv - WCInv$$

When calculating FCFF from EBIT, do not make any adjustments for interest expense. Further, the above formula assumes that apart from depreciation, non-cash charges in the income statement are made after the calculation of operating earnings (EBIT).

Computing FCFF from EBITDA

$$FCFF = EBITDA\ (1 - Tax\ rate) + Depreciation\ (Tax\ rate) - FCInv - WCInv$$

Computing FCFE

Computing FCFE from FCFF

$$\text{FCFE} = \text{FCFF} - \text{Int} \ (1 - \text{Tax rate}) + \text{Net borrowing}$$

Computing FCFE from Net Income

$$\text{FCFE} = \text{NI} + \text{NCC} - \text{FCInv} - \text{WCInv} + \text{Net borrowing}$$

Computing FCFE from CFO

$$\text{FCFE} = \text{CFO} - \text{FCInv} + \text{Net borrowing}$$

Computing FCFE from EBIT

$$\text{FCFE} = \text{EBIT} \ (1 - \text{Tax rate}) - \text{Int} \ (1 - \text{Tax rate}) + \text{Depreciation} - \text{FCInv} - \text{WCInv} + \text{NB}$$

Computing FCFE from EBITDA

$$\text{FCFE} = \text{EBITDA} \ (1 - \text{Tax rate}) - \text{Int} \ (1 - \text{Tax rate}) + \text{Dep} \ (\text{Tax rate}) - \text{FCInv} - \text{WCInv} + \text{NB}$$

Computing FCFF and FCFE on a Uses-of-Free-Cash-Flow Basis

A firm generally has the following uses of positive FCFF:

- Retain it to increase its balances of cash and marketable securities.
- Make payments to providers of debt capital.
- Make payments to providers of equity capital (e.g. cash dividends or share repurchases).

Increases in cash balances
Plus: Net payments to providers of debt capital
  + Interest expense (1 – tax rate)
  + Repayment of principal
  – New borrowings
Plus: Net payments to providers of equity capital
  + Cash dividends
  + Share repurchases
  – New equity issues
  = Uses of FCFF

FCFE is usually only used to make payments to providers of equity capital.

Increases in cash balances
Plus: Net payments to providers of equity capital
  + Cash dividends
  + Share repurchases
  – New equity issues
  = Uses of FCFE

Forecasting FCFF and FCFE

- Calculate the current level of free cash flow and apply a specific growth rate assuming that free cash flow will grow at a constant growth rate, and that the historical relationship between free cash flow and fundamental factors is expected to continue.

- Forecast the individual components of free cash flow. For example, analysts may forecast EBIT, net non-cash charges, investments in fixed capital, and working capital and use these figures to calculate free cash flow.

Important

- Dividends, share repurchases, and share issues have no effect on FCFF and FCFE.
- Changes in leverage have a minor effect on FCFE and no impact on FCFF.

Net Income as a Proxy for Cash Flow

Net income is a poor proxy for FCFE for use in valuation because it:
- Includes the effects of non-cash charges like depreciation that should be added back to compute cash flow available to equity holders.
- Ignores cash outflow for investment in fixed and working capital.
- Ignores cash inflow from net borrowings.

EBITDA as a Proxy for Cash Flow

EBITDA is a poor proxy for FCFF for use in valuation because it:

- Does not account for cash outflow from taxes paid.
- Does not account for the contribution of the depreciation tax shield to FCFF.
- Ignores cash outflow for investment in fixed and working capital.

Free Cash Flow Model Variations

Single-Stage Valuation Model

$$\text{Value of the firm} = \frac{FCFF_1}{WACC - g}$$

$$\text{Value of equity} = \frac{FCFE_1}{r - g}$$

Multi-Stage Valuation Models

There can be many different patterns of future growth rates depending on a firm's prospects. However, the same discounting principles are applied for valuing firms over multiple holding periods. In order to estimate the value of the firm, we first estimate the free cash flows that will be generated by the firm each year and then discount these expected cash flows at the appropriate rate.

Non-operating assets (e.g. excess cash and marketable securities) are separated from the company's operating assets. They are valued separately and their value is then added to the calculated value of the company's operating assets to determine total firm value.

General expression for the two-stage FCFF model:

$$\text{Firm value} = \sum_{t=1}^{n} \frac{\text{FCFF}_t}{(1+\text{WACC})^t} + \frac{\text{FCFF}_{n+1}}{(\text{WACC}-g)} \frac{1}{(1+\text{WACC})^n}$$

Firm value = PV of FCFF in Stage 1 + Terminal value × Discount Factor

General expression for the two-stage FCFE model:

$$\text{Equity value} = \sum_{t=1}^{n} \frac{\text{FCFE}_t}{(1+r)^t} + \frac{\text{FCFF}_{n+1}}{r-g} \frac{1}{(1+r)^n}$$

Equity value = PV of FCFE in Stage 1 + Terminal value × Discount Factor

Importance of Sensitivity Analysis

There are two major sources of errors in the valuation exercise.

1. Errors in estimating growth rates of FCFE and FCFF. These growth forecasts are dependent on a variety of factors including the company's sales growth, net profit margins, capital requirements, and industry profitability.
2. Errors in estimating the base-year values of FCFF and FCFE. Given the same set of growth forecasts, the estimate of value obtained from the model will vary with different base year values for FCFF and FCFE.

MARKET-BASED VALUATION: PRICE AND ENTERPRISE VALUE MULTIPLES
Cross-Reference to CFA Institute Assigned Reading #35

The Method of Comparables

- Based on the law of one price i.e., two identical assets should sell at the same price.
- Values an asset based on multiples of comparable (similar) assets.
- Is a relative valuation method, so the stock is evaluated relative to a benchmark.

The Method of Forecasted Fundamentals

- Uses multiples that are derived from forecasted fundamentals.
- These fundamentals may be related to the company's earnings, growth, or financial strength.

Price Multiples

Price to Earnings

Advantages:
- Earnings are key drivers of stock value.
- The ratio is simple to calculate and widely used in the industry.
- According to empirical research, differences in P/E ratios are significantly related to long-term stock returns.

Disadvantages:
- Companies that make losses have negative EPS. Negative P/E ratios are useless as far as relative valuation is concerned.
- It can be difficult to separate recurring components of earnings from transient components.
- Management may use different accounting standards and assumptions to prepare financial statements, which reduces the comparability of P/E ratios across companies.

Versions of the P/E ratio

- The trailing P/E ratio divides the current stock price by earnings over the most recent four quarters.
  - It is used when future earnings are expected to be volatile and cannot be forecasted accurately.
- The leading P/E ratio divides the current stock price by expected earnings over the next year.
  - It is used if a company's business has changed fundamentally in the recent past (e.g. due to an acquisition).

Issues to consider in calculating trailing P/E

- Potential dilution of EPS.
  - This is not such a major problem as companies now report both basic and diluted EPS.
- Transitory, non-recurring components of earnings that are company specific.
  - Analysts aim to estimate underlying or persistent earnings (that exclude nonrecurring components). Financial statement footnotes and the MD&A section are important sources of information in this exercise.
- Transitory components of earnings related to business or industry cycle.
  - In order to eliminate the effects of business cycles on P/E ratios, analysts usually calculate normalized earnings.
- Differences in accounting methods.

Calculating Underlying or Persistent Earnings

- There are no prescribed rules for calculating underlying earnings.
- Analysts should not rely on company-reported core or continuing earnings.
- Analysts should compute the adjusted P/E ratio based on their own judgment regarding how the company's underlying earnings should be calculated, and the same basis should then be applied for all stocks under review.
- Non-recurring components of earnings cannot easily be identified by just looking at the income statement. The financial statement footnotes and the MD&A section can be important sources of information in this regard.
- Earnings may also be segregated into their cash flow and accrual component. A higher P/E should be assigned to the cash flow component when calculating P/Es.

Calculating Normalized Earnings

- Under the method of historical average EPS, normalized EPS is calculated as average EPS over the most recent full cycle.
  - This method does not account for changes in a company's size over the period.
- Under the method of average return on equity, normalized EPS is calculated as current book value per share times the average return on equity over the most recent full cycle.
  - This method does account for changes in a company's size.
- Other methods (that are particularly useful when a cyclical company reports a loss) include (1) multiplying total assets by estimated long run return on assets, and (2) multiplying shareholders' equity by estimated long run return on equity.

The Earnings Yield

- Earnings may sometimes be zero or negative, which makes the P/E ratio useless.
- In such cases, analysts use the reciprocal of the P/E ratio to rank investments. The earnings-to-price ratio is known as the earnings yield.
- Securities may be ranked based on earnings yield from highest to lowest i.e., from cheapest to most costly in terms of the amount of earnings per unit of price.

P/E based on the method of forecasted fundamentals:

$$\text{Leading P/E} = \frac{P_0}{E_1} = \frac{D_1/E_1}{r-g} = \frac{(1-b)}{r-g}$$

$$\text{Trailing P/E} = \frac{P_0}{E_0} = \frac{D_0(1+g)/E_0}{r-g} = \frac{(1-b)(1+g)}{r-g}$$

P/E's based on cross-sectional regression:

P/E ratios may also be calculated based on cross-sectional regression. However, such a model has the following limitations:

- It is only applicable for a specific stock for a specific time period.
- The relationships between P/E and fundamentals may change over time.
- The regression may suffer from multicollinearity.

The P/E-to-Growth (PEG) Ratio

The impact of earnings growth on the P/E ratio is captured by the P/E-to-growth (PEG) ratio. This ratio is calculated as the stock's P/E divided by the expected earnings growth rate in percent. All else being equal, investors prefer stocks with *lower* PEGs over stocks with higher PEGs. The PEG ratio has the following drawbacks:

- It incorrectly assumes a linear relationship between P/E and growth.
- It does not account for the different risks in different stocks.
- It does not account for differences in the duration of growth.

Price to Book Value

$$\text{P/B ratio} = \frac{\text{Market price per share}}{\text{Book value per share}}$$

Book value of equity = Common shareholders' equity = Shareholders' equity − Total value of equity claims that are senior to common stock

Book value of equity = Total assets − Total liabilities − Preferred stock

Advantages:
- Book value usually remains positive even when the company reports negative earnings.
- Book value is typically more stable than reported earnings.
- For financial sector companies that have significant holdings of liquid assets, P/B is more meaningful as book values reflect recent market values.
- P/B is useful in valuing a company that is expected to go out of business.
- Studies suggest that differences in P/B ratios over time are related to differences in long term average returns on stocks.

Disadvantages:

- Book values ignore non-tangible factors such as the quality of a company's human capital and brand image.
- P/B can lead to misleading valuations, if significantly different levels of assets are being used by the companies being studied.
- Accounting differences can impair the comparability of P/B ratios across companies.
- Inflation and changes in technology may result in significant differences between accounting book values and actual fair values of a company's assets.
- Share repurchases or issuances may distort historical comparisons.

Analysts usually make the following adjustments to book value in order to increase its comparability with other companies:

- They use tangible book value per share, which is calculated as common shareholders' equity less certain intangible assets (goodwill).
- They adjust reported financials to eliminate the effects of differences in accounting standards.
- They adjust the balance sheet for off-balance sheet items.
- They adjust certain balance sheet (historical) values to reflect current fair values.

P/B based on the method of forecasted fundamentals:

$$\frac{P_0}{B_0} = \frac{ROE - g}{r - g}$$

Price to Sales

$$P/S \text{ ratio} = \frac{\text{Market price per share}}{\text{Sales per share}}$$

Advantages:

- Sales are less prone to manipulation by management than earnings, and book values.
- Sales are positive even when EPS is negative.
- The P/S ratio is usually more stable than the P/E ratio.
- Price to sales is considered an appropriate measure for valuing mature, cyclical and loss-making companies.
- Studies have shown that differences in price to sales ratios are related to differences in long-term average returns on stocks.

Disadvantages:

- Sales reveal no information about the operating profitability of a company.
- Using the P/S ratio does not reflect the differences in cost structure and operating efficiency between companies.
- Revenue recognition practices may allow management to distort revenue figures.

P/S ratio based on the method of forecasted fundamentals:

$$\frac{P_0}{S_0} = \frac{(E_0/S_0)(1-b)(1+g)}{r-g}$$

Price to Cash Flow

$$P/CF \text{ ratio} = \frac{\text{Market price per share}}{\text{Free cash flow per share}}$$

Advantages:
- Cash flows are less susceptible to management manipulation than earnings.
- P/CF is more stable than the P/E ratio.
- Using the price to cash flow ratio gets around the problem related to differences in accounting methods used by companies.
- Differences in price to cash flow ratio over time are related to differences in long term average returns on stocks.

Disadvantages:
- When "EPS plus noncash charges" is used as the definition for cash flow, noncash revenue and changes in working capital items are ignored.
- FCFE is more appropriate for valuing a company than operating cash flow. However, FCFE has the following drawbacks:
  - For many businesses, it is more volatile than operating cash flow.
  - It is more frequently negative than operating cash flow.
- Companies may inflate certain cash flow measures (e.g. CFO).

Justified P/CF Multiple Based on Fundamentals

The justified P/CF multiple based on fundamentals can be determined by first computing the intrinsic value of the stock using a discounted cash flow model and then dividing the intrinsic value estimate by the chosen definition of cash flow.

For example, the constant growth FCFE model is given as:

$$V_0 = \frac{FCFE_0(1+g)}{(r-g)}$$

We could divide both sides of this equation by our desired definition of cash flow to obtain the justified P/CF multiple for a stock.

- The justified P/CF multiple is positively related to the growth rate of cash flows (g).
- The justified P/CF multiple is inversely related to stock's required rate of return (r).

Price-to-Dividends and Dividend Yield

Dividend yield = Dividend per share / Price per share

Advantages:
- The dividend yield is a component of total return.
- The dividend yield component of total return is less risky than the capital gains component.

Disadvantages:
- The dividend yield is only one of the (two) components of total return. Ignoring the capital appreciation component in valuation is risky.
- Dividends paid now "displace" earnings in future periods. A higher dividend yield usually implies a lower earnings growth rate going forward.
- The argument that dividends are relatively safe (less risky) assumes that the market prices reflect differences in relative risk between the two components of total return.
- Trailing dividend yield is calculated by dividing the annualized amount of the most recent dividend by the current market price per share.
- Leading dividend yield is calculated by dividing next year's forecasted dividend per share by the current market price per share.

Dividend yield using the method based on forecasted fundamentals:

$$\frac{D_0}{P_0} = \frac{r-g}{1+g}$$

- The dividend yield is positively related to the required rate of return on equity (r).
- The dividend yield is negatively related to the expected rate of growth in dividends (g). This implies that investing in a low dividend yield stock reflects a growth rather than a value strategy.

Enterprise Value Multiples

Enterprise Value to EBITDA

Enterprise value = Market value of common equity + Market value of preferred stock
            + Market value of debt + Minority interest
            − Value of cash and short-term investments

Advantages:
- The EV/EBITDA multiple is appropriate for comparing companies with different levels of financial leverage.
- Unlike net income, EBITDA controls for differences in depreciation and amortization among companies and therefore, is more appropriate for valuing capital-intensive businesses.
- EBITDA is often positive when EPS is negative.

Drawbacks:
- EBITDA ignores the effects of differences in revenue recognition policies on cash flow from operations.
- EBITDA may overstate CFO if working capital is growing.
- Free cash flow to the firm (FCFF) can have a stronger link to company value than EBITDA.

Other enterprise value multiples, such as EV/FCFF and EV/Sales are also frequently used.

Alternative Definitions of Cash Flow for EV Multiples

EPS-plus non-cash charges (CF)
- Calculated as EPS + Depreciation + Amortization.
- Ignores noncash revenue and changes in working capital items.

Cash flow from operations (CFO)
- May require adjustments for nonrecurring components of cash flow.
- Adjustments may be required when comparing companies that use different accounting standards.

Free cash flow to equity (FCFE)
- Calculated as CFO − FCInv + Net borrowing
- Theoretically, it is the most suitable definition for free cash flow.
- However, it may be more volatile than CFO and may also be more frequently negative than CFO.

EBITDA
- Calculated by adding depreciation and amortization to EBIT.
- Since it represents a flow available to both equity holders and bond holders, it is more suited for calculating the value of the company; not the value of equity.

Valuation Based on Forecasted Fundamentals

All other things remaining the same, the justified EV/EBITDA multiple based on fundamentals is:
- Positively related to the expected growth rate of FCFF.
- Positively related to the return on invested capital, ROIC (expected profitability).
  - ROIC is calculated as operating profit after tax divided by total invested capital.
- Negatively related to the WACC.

Momentum Valuation Indicators

Unexpected earnings is the difference between a company's reported earnings and its expected earnings.

$$UE_t = EPS_t - E(EPS_t)$$

- Standardized unexpected earnings is calculated by dividing a company's unexpected earnings by the standard deviation of past unexpected earnings over a period of time.

$$SUE_t = \frac{EPS_t - E(EPS_t)}{\sigma[EPS_t - E(EPS_t)]}$$

- Relative-strength indicators compare a stock's performance during a particular period, either with its own past performance, or with the performance of a group of comparable stocks.

Valuation Indicators: Issues in Practice

Average Multiples: The Harmonic Mean

The P/E for a portfolio or an index is most accurately calculated through the harmonic mean and the weighted harmonic mean.

Simple harmonic mean: $X_H = \dfrac{n}{\sum_{i=1}^{n} (1/X_i)}$

Weighted harmonic mean $= X_{WH} = \dfrac{1}{\sum_{i=1}^{n} (w_i / X_i)}$

- The simple harmonic mean inherently gives a lower weight to higher P/Es and a higher weight to lower P/Es.
- Using the median (as opposed to the mean) mitigates the effect of outliers.
- The harmonic mean may also be used to reduce the impact of outliers. However, while the harmonic mean mitigates the impact of large outliers, it may actually aggravate the impact of small outliers.
- For an equal-weighted index, simple harmonic mean, and weighted harmonic mean are equal.

Using Multiple Valuation Indicators

- When back-testing, analysts should be wary of look-ahead bias.
- Stock screens usually define criteria (based on valuation indicators) for including stocks in an investor's portfolio and provide an efficient way to narrow a search for investments.

RESIDUAL INCOME VALUATION
Cross-Reference to CFA Institute Assigned Reading #36

Residual Income

Residual income, or economic profit, recognizes the cost of equity capital. It is calculated by deducting a charge for equity capital from net income.

$$\text{Residual income} = \text{Net income} - \text{Equity charge}$$

$$\text{Equity charge} = \text{Cost of equity capital} \times \text{Equity capital}$$

- Companies with positive RI create value as they generate more income than their cost of obtaining capital.
- Companies with negative RI effectively destroy value as they do not generate sufficient income to cover their cost of capital.
- Companies with higher (lower) residual income should be associated with higher (lower) valuations.

Economic Value Added (EVA)

EVA measures the value added for shareholders by the management of a company during a given year.

$$\text{EVA} = [\text{EBIT}\,(1 - \text{Tax rate})] - (C\% \times TC)$$

$$\text{EVA} = \text{NOPAT} - \$\text{WACC}$$

Market Value Added (MVA)

Market value added (MVA) measures the value created by management for the company's investors by generating economic profits over the life of the company.

$$\text{MVA} = \text{Market value of the company} - \text{Book value of invested capital}$$

$$\text{Market value of company} = \text{Market value of debt} + \text{Market value of equity.}$$

The Residual Income Model

The residual income (RI) model breaks the intrinsic value of a stock into the following two components:

- Current book value of equity
- Present value of expected future residual income

The intrinsic value of a stock can be calculated as:

$$V_0 = B_0 + \sum_{t=1}^{\infty} \frac{RI_t}{(1+r)^t} = B_0 + \sum_{t=1}^{\infty} \frac{E_t - rB_{t-1}}{(1+r)^t}$$

The general residual income model may also be expressed as:

$$V_0 = B_0 + \sum_{t=1}^{\infty} \frac{(ROE_t - r)B_{t-1}}{(1+r)^t}$$

The intrinsic value of a stock under the residual income model can be expressed as:

$$V_0 = B_0 + \frac{ROE - r}{r - g} B_0$$

Under this constant-growth residual income model, the intrinsic value of a stock equals the sum of:
- Its current book value (B_0); and
- The present value of its expected stream of residual income [(ROE − r) × B_0/(r − g)]. This term represents the additional value created as a result of the company's ability to generate returns in excess of its cost of equity.

Also note that:

- If the return on equity (ROE) equals the required return on equity (r), the intrinsic value of the stock would equal its book value.
- If the return on equity (ROE) is greater than the required return on equity (r), the present value of the expected stream of residual income will be positive, the intrinsic value of the stock will be greater than its book value, and the justified P/B ratio will be greater than 1.
- If the return on equity (ROE) is less than the required return on equity (r), the present value of the expected stream of residual income will be negative, the intrinsic value of the stock will be lower than its book value, and the justified P/B ratio will be less than 1.

Therefore, a stock's justified P/B ratio is directly related to the company's expected future residual income.

Tobin's q

$$\text{Tobin's q} = \frac{\text{Market value of debt and equity}}{\text{Replacement cost of total assets}}$$

Tobin's q is different from the P/B in the following respects:
- It uses the market value of equity and debt (rather than just equity) in the numerator and uses total assets (rather than equity) in the denominator.
- Assets are valued at replacement cost (as opposed to book or accounting values).

All else equal, the greater the productivity of a firm's assets, the higher the Tobin's q.

Single-Stage Residual Income Model

The single-stage residual income model makes the following simplifying assumptions:

- The company earns a constant return on equity.
- The earnings growth rate is constant at a level that is lower than the required return on equity.

$$V_0 = B_0 + \frac{ROE - r}{r - g} B_0$$

- If the return on equity (ROE) equals the required return on equity (r), the intrinsic value of the stock would equal its book value.
- If the return on equity (ROE) is greater than the required return on equity (r), the intrinsic value of the stock would be greater than its book value.
- If the return on equity (ROE) is less than the required return on equity (r), the intrinsic value of the stock would be less than its book value.

The single-stage RI model assumes that the return on equity will remain in excess of the required rate of return on equity (resulting in positive RI) for an indefinite period of time. This assumption is a bit unrealistic as residual income will likely fall to zero at some point in time.

Multi-Stage Residual Income Valuation

In the multi-stage residual income model, the intrinsic value of a stock has three components:

$V_0 = B_0 + $ (PV of future RI over the short-term) + (PV of continuing RI)

$$V_0 = B_0 + \sum_{t=1}^{T} \frac{(ROE_t - r)B_{t-1}}{(1+r)^t} + \frac{P_T - B_T}{(1+r)^T}$$

Analysts may make any one of the following assumptions regarding continuing residual income:
- It continues indefinitely at a positive level.
- It is zero from the terminal year forward.
- It declines to zero as ROE reverts to the cost of equity over time.
- It reflects the reversion of ROE to some mean level.

The more sustainable a company's competitive advantage and the brighter the industry's prospects, the higher the persistence factor.

$$V_0 = B_0 + \sum_{t=1}^{T-1} \frac{(E_t - rB_{t-1})}{(1+r)^t} + \frac{E_T - rB_{T-1}}{(1+r-\omega)(1+r)^{T-1}}$$

Implied Growth Rate

$$g = r - \left[\frac{(ROE - r) \times B_0}{V_0 - B_0} \right]$$

Advantages and Disadvantages of the Residual Income Model

Advantages:
- Unlike DDM and FCF valuation models, the terminal value estimate (which has a significant amount of uncertainty associated with it) does not constitute a significant proportion of intrinsic value in the RI model. Most of the value under the RI model comes from current book value, which leads to earlier recognition of value relative to other valuation models.
- It uses accounting data which is easily available.
- It is applicable to companies that do not pay any dividends or have negative free cash flows.
- It is applicable to companies with uncertain cash flows.
- It focuses on economic profitability.

Disadvantages:
- It is based on accounting data which can be manipulated by management.
- Accounting data must be adjusted to be used in the model.
- It assumes that the clean-surplus relation holds i.e., ending book value of equity equals beginning book value plus earnings less dividends.
- It assumes that interest expense appropriately reflects the cost of debt capital.

Scenarios when the residual income model is appropriate:
- The company does not have a history of paying dividends, or dividends cannot be predicted with certainty.
- The company's free cash flows are expected to remain negative for the foreseeable future.
- The estimates of terminal value using alternative valuation models entail a great amount of uncertainty.

Scenarios when the residual income model is not appropriate:
- There are significant violations of the clean surplus relation.
- It is difficult to predict the main determinants of residual income i.e., book value and ROE.

Important Considerations in RI Valuation

- Analysts should ensure that the clean-surplus relation holds. The clean surplus relation may be violated if items are charged directly to equity without going through the income statement. If the clean-surplus relation does not hold, forecasted value of ROE obtained through the RI model will not be accurate.
- The book values of many balance sheet items may be significantly different from their fair values. If this is the case, analysts need to make adjustments to these items to reflect fair value.
- The balance sheet may contain intangible assets. These items require close attention as they can have a significant effect on book value.
- The book value of common equity should be adjusted for off-balance sheet items and amortization of certain intangible assets.
- Non-recurring items should be excluded when forecasting residual income.
- Analysts need to consider the reliability of earnings estimates, and whether "poor quality" accounting rules result in delayed recognition of value changes.

PRIVATE COMPANY VALUATION
Cross-Reference to CFA Institute Assigned Reading #37

Private versus Public Company Valuation

Company-Specific Factors

- Private companies are typically in an earlier stage of their life cycle compared to public companies, which generally tend to be more mature.
- Private companies are usually smaller in size than public companies, which is why they are more risky investments.
- Owners of private companies are usually also involved in the management of the company. In public companies, there is a distinction between owners and management, which gives rise to agency problems.
- Public companies are usually able to attract better quality management than private companies.
- Public companies are required by regulatory authorities to publish their financial statements regularly. This is not a requirement for private firms, which increases the level of risk for investors as they do not have access to credible financial information regarding the company. Higher risk results in lower valuations.
- Managers in public companies constantly face pressure to maintain or increase the company's stock price, which makes them focus on short-term goals. Managers of private companies do not face such pressures and therefore, pursue profitable long-term strategies even if they may have a negative short-term impact.
- Private companies are usually more concerned about taxes than public companies.

Stock-Specific Factors

- Private company shares are usually less liquid than public company shares.
- Control of private companies is generally concentrated in the hands of a few shareholders, who may pursue activities that benefit a few shareholders at the cost of others.
- Private companies may restrict shareholders from selling their stakes in the company, which further reduces the marketability of their equity interests.

Reasons for Performing Valuations

- Transaction-related valuations refer to valuations for:
  - Private financing
  - Initial public offering (IPO)
  - Acquisition
  - Bankruptcy
  - Share-based payment (compensation)
- Compliance-related valuations may be required by law and primarily focus on financial reporting and tax reporting.
- Litigation-related valuations arise from shareholder disputes, damage claims, etc.

Definitions of Value

Fair market value (FMV): The price that similarly-informed buyers and sellers would agree to trade an asset where the trade must be an arm's length transaction and neither the buyer nor seller is under any external pressure to trade.
- Fair market value is mostly used for tax reporting purposes.

Market value: The estimated amount for which a property should exchange on the date of valuation between a willing buyer and willing seller in an arm's length transaction after proper marketing wherein the parties had each acted knowledgeably, prudently, and without compulsion.
- Market value is frequently used in appraisals of real estate and tangible assets when they are used as collateral for borrowings.

Fair value (financial reporting): Under IFRS, fair value is defined as "the price that would be received for an asset or paid to transfer a liability in a current transaction between two marketplace participants in the reference market for the asset or liability". Under U.S. GAAP, fair value is defined as "the price that would be received to sell an asset or paid to transfer a liability in an orderly transaction between market participants at the measurement date".
- This value is used in financial reporting and is very similar to the fair market value.

Fair value (litigation): The definition of fair value in a legal setting is generally similar to the definitions of fair value for financial reporting.

Investment value: The value of an asset to a particular buyer based on her investment requirements and expectations.
- Investment value is important in acquisitions of private companies.

Intrinsic value: The "true" or "real" value of an asset based on its risk-return expectations absent short-term mispricings.
- Intrinsic value is often used in investment analysis.

Private Company Valuation Approaches

- The income approach values a private company based on the present value of its expected future income.
- The market approach values a private company based on price multiples derived from sales of comparable companies.
- The asset-based approach values a private company based on the value of its underlying net assets.

Factors to Consider when Deciding on a Valuation Approach

Nature of operations and life cycle stage: Generally speaking:
- A company in the earliest stages of development should be valued using the asset-based approach as future cash flows might be too unpredictable and there is no guarantee that the company will be able to operate as a going concern for the foreseeable future.
- A company that has successfully negotiated the early development stage and is witnessing high growth should be valued using the income approach (based on discounted expected future cash flows).
- A stable, relatively mature company should be valued using the market approach.

Company size: Generally speaking:

- Use of multiples from larger public companies is not appropriate for smaller, relatively mature private firms with limited growth prospects.
- Use of multiples from large public companies is not appropriate for smaller private firms that entail significantly more risk.

Finally, note that non-operating assets (e.g. excess cash and investments) which are not part of the firm's core business should be accounted for in the valuation of an entity regardless of the valuation approach or method used.

Earnings Normalization Issues in Private Companies

Analysts may sometimes need to make significant adjustments to a private company's earnings due to the following reasons:

- There is concentration of control which may lead to significant discretionary and tax-motivated expenses being recognized on the income statement.
- Personal expenses may be included as company expenses.
- The effects of significant related-party transactions (which may be recorded at inflated or deflated prices) must be accounted for.
- The company's profitability may suffer if excessive compensation is being paid out to senior managers (owners).
- Revenues and expenses related to company-owned real estate should be removed from the company's income statement, and a market estimate for rent should be recognized instead. The property should be treated as a non-operating asset.
- In estimating normalized earnings for strategic buyers, the effects of synergies should be incorporated.

Cash Flow Estimation in Private Companies

Calculating free cash flow for private companies is a challenging process given the uncertainty of future cash flows. Further, company projections may be biased as they are usually prepared by managers who are also owners.

- Analysts may develop a number of scenarios to forecast cash flows and discount future cash flows in each scenario using an appropriate risk-adjusted discount rate. They can then calculate the value of the company as the weighted-average of the value in each scenario.
- Alternatively, they may forecast future cash flows in a single scenario considering all the associated risks and discount them at an appropriate risk-adjusted discount rate to calculate the value of the firm.
- Use of FCFF is preferred over FCFE when the company's capital structure is expected to change going forward as the WACC is less sensitive to leverage changes than the cost of equity capital.

Income Approach Methods of Private Company Valuation

- The free cash flow method calculates the value of a firm as the present value of future free cash flows expected to be generated by the firm discounted at an appropriate risk-adjusted discount rate.

- The capitalized cash flow method calculates firm value by dividing a single representative estimate of economic benefits by a capitalization rate, where the capitalization rate is calculated as an appropriate discount rate minus a growth rate.

- The excess earnings method calculates firm value by adding the value of the firm's intangible assets to the value of working capital and fixed assets. The value of intangible assets is calculated by capitalizing future earnings of the firm in excess of the estimated return requirements associated with working capital and fixed assets.

Challenges in Determining the Required Rate of Return

- A size premium must be added to the discount rate in valuing small private firms. Size premiums based on public company data can capture premiums for distress which may not be relevant for private companies.
- The use of the CAPM may not be appropriate for estimating the cost of equity for private firms (especially if they have slim chances of going public or being acquired by a public company).
- If the build-up approach is used, an industry risk premium must be included in the model. This premium may be difficult to determine.
- It may be more difficult for private companies to raise debt capital than for public companies. This makes them more reliant on equity financing, which results in a larger WACC. Further, the cost of debt is higher for private companies due to their smaller size and higher operating risk.
- When acquiring a private firm, the acquirer should use the target's capital structure and cost of capital to determine the WACC applicable to the target's cash flows.
- A premium for projection risk (the risk that arises due to uncertainty involved in projecting future cash flows of private firms) and managerial inexperience may be added to the required rate of return.

Market Approach Methods of Private Company Valuation

- The guideline public company method calculates the value of a private company based on price multiples from trading data of comparable public companies. The price multiple is adjusted to reflect the differences in the relative risk and growth prospects between the companies. Factors that require consideration include:
    - Type of transaction
    - Industry factors
    - Form of consideration
    - Reasonableness
- The guideline transaction method calculates the value of a private company based on price multiples obtained from past acquisitions of entire public or private companies. The multiples used must consider the following factors:
    - Synergies
    - Contingent consideration
    - Noncash consideration
    - Availability of transactions
    - Changes between the transaction date and valuation date

- The prior transaction method calculates the value of a private company based on actual transactions in the stock of the subject private company.

Asset-Based Approach

This approach values a private company based on the fair value of its underlying net assets. This method is not appropriate for valuing going-concerns and is only suitable for valuing:
- Small firms that are in the early stages of their life-cycle.
- Firms with minimal profits, with no prospects for doing better in the future.
- Firms whose assets and liabilities are based on market values (e.g. banks).
- Investment companies where the value of underlying assets is determined using the market or income approaches (e.g. REITs).
- Firms with natural resources whose assets can be valued using data from comparable sales.

Valuation Discounts and Premiums

Discount for Lack of Control (DLOC)

A discount for lack of control is applied to the pro rate share of the value of an equity interest in a business to reflect the absence of all or some of the powers on control.

$$DLOC = 1 - \left[\frac{1}{1 + \text{Control Premium}} \right]$$

The application of DLOC varies with the method and basis used to value the equity interest:

- The guideline public company method values a company from a non-controlling perspective and therefore, a DLOC must not be applied.
- The guideline transaction method values a company from a control perspective and therefore, a DLOC should be applied.
- The application of DLOC in the capitalized cash flow or the free cash flow method depends on the type of cash flows used.
  - Generally speaking, the CCM and FCF models use cash flows and discount rates that are estimated on a controlling interest basis so a DLOC is applied to the results of the model.
  - However, if control cash flows are not used and/or the discount rate does not reflect an optimal capital structure, a DLOC must not be applied.

Discount for Lack of Marketability (DLOM)

A discount for lack of marketability is applied to the value of an ownership interest to reflect the relative absence of marketability. The DLOM is affected by the following variables:

- Prospects for liquidity
- Contractual arrangements affecting marketability
- Restrictions on transferability
- Pool of potential buyers
- Risk or volatility
- Size and timing of distributions
- Uncertainty of value
- Concentration of ownership

The DLOM may be estimated based on:

- Private sales of restricted stock in public companies relatively to their freely-traded stock price.
- Private sales of a company's stock prior to an IPO.
- The pricing of put options.

The relationship between DLOC and DLOM is not additive, so you should compound when both exist. For example, if the DLOC is 5% and the DLOM is 3%, the total discount is not 8%, but:

$$1 - [(1 - 0.05)(1 - 0.03)] = 7.85\%$$

Important:

- If publicly traded shares are used as the basis for price multiples, control premiums should be added when measuring the total value of a private company.
- A DLOM may not need to be applied when there is a high likelihood of a liquidity event in the near future.

PRIVATE REAL ESTATE INVESTMENTS
Cross-Reference to CFA Institute Assigned Reading #38

Real Estate Investment: Basic Forms

Real estate investments can be classified into different forms on the basis of:

- Whether the investment is being made in the private or public market.
  - Investments in private markets can be made either directly or indirectly.
  - Investments in public markets are usually made *indirectly* through ownership of securities that serve as claims on the underlying assets.
- Whether the investment is structured as equity or debt.
  - An equity investor has an ownership interest in real estate or in securities of an entity that owns real estate.
  - A debt investor is a lender who owns a mortgage loan or mortgage securities.

Table 1: Examples of the Basic Forms of Real Estate Investment

	Equity	Debt
Private	Direct investments in real estate. This can be through sole ownership, joint venture, real estate limited partnerships or other forms of commingled funds.	Mortgages
Publicly traded	Shares of real estate operating companies and shares of REITs.	Mortgage-backed securities (Residential and commercial)

Each form of real estate investment has its own risks, expected returns, regulations, legal structures, and market structures:

- Private real estate investments are indivisible and therefore, tend to involve larger amounts.
- Public real estate investments allow the ownership or claim on the property to be divided, which makes them more liquid than private real estate investments, and also allows investors to diversify by purchasing ownership interests across several properties.
- Private equity investment in real estate requires the owner to manage the property herself or to hire a property manager. REOCs and REITs have professional teams to manage their real estate investments, so investors in publicly traded real estate investments do not require real estate management expertise.
- Equity investors usually require a higher rate of return than debt investors as they take on greater risk. Their claim on the interim cash flows and proceeds from sale of real estate property is subordinate to that of debt holders. However, debt investors usually do not participate in any upside in the value of the underlying real estate.
- The return to equity investors in real estate has two components: an income stream (e.g. rental income) and a capital appreciation component.

Real Estate Characteristics

- Heterogeneity and fixed location
- High unit value
- Management intensive
- High transaction costs
- Depreciation
- Need for debt capital
- Illiquidity
- Difficulties in price determination

Real Estate Classifications

Real estate investments may be classified as residential or non-residential properties. Another potential classification is single-family residential, commercial, farmland and timber.

Benefits of Real Estate Equity Investments

- Real estate investments can generate current income by letting, leasing, or renting the property.
- Real estate prices may increase over time, so capital appreciation can contribute to an investors' total return.
- Real estate values usually rise in an inflationary environment, so real estate investments serve as an inflation hedge.
- Investments in real estate provide diversification benefits to investors.
- Investors in real estate may receive favorable tax treatment.

Risks Factors

- Business conditions: Changes in economic factors such as GDP growth, employment, household income, interest rates, and inflation rates affect both (1) real estate values and (2) rental income.
- Long lead time for new developments: Real estate projects take a long time to be completed and market conditions can change significantly during their development.
- Cost and availability of capital: Scarcity of capital and high financing costs lead to lower real estate values.
- Unexpected inflation: If the real estate market is relatively weak, high vacancy rates and low rents could mean that real estate values may not keep up with inflation.
- Demographics: The demand for real estate is also affected by factors such as the size and age distribution of the population in the local market, the distribution of socio-economic groups, and the rate of new household formation.
- Lack of liquidity: Real estate investments tend to have poor liquidity due to (1) the large outlays required and (2) the time taken and costs incurred to sell.
- Environmental: Poor environmental conditions (e.g. contaminants related to a prior owner or an adjacent property owner) can have an adverse impact on the value of a property.
- Availability of information: There is a risk of overpaying for a property if the owner makes the investment decision based on insufficient or inaccurate information.

- Management: Management risk reflects the ability of both asset managers and property managers to make the right decisions regarding the operation of the property.
- Leverage: A small decrease in NOI can have a significant negative impact on the cash flow available to equity investors after meeting debt servicing obligations.
- Other risk factors: Other risk factors include unobserved physical defects in the property, natural disasters, and acts of terrorism.

Investment Characteristics of Commercial Property Types

Office

The demand for office buildings is influenced by employment growth, especially in industries that are heavy users of office space. Lease lengths are generally influenced by (1) the desirability of the property, (2) the financial strength of the tenant and (3) other terms in the lease such as future rent changes and whether there is an option to extend the lease.

An important consideration in office leases is whether it is the owner or the tenant who bears the risk of operating expenses (e.g. utilities) increasing in the future.

Industrial and Warehouse

The demand for industrial and warehouse properties is heavily influenced by the strength of the overall economy, prospects for growth, and import and export activity. Leases for industrial and warehouse properties may be structured as net leases, gross leases or leases with expense reimbursements.

Retail

The demand for retail space is primarily influenced by consumers' willingness to spend, which in turn is influenced by the strength of the overall economy, job growth, population growth, and savings rates.

Lease terms for retail space are influenced by the quality of the property as well as by the size and importance of the tenant.

Multi-Family

The demand for multi-family space depends on demographic factors such as population growth, relevant age segment for renters, and propensity to rent. Demand also depends on the cost of ownership relative to the cost of renting i.e., the ratio of home prices to rents. If home prices rise, people will lean towards renting, and vice-versa. Home prices are also influenced by the level of interest rates. Higher mortgage rates make purchases more expensive to finance so people shift towards renting.

Appraisals and Value

Since real estate properties are traded relatively infrequently and are unique, appraisals (estimates of value) are important for performance measurement and evaluation. In most cases, appraisals aim to estimate the market value of a property, which can be defined as the amount a *typical* investor would be willing to pay for the property.

Highest and Best Use

The highest and best use of a vacant site refers to the use that would result in the highest implied value for a property, irrespective of what it is currently being used for. Implied value equals the value of the property after construction less costs to construct the building.

- Value after construction refers to what the property would sell for once it is constructed and leased.
- The cost to construct the building includes profit to the developer for handling construction and getting the property leased.

The value of a piece of land should be based on its highest and best use even if there is an existing building on the site. If there is an existing building that is not the highest and best use, then the value of the building will be lower, not the value of the land.

THE INCOME APPROACH TO VALUATION

The direct capitalization method and discounted cash flow method are two income approaches used to estimate the value of commercial (income-producing) property. Both these methods focus on net operating income (NOI) as a measure of income and a proxy for cash flow.

Net Operating Income

> Rental income at full occupancy
> + Other income (such as parking)
> = Potential gross income (PGI)
> – Vacancy and collection loss
> = Effective gross income (EGI)
> – Operating expenses (OE)
> = **Net operating income (NOI)**

- Operating expenses include items such as property taxes, insurance, maintenance, utilities, repairs, and insurance.
- NOI is a before-tax unleveraged measure of income. It is calculated before deducting financing costs and federal income taxes on income generated from the property.
- Sometimes leases may be structured such that tenants are responsible for paying operating expenses. In such cases, those operating expenses are not deducted from income when calculating NOI. In case they have been deducted, the additional income received from the tenants as expense reimbursements would be included in the calculation of NOI.

The Direct Capitalization Method

Under this method, the value of a property is estimated by capitalizing its current NOI at a rate referred to as the capitalization rate (or cap rate).

The cap rate is applied to first-year NOI, while the discount rate is applied to current and future NOI. Generally, **when income and value are growing constantly at the same rate**, the relationship between the cap rate and discount rate can be expressed as:

$$\text{Cap rate} = \text{Discount rate} - \text{Growth rate}$$

The term going-in cap rate is sometimes used to clarify that the cap rate is based on the first year of ownership.

$$\text{Value} = \frac{\text{NOI}_1}{\text{Cap rate}}$$

An estimate of the appropriate cap rate for a property can be obtained from the selling price of similar or comparable properties.

$$\text{Cap rate} = \frac{\text{NOI}_1}{\text{Sale price of comparable property}}$$

Other Forms of the Income Approach: Gross Income Multiplier

$$\text{Gross income multiplier} = \frac{\text{Selling price}}{\text{Gross income}}$$

$$\text{Value of subject property} = \text{Gross income multiplier} \times \text{Gross income of subject property}$$

A drawback of this approach is that it does not explicitly consider vacancy rates and operating expenses.

The Discounted Cash Flow Method (DCF)

Under this method, the value of a property is estimated by projecting income beyond the first year and then discounting the income stream (using an appropriate discount rate).

The investor's total return (discount rate) comes from (1) the return on first-year income (cap rate) and (2) growth in income and value over time (growth rate). If NOI for the property is expected to grow at a constant rate, then the value of the property can be calculated as:

$$\text{Value} = \frac{\text{NOI}_1}{(r - g)}$$

If NOI is expected to remain constant (growth rate = 0) like a perpetuity, then the cap rate and discount rate will be the same.

The Terminal Capitalization Rate

If the growth rate in NOI is not expected to remain constant, investors forecast (1) NOI for each year during a specific holding period and (2) a terminal value (estimated sale price) at the end of the holding period (instead of projecting NOI into infinity). The sum of the present values of these amounts (discounted at the required rate of return) is used as an estimate of the value of the property.

The direct capitalization method is used to estimate terminal value at the end of the holding period.

$$\text{Terminal value} = \frac{\text{NOI for the first year of ownership for the next investor}}{\text{Terminal cap rate}}$$

The terminal cap rate (also called residual cap rate) is selected at the time of valuation and refers to the cap rate that is applied to expected income for the first year after the anticipated sale of the property.

- The terminal cap rate is usually higher than the going-in cap rate as it is applied to an income stream that is more uncertain. Other reasons for a higher terminal cap rate include higher expected future interest rates (discount rates) or lower growth in NOI.
- The terminal cap rate can be lower than the going-in cap rate if investors expect interest rates to be lower and/or growth in NOI to be higher in the future.

Adopting to Different Lease Structures

- The term and reversion approach splits total value into two components (1) term rent and (2) reversion. The value of each component is appraised separately by applying different capitalization rates.
- The layer method assumes that one component of income is the current contract rent, which will continue indefinitely (like a perpetuity), and then adds a second component which comes from the value of the incremental rent expected to be received after the rent review.

General Steps to a DCF Analysis

- Project income from existing leases
- Make assumptions about lease renewals
- Make assumptions about operating expenses
- Make assumptions about capital expenditures
- Make assumptions about absorption of any vacant space
- Estimate resale value (reversion)
- Select discount rate to find PV of cash flows

Direct Capitalization Method versus Discounted Cash Flow Method

- Under the direct capitalization approach, a capitalization rate or income multiplier is applied to first-year NOI. Any growth in NOI is *implicit* in the capitalization rate. The higher the expected growth, the lower the capitalization rate, and the higher the value of the property.
- Under the DCF approach, the future income pattern, including the effects of growth, is *explicitly* considered. Further, DCF valuation can incorporate other cash flows that might occur in the future and are not reflected in NOI, such as capital expenditures.

Advantages and Disadvantages of the Income Approach

- The advantage of using income approach, such as DCF analysis, is that it considers **all** the cash flows that investors are concerned with. Further, it is not dependent on current transactions from comparable sales as long as an appropriate discount rate is selected.

- The disadvantage of the income approach is that it requires detailed information and assumptions regarding the growth rate of NOI, and detailed lease-by-lease analysis. Further, selecting an appropriate discount rate and terminal cap rate is critical to the valuation because slight changes in these assumptions have a significant impact on the property's estimated value.

THE COST APPROACH

The cost approach is based on the view that a buyer would not pay more for a property than it would cost to purchase the land and construct a comparable building on it. This approach is generally used to value unique properties or those with a specialized use for which it is relatively difficult to obtain market comparables. Under the cost approach, the value of a property is estimated as the sum of:

- The value of the land, which is usually determined using the sales comparison approach; and
- The value of the building, which is based on adjusted replacement cost.

Replacement cost refers to the cost of constructing the building today using current construction costs and standards. This replacement cost is then *adjusted* for different types of depreciation (loss in value) to arrive at adjusted or depreciated replacement cost.

The different types of depreciation include:

- Physical deterioration: This refers to the physical wear and tear of the property as it ages over time.
  - *Curable physical deterioration* refers to a problem whose fixing/repairing will add at least as much to the value of the building as it costs to repair. The cost of fixing curable items is deducted from replacement cost.
  - *Incurable physical deterioration* refers to a problem whose cost of repair would exceed the increase in value resulting from the repair, making it unfeasible to fix the problem. Since the costs of repairing such deterioration are not actually borne (since the problem is not repaired) analysts account for the affect of the property's age on its value through a depreciation charge. This depreciation charge is based on the effective age of the property relative to its economic life. The loss from incurable physical deterioration (depreciation) is estimated by applying this ratio to replacement cost *after* deducting the cost of curable physical deterioration.
- Functional obsolescence: This refers to the loss in the value of a building because its current design is not ideally suited for its intended use.
- External obsolescence: This refers to the loss in the value of a building due to external factors, such as the location of the property or economic conditions.
  - *Locational obsolescence* occurs when the location of the building is no longer optimal for its intended use.
  - *Economic obsolescence* occurs when it is not feasible to construct a new building under current economic conditions. This can happen when rent levels are not high enough to generate a value for a newly-constructed property that is at least equal to development costs (including profit to the developer).

Advantages and Disadvantages of the Cost Approach

- The cost approach can be used to determine the upper limit on the value of a property as an investor would never pay more for a property than it costs to purchase the land and construct a comparable building.
- The main disadvantage of this approach is that it is difficult to estimate depreciation for a property that is older and/or has much obsolescence. Therefore, the cost approach is most appropriate for newer properties that have a relatively modern design in a stable market.

THE SALES COMPARISON APPROACH

The sales comparison approach is based on the view that the value of a property depends on what investors are paying for similar properties in the current market. Since it is impossible to find a comparable property that (1) is exactly the same as the subject property in all respects and (2) is sold on the same date as the date of appraisal of the subject property, adjustments must be made for differences between the subject property and comparable properties relating to size, age, location, property condition and market conditions at the time of sale. The idea is to determine what comparable properties would have sold for if they were like the subject property.

The quality of the value estimate from the sales comparison approach depends on the number of recent transactions involving comparable properties. Application of this approach is relatively easy when the market is active, but difficult when the market is weak. Even in an active market, it might be difficult to find comparable sales for some properties (e.g. regional malls and special purpose properties).

Further, the sales comparison approach assumes that purchasers behave rationally i.e., the prices they pay reflect current market values. However, this may not always be the case as the investment value of a property to a particular investor may exceed its market value. Further, in times of exuberance when real estate markets are in a "bubble", the sales comparison approach can lead to inflated valuations, especially when considered in light of values in more "normal" market conditions.

The sales comparison approach is generally used to value single-family homes for which income is not relevant and there is availability of sales data for reasonable comparisons.

Due Diligence in Private Equity Real Estate Investment

Due diligence usually includes the following:
- Review of the lease and history of rental payments.
- Review of operating expenses by obtaining copies of bills (e.g. utility bills).
- Review of cash flow statements of the previous owner.
- An environmental inspection to ensure that there are no contaminant materials on the site.
- A physical/engineering inspection to ensure that there are no structural issues with the property and to check the condition of the building systems, structures, foundation, and adequacy of utilities.

- Review of ownership history to ensure that there are no issues related to the seller's ability to transfer free and clear title that is not subject to any previously unidentified liens.
- Review of service and maintenance agreements.
- A property survey to ensure that any physical improvements are within boundary lines and to identify any easements that may affect value.
- Verification that the property is compliant with zoning, environmental regulations, parking ratios, etc.
- Verification of payment of property taxes, insurance, special assessments, etc.

While due diligence can be costly, it lowers the risk of unidentified legal and physical problems.

PRIVATE EQUITY REAL ESTATE INVESTMENT INDICES

Appraisal-Based Indices

These indices rely on appraisals of value (rather than prices from actual transactions) to estimate changes in the value because real estate transactions involving a specific property occur relatively infrequently. Appraisal-based indices combine valuation information from individual properties to provide a measure of market movements.

The return for all the properties is calculated as:

$$\text{Return} = \frac{\text{NOI} - \text{Capital expenditures} + (\text{Ending market value} - \text{Beginning market value})}{\text{Beginning market value}}$$

- Beginning and ending market values are based on appraisals of the properties.
- The return computed from the formula is the holding period return or the single-period IRR.

The returns on all the properties in the index are then value-weighted to get the index return.

Appraisal-based indices allow investors to compare the performance of real estate relative to other asset classes such as stocks and bonds. Further, the quarterly returns can be used to measure risk (standard deviation). Investors may also use appraisal-based indices to benchmark returns on their real estate portfolios.

One of the disadvantages associated with appraisal-based indices is the appraisal lag as appraised values tend to lag transaction prices when there are sudden shifts in the market.

Transaction-Based Indices

These indices are based on actual transactions rather than appraised values.

- A repeat sales index relies on the repeat sales of the same property. The idea is that if a specific property is sold twice in a given period, its change in value between the two sale dates indicates how market conditions have changed over time. Regression analysis is then used to allocate the change in value to each quarter.

- A hedonic index requires only one sale (instead of repeat sales of the same property). In order to account for the fact that different properties are being sold each quarter, it includes (independent) variables in the regression that control for differences in the characteristics of each property, such as size, age, quality of construction and location. The unexplained variation in the regression reflects the impact of changes in overall market conditions on values.

Transaction-based indices are considered better than appraisal-based indices. However, the need to use statistical techniques to estimate the index can lead to random elements in the observations (noise).

Private Market Real Estate Debt

The amount of debt an investor can obtain to finance the purchase of commercial real estate is usually limited by (1) the loan to value ratio (LTV ratio) or (2) the debt service coverage ratio (DSCR), depending on which measure results in a lower loan amount.

$$\text{LTV ratio} = \frac{\text{Loan amount}}{\text{Appraised value}}$$

$$\text{DSCR} = \frac{\text{NOI}}{\text{Debt service}}$$

Debt service (also referred to as the loan payment) includes both interest payments and principal payments (if required).

When investors use debt to finance the purchase of a property, they often calculate the equity dividend rate to measure how much cash flow they are getting as a percentage of their equity investment. This is also referred to as the cash-on-cash return.

$$\text{Equity dividend rate} = \frac{\text{First year cash flow}}{\text{Equity investment}}$$

PUBLICLY TRADED REAL ESTATE SECURITIES
Cross-Reference to CFA Institute Assigned Reading #39

Investment Characteristics of REITs

Exemption from income taxes: REITs are typically exempt from income taxes at the corporate/trust level if (1) a specified majority of their income and assets relate to income-producing property and (2) they distribute all their potentially taxable income to shareholders.

High income distributions: Due to the fact that REITs must distribute virtually all their income to shareholders in order to qualify for income tax exemption, they typically offer higher dividend yields than most publicly traded equities.

Relatively low volatility of reported income: Due to the fact that they must generate most of the earnings from income-producing property (rental income) to qualify for income tax exemption, REITs typically use conservative, rental-property focused business models, which result in relatively stable revenue streams (except in the case of hotel REITs).

More frequent secondary equity offerings compared with industrial companies: Due to the distribution requirement, REITs are not able to retain earnings to finance growth. Therefore, they rely on new equity issues to finance property acquisitions.

Advantages of Publicly Traded Equity Real Estate Securities

- Greater liquidity
- Lower investment requirements
- Limited liability
- Access to superior quality properties and a range of properties
- Active professional management
- Diversification
- Protection

Advantages of Investing in REITs as Opposed to Publicly Traded REOCs

- Exemption from taxes
- Earnings predictability
- High income payout ratios and yields

Advantage of Investing in REOCs as Opposed to REITs

- Operating flexibility

Disadvantages of Publicly Traded Equity Real Estate Securities

- Taxation
- Control
- Costs
- Stock market determined pricing
- Structural conflicts
- Moderate income growth potential
- Potential for forced equity issuance at disadvantaged pricing

Considerations in Analysis and Due Diligence of Equity REITs

- Remaining lease term
- Inflation protection
- Market rent analysis
- Cost of re-leasing space
- Tenant concentration
- Availability of new competitive supply
- Balance sheet/leverage analysis
- Management

Characteristics of REIT property subtypes

REIT Type	Economic Value Determinants	Investment Characteristics
Retail	• Growth in National GDP • Retail sales growth • Job creation	• Stable revenue stream over the medium term
Office	• Growth in National GDP • Job creation	• Long lease terms • Stable year-to-year income
Residential	• Growth in National GDP • Population growth • Job creation	• Short term one-year leases • Relatively stable demand • Typically structured as gross leases
Health care	• Growth in National GDP • Population growth	• REITs lease facilities to health care providers. • Typically structured as net leases
Industrial	• Growth in National GDP • Retail sales growth • Population growth	• Less cyclical than some other REIT types • Typically structured as long-term net leases • Can be preleased
Hotel	• Growth in National GDP • Job creation • New space supply relative to demand.	• REITs lease facilities to taxable subsidiaries • Volatile income
Storage	• Growth in National GDP • Population growth • Job creation	• Space is leased under gross leases and on a monthly basis

Principal Risks	Due Diligence Considerations
• Trends in consumer spending	• Rental rates and sales per-square-foot
• Changes in office market vacancy and rental rates • Dislocations between supply and demand • Office industry cycle	• New space under construction • Quality of office space • Site location and access to public transport • Business conditions
• Competition • Tenant inducements • Regional economic strength and weakness • Effects of inflation on operating costs • Taxes and maintenance cost	• Demographics and income trends • Age and competitive appeal • Cost and availability • Rent controls • Fuel and energy costs
• Demographics • Government funding • Construction cycles • Financial conditions of operators • Tenant litigation • Dislocations between supply and demand	• Operating trends • Government funding trends • Litigation settlements • Insurance costs • Development of competing facilities
• Shifts in the composition of local and national industrial bases and trade.	• Tenants' requirements • Obsolescence of existing space • Need for new types of space • Access to transportation links • Trends in local supply and demand
• Changes in business and leisure travel • Dislocations between supply and demand	• Occupancy, room rates, and profit margins relative to industry averages • Revenue per available room (RevPAR) • Trends in forward bookings • Maintenance expenditures • New construction in local markets • Financial leverage
• Ease of entry can lead to overbuilding	• Construction of competing facilities • Trends in housing sales • Local demographic trends • Business start-up activity • Seasonal trends in demand for storage facilities

Economic Value Determinants of REITs

Table 1: Importance of Factors Affecting Economic Value for Various Property Types[1]

	National GDP Growth	Job Creation	Retail Sales Growth	Population Growth	New Space Supply vs. Demand
Retail	1	3	2	4	4
Office	1	2	5	4	3
Industrial	1	5	2	3	4
Multi-family	1	2	5	2	4
Storage	1	3	5	2	4
Health care	1	4	5	2	3
Hotels	1	2	5	4	3

Note 1: = most important, 5 = least important
Source: Based on data from the authors' research

The largest driver of economic value for all REIT types is growth in the overall economy or national GDP. Economic growth leads to the creation of more jobs, which leads to higher demand for office space. Economic growth also leads to more disposable income, higher demand for multi-family accommodation, hotel rooms, storage space and retail space.

Principal Risks

Risks tend to be highest for REITs that concentrate on properties (1) where demand for rental space can fluctuate widely in the short term (especially hotels), and (2) in which dislocations between demand and supply are likely to happen (especially offices, hotels and healthcare). Further, a REIT's risk profile is also determined by the quality and location of the properties it holds, and their leasing and financing status.

VALUATION: NET ASSET VALUE APPROACH

Analysts generally use net asset value per share (NAVPS) for valuing REITs and REOCs. NAVPS is the amount (on a per share basis) by which the current market value of a company's assets exceeds the current market value of its liabilities.

In cases where reliable appraisals are not available, analysts estimate the value of operating real estate by capitalizing net operating income (NOI). The cap rate is estimated based on recent comparable transactions.

$$\text{Capitalizaton rate} = \frac{\text{NOI of a comparable property}}{\text{Total value of comparable property}}$$

1 - Exhibit 6, pg 97, Vol 4, CFA Program Curriculum 2014

In order to compute **expected NOI for the coming year**, the following adjustments must be performed on current year actual NOI:

- **Non-cash rents** should be deducted from current period NOI.
- Current-year NOI must also be increased to reflect a full year's rent for properties acquired during the year.
- An expected growth rate may then be applied to estimate NOI for the coming year.

Once next year's expected NOI is capitalized at the appropriate cap rate to compute the value of the REIT's operating real estate, the value of other tangible assets (e.g. prepaid expenses, cash, accounts receivable, land for future development, etc.) is added, and the value of liabilities subtracted, to compute the REITs total net asset value. This total net asset value is then divided by the total number of shares outstanding to calculate NAVPS.

Important Considerations in a NAV-Based Approach to Valuing REITS

- NAV reflects the value of the REIT's assets to a private market buyer, which is usually different from the value that public equity investors ascribe to the business.
- NAV implicitly treats a company as an individual asset or as a static pool of assets. This treatment is not consistent with the going-concern assumption.
- NAV estimates can be quite subjective in times when property markets are illiquid and/or there are few comparable transactions.

VALUATION: RELATIVE VALUATION (PRICE MULTIPLE) APPROACH

Analysts commonly use (1) the price to funds from operations ratio, (2) the price to adjusted funds from operations ratio and (3) enterprise value to EBITDA ratio to value shares of REITs and REOCs.

Funds from operations (FFO) is calculated as:

> Accounting net earnings
> Add: Depreciation charges on real estate
> Add: Deferred tax charges
> Add (Less): Losses (gains) from sale of property and debt restructuring
> **Funds from operations**

Adjusted funds from operations (AFFO) (also referred to as **funds available for distribution** or **cash available for distribution**) is considered a more accurate measure of current economic income. It is calculated as:

> Funds from operations
> Less: Non-cash rent
> Less: Maintenance-type capital expenditures and leasing costs
> **Adjusted funds from operations**

AFFO is preferred over FFO as it takes into account the capital expenditures necessary to maintain the economic income of a property portfolio. Practically however, FFO is more commonly used because AFFO is subject to more variation and error in estimation.

For a REIT, EBITDA can be computed as NOI minus general and administrative (G&A) expenses.

Factors Affecting Valuation Multiples

- Expectations for growth in FFO/AFFO
- Risk associated with the underlying real estate
- Risk associated with the company's capital structures and access to capital

P/FFO and P/AFFO multiples: Advantages and Drawbacks

Advantages:
- Earnings multiples are widely accepted in evaluating shares across global stock markets and industries.
- They enable portfolio managers to put the valuation of REITs and REOCs into context with other investment alternatives.
- Estimates for FFO are readily available through market data providers.
- They can be used in conjunction with expected growth and leverage levels to deepen the relative analysis among REITs and REOCs.

Drawbacks:
- They may not capture the intrinsic value of all real estate assets (e.g. land parcels and empty buildings that are currently not producing any income) held by the REIT or REOC.
- P/FFO does not adjust for the impact of recurring capital expenditures needed to keep properties operating smoothly.
- New revenue recognition rules and increased levels of one-time gains and accounting charges in recent times have made P/FFO and P/AFFO more difficult to calculate and compare across companies.

VALUATION: DISCOUNTED CASH FLOW APPROACH

REITs and REOCs return a significant portion of their income to their investors in the form of dividends, which makes dividend discount models appropriate for valuing their shares.

Considerations when Forecasting Long-Term Growth Rates

- Internal growth potential resulting from rent increases over time.
- Impact of investment activities (e.g. acquisitions and new development) on the long-term growth rate.
- Impact of changes in capital structure on growth.
- Contribution of retaining and reinvesting a portion of free cash flow on the growth rate.

PRIVATE EQUITY VALUATION
Cross-Reference to CFA Institute Assigned Reading #40

Valuation Methodologies[1]

Valuation Technique	Brief Description	Application
Income approach: Discounted cash flows (DCF)	Value is obtained by discounting expected future cash at an appropriate cost of capital.	Generally applies across the broad spectrum of company stages. Given the emphasis on expected cash flows, this methodology provides the most relevant results when applied to companies with a sufficient operating history. Therefore, most applicable to companies operating from the expansion up to the maturity phase.
Relative values: Earnings multiples	Application of an earnings multiple to the earnings of a portfolio company. The earnings multiple is frequently obtained from the average of a group of public companies operating in a similar business and of a comparable size. Commonly used multiples include: Price/Earnings (P/E), Enterprise Value/EBITDA, Enterprise Value/Sales.	Generally applies to companies with a significant operating history and predictable stream of cash flows. May also apply with caution to companies operating at the expansion stage. Rarely applies to early stage or start-up companies.
Real option	The right to undertake a business decision (call or put option). Requires judgmental assumptions about key operational parameters.	Generally applies to situations in which the management or shareholders have significant flexibility in making radically different strategic decisions (i.e., option to undertake or abandon a high risk, high return project). Therefore, generally applies to some companies operating at the seed or start-up phase.
Replacement cost	Estimated cost to recreate the business as it stands as of the valuation date.	Generally applies to early (seed and start-up) stage companies or companies operating at the development stage and generating negative cash flows. Rarely applies to mature companies as it is difficult to estimate the cost to recreate a company with a long operating history. For example, it would be difficult to recreate a long established brand like Coca-Cola, whereas the replacement cost methodology may be used to estimate the brand value for a recently launched beverage (R&D expenses, marketing costs, etc.).

1 - Exhibit 2, pg 143, Vol 5, CFA Program Curriculum 2014

Important Considerations in Private Equity Valuation

- How the PE firm can improve the business's financing, operations, management and marketing.
- Exogenous factors and drivers of business value.
- Valuation of control premium.
- Determination of discounts for lack of liquidity and marketability.
- Evaluation of country risk.

Value Creation in Private Equity

- PE companies have the expertise to re-engineer and reorganize investee companies.
- They are more capable of raising higher levels of debt as they have a reputation for having raised and successfully repaid high levels of debt in past transactions.
- They are better at aligning interest of management with their own and incentivizing management to focus more on long term performance.

Aligning Management Interests with those of the PE Firm

Private equity firms retain control over the management of investee companies through the following control mechanisms:

- Results-driven management pay packages.
- Contractual provisions (e.g. tag-along, drag-along rights) that enable management to participate in the upside in value from a successful exit from the portfolio company.
- Provisions that ensure that the PE firm attains control through board representation if the company experiences a major corporate event (e.g. takeover, restructuring, IPO, bankruptcy or liquidation).
- Non-compete clauses that restrict founders of portfolio companies from launching competing companies for a predefined period of time.
- Clauses that entitle the PE firm to preference dividends, and guarantee the PE firm a multiple of its original investment in the company before other shareholders receive any returns.
- Clauses that make certain important matters (e.g. changes in business plan, acquisitions and divestures) subject to approval or veto by the PE firm.
- Mechanisms (known as earn-outs) that link the acquisition price paid by the PE firm to the portfolio company's future financial performance.

Contrasting Valuation in Venture Capital and Buyout Settings[2]

Buyout Investments:	Venture Capital Investments:
• Steady and predictable cash flows	• Low cash flow predictability, cash flow projections may not be realistic
• Excellent market position (can be a niche player)	• Lack of market history, new market and possibly unproven future market (early stage venture)
• Significant asset base (may serve as basis for collateral lending)	• Weak asset base
• Strong and experienced management team	• Newly formed management team with strong individual track record as entrepreneurs
• Extensive use of leverage consisting of a large proportion of senior debt and significant layer of junior and/or mezzanine debt	• Primarily equity funded. Use of leverage is rare and very limited
• Risk is measurable (mature businesses, long operating history)	• Assessment of risk is difficult because of new technologies, new markets, lack of operating history
• Predictable exit (secondary buyout, sale to a strategic buyer, IPO)	• Exit difficult to anticipate (IPO, trade sale, secondary venture sale)
• Established products	• Technological breakthrough but route to market yet to be proven
• Potential for restructuring and cost reduction	• Significant cash burn rate required to ensure company development and commercial viability
• Low working capital requirement	• Expanding capital requirement if in the growth phase
• Buyout firm typically conducts full blown due diligence approach before investing in the target firm (financial, strategic, commercial, legal, tax, environmental)	• Venture capital firm tends to conduct primarily a technology and commercial due diligence before investing; financial due diligence is limited as portfolio companies have no or very little operating history.
• Buyout firm monitors cash flow management, strategic, and business planning	• Venture capital firm monitors achievement of milestones defined in business plan and growth management

2 - Exhibit 3, pg 149, Vol 5, CFA Program Curriculum 2014

Buyout Investments:	Venture Capital Investments:
• Returns of investment portfolios are generally characterized by lower variance across returns from underlying investments; bankruptcies are rare events	• Returns of investment portfolios are generally characterized by very high returns from a limited number of highly successful investments and a significant number of write-offs from low performing investments or failures
• Large buyout firms are generally significant players in capital markets	• Venture capital firms tend to be much less active in capital markets
• Most transactions are auctions, involving multiple potential acquirers	• Many transactions are "proprietary", being the result of relationships between venture capitalists and entrepreneurs
• Strong performing buyout firms tend to have a better ability to raise larger funds after they have successfully raised their first funds	• Venture capital firms tend to be less scalable relative to buyout firms; the increase in size of subsequent funds tend to be less significant
• Variable revenue to the general partner (GP) at buyout firms generally comprise the following three sources: carried interest, transaction fees, and monitoring fees.	• Carried interest (participation in profits) is generally the main source of variable revenue to the general partner at venture capital firms; transaction and monitoring fees are rare in practice

Private Equity Valuation Techniques

There are six techniques that are generally used to value private equity portfolio companies.

- The income approach (discounted cash flows) is generally applied to companies with sufficient operating history (typically expansion to mature stage companies).
- Relative valuation (using earnings multiples) is generally applied to companies with significant operating history and a predictable stream of cash flows.
- Real option valuation is applied in situations where management/shareholders have significant flexibility in decision-making. It is generally applied to companies in the seed or start-up phase.
- Replacement cost is applied to early-stage companies that are in the development stage and are currently generating negative cash flow. It rarely applies to mature companies.
- The venture capital method and the leveraged buyout model are discussed later in this reading.

Using Market Data in Private Company Valuation

- Valuation ratios (e.g. EV/EBITDA) for publicly-traded comparable firms are used to value private companies.
- The WACC for public companies is used to estimate the discount rate when valuing private companies (in DCF approaches).
- The beta of public comparable companies is adjusted for financial and operating leverage to estimate beta for private companies.
- The terminal value of an investment in a private company is determined based on trading multiples in public markets.

Challenges in Private Equity Valuation

- Forecasting the company's future profitability and cash flows based on expectations of exogenous factors (e.g. interest rates, exchange rates, etc.) and value drivers for the business (sales margins, etc.).
- Incorporating ways through which the PE firm can enhance financing, operations, management and marketing of the portfolio company into those forecasts.
- Determining the appropriate (1) premium for control, (2) lack of liquidity discount (as investments in portfolio companies are typically not readily convertible into cash) and (3) lack of marketability discount (as investors usually face restrictions on the sale of shares).
- Estimating the country risk premium (when valuing companies in emerging markets).

Valuation Issues in Buyout Transactions

The LBO Model

In LBO transactions buyers use a significant amount of debt to finance their purchase of the target company. The LBO model is used to determine the impact of capital structure, purchase price, and various other factors on expected return for the private equity firm from the transaction. It has three main inputs:

- Forecasted cash flows of the target company.
- Expected returns for providers of various types of capital.
- The amount of financing available for the transaction.

Value creation comes from:

- Earnings growth from operational improvements.
- Multiple expansion depending on potential exit.
- Optimal financial leverage and debt repayment with operating cash flow before exit.

Exit value = Initial cost + Earnings growth + Multiple expansion + Debt reduction

Venture Capital Transactions

- Pre-money valuation (PRE) refers to the agreed value of the company prior to a round of financing.
- Post-money valuation (POST) refers to the value of the company after the round of financing.

$$POST = PRE + I$$

The proportionate ownership of the VC investor is calculated as: $I \,/\, POST$

Importance of Exit Routes

- Because private equity investments are not very liquid, it is extremely important for private equity investors to consider exit strategies before making an investment.
- The timing of exit also has an impact on firm value and therefore, is an important consideration.

Types of Exit

Initial Public Offerings (IPO)
An IPO is an appropriate exit route for large companies with excellent growth prospects.

Advantages:
- Generally results in highest valuation for the company.
- Increases liquidity of company shares.
- Gives the company access to large amounts of capital.
- Enables the company to attract higher-caliber managers.

Disadvantages:
- The process of taking the company public can be quite cumbersome.
- The company is left with less flexibility.
- It entails significant costs.

Secondary Market Sale
This involves a private sale of an ownership stake in the company to other financial or strategic investors.

Advantages:
- Typically results in highest valuation for the company outside of an IPO.
- Specialized PE firms can create additional value for the company.

Management Buyout (MBO)
This involves the purchase of the company by its management. Although this method results in the best alignment of interests, the company suffers from reduced flexibility due to significant financial leverage.

Liquidation
This involves an outright sale of the company's assets and results in the lowest value for the company.

Private Equity Fund Structures

One of the most common forms of private equity structures is the limited partnership.

- Limited partners (LPs) are the providers of funds that are invested in target companies. They are only liable for losses up to the amount of funds invested by them.
- General partners (GPs) manage the fund and are liable for all of the firm's debt.

Private Equity Fund Terms

Economic Terms
- Management fees
- Transaction fees
- Carried interest
- Ratchet
- Hurdle rate
- Target fund size
- Vintage year
- Term of the fund

Corporate Governance Terms
- Key man clause
- Disclosure and confidentiality
- Clawback provision
- Distribution waterfall
- Tag-along, drag-along rights
- No-fault divorce clause
- Removal for "cause"
- Investment restrictions
- Co-investment

Due Diligence Investigations by Potential Investors

Prior to investing in a private equity fund, prospective investors should conduct a thorough due diligence of the fund because:

- Their investments are locked in for the long-term.
- Returns of the funds tend to persist over time.
- The difference in returns between well-performing funds and poor-performing funds is significant.

Determining a Private Equity Fund's Value

A fund's NAV can be determined in the following ways:

- At cost with significant adjustments for subsequent financing events or deterioration.
- At lower of cost or market value.
- By revaluing a portfolio company whenever a new financing round involving new investors takes place.
- At cost with no interim adjustment until exit.
- With a discount for restricted securities.
- Marked to market by reference to a peer group of public comparables and applying illiquidity discounts.

Issues in Calculating a PE Fund's NAV

- If value is only adjusted when a new round of financing occurs, the NAV will be out-dated if there is an extended period with no financing round.
- The value of investments in target companies cannot be calculated with certainty before exit as there is no market for them.
- Undrawn LP commitments represent liabilities of the LP, but they are not accounted for in the calculation of NAV.
- Market multiples that are used to value portfolio companies may be inflated during bubbles.
- Valuations are usually performed by GPs.

Differences between Private and Public firms

- Unlike public firms, whose shares are available for purchase to the general public, private equity investments are often only available to qualified investors.
- In public firms, the capital acquired from the sale of shares is almost immediately invested in the business. On the other hand, the capital committed by investors to private equity firms is drawn down in stages as it is invested in target companies.
- Private equity firms typically experience the J-curve effect in their earnings. This refers to the low or negative earnings in the early years of the private equity fund, followed by increased earnings in the later years.

Risks and Costs of Investing in Private Equity

Risks

- Illiquidity of investments
- Unquoted investments
- Competition for attractive investment opportunities
- Reliance on the management of investee companies (agency risk)
- Loss of capital
- Adverse impact of government regulations
- Taxation risk
- Valuation of investments
- Lack of investment capital
- Lack of diversification
- Market risk i.e., adverse impact of changes in general market conditions (interest rate, currency exchange rates, etc.).

Costs

- Transaction fees
- Investment vehicle fund setup costs
- Administrative costs
- Audit costs
- Management and performance fees
- Dilution
- Placement fees

Evaluating Fund Performance

Internal Rate of Return (IRR)

- Gross IRR reflects cash flows between the private equity fund and its portfolio companies and is thus a relevant measure for evaluating the investment management team's performance.
- Net IRR reflects cash flows between the private equity fund and LPs and is thus a relevant measure for return to investors.

IRR should be interpreted with caution because investments in private equity are quite illiquid, while IRR assumes that interim cash flows are reinvested at the IRR.

Multiples

- PIC (Paid-in capital): Ratio of invested capital to committed capital.
- DPI (Distributed to paid-in): Ratio of cumulative distributions paid to LPs to cumulative invested capital.
- RVPI (Residual value to paid-in): Ratio of LPs' holdings held with the fund to cumulative invested capital.
- TVPI (Total value to paid-in): Sum of DPI and RVPI.

Qualitative Measures

- Analysis of investments realized since inception, evaluating all successes and failures.
- Analysis of unrealized investments, highlighting red flags and expected times to exit each investment.
- Cash flow forecasts at the portfolio company level as well as for the entire portfolio.
- Analysis of portfolio valuation, NAV and audited financial statements.

The Basic Venture Capital Method (in Terms of NPV)

Step 1: Determine the post-money valuation.

$$\text{Post-money value} = \frac{\text{Exit value}}{(1+\text{Required rate of return})^{\text{Number of years to exists}}}$$

Step 2: Determine the pre-money valuation.

$$\text{Pre-money value} = \text{Post-money value} - \text{Investment}$$

Step 3: Calculate the ownership percentage of the VC investor.

$$\text{Ownership proportion of VC investor} = \frac{\text{Investment}}{\text{Post-money value}}$$

Step 4: Calculate the number of shares to be issued to the VC investor.

$$\text{Shares to be issued} = \frac{\text{Proportion of venture capitalist investment} \times \text{Shares held by company founders}}{\text{Proportion of investment of company founders}}$$

Step 5: Calculate the price of shares.

$$\text{Price per share} = \frac{\text{Amount of venture capital investment}}{\text{Number of shares issued to venture capital investment}}$$

Venture Capital Method (in Terms of the IRR)

The venture capital method can also be explained in terms of the IRR. Whether based on NPV or IRR, the venture capital method gives exactly the same answer. The IRR method involves the following steps.

Step 1: Calculate the future wealth required by the VC investor to achieve its desired IRR.

$$\text{Required wealth} = \text{Investment} \times (1 + \text{IRR})^{\text{Number of years to exit}}$$

Step 2: Calculate the ownership percentage of venture capital investor.

$$\text{Required wealth} = \text{Investment} \times (1 + \text{IRR})^{\text{Number of years to exit}}$$

Step 3: Calculate the number of shares to be issued to the venture capital investor.

$$\text{Shares to be issued} = \frac{\text{Proportion of venture capitalist investment} \times \text{Shares held by company founders}}{\text{Proportion of investment of company founders}}$$

Step 4: Calculate the price of shares.

$$\text{Price per share} = \frac{\text{Amount of venture capital investment}}{\text{Number of shares issued to venture capital investors}}$$

Step 5: Determine the post-money valuation.

$$\text{Post-money value} = \text{Investment} / \text{VC's ownership proportion}$$

Step 6: Determine the pre-money valuation.

$$\text{Pre-money valuation} = \text{Post-money valuation} - \text{Investment}$$

Venture Capital Method with Multiple Rounds of Financing

When there are 2 rounds of financing, the venture capital method requires the following steps:

Step 1: Define appropriate compound interest rates between each financing round.

Step 2: Determine the post-money valuation after the second round.

Step 3: Determine the pre-money valuation after the second round.

Step 4: Determine the post-money valuation after the first round.

Step 5: Determine the pre-money valuation after the first round.

Step 6: Determine the required ownership percentage for second round investors.

Step 7: Determine the required ownership percentage for first round investors. Note that this is not their final ownership percentage as their equity interest will be diluted in the second round.

Step 8: Determine the number of shares that must be issued to first round investors for them to attain their desired ownership percentage.

Step 9: Determine price per share in the first round.

Step 10: Determine the number of shares at the time of the second round.

Step 11: Determine the number of shares that must be issued to second round investors for them to attain their desired ownership percentage.

Step 12: Determine price per share in the second round

Accounting for Risks

Venture capitalists typically apply very high discount rates when evaluating target companies for the following reasons:
- VC firms must be compensated for the significant non-diversifiable risk inherent in portfolio companies.
- Estimates of terminal value do not necessarily reflect *expected earnings*. They reflect future earnings in some kind of *success scenario*.

These risks may be accounted for in the following two ways:

- By adjusting the discount rate.

$$\text{Adjusted discount rate} = \frac{1 + \text{Unadjusted discount rate}}{1 - \text{Probability of failure}} - 1$$

- By adjusting the terminal value using scenario analysis.

A PRIMER ON COMMODITY INVESTING
Cross-Reference to CFA Institute Assigned Reading #41

Participants in the Commodity Futures Market

- **Hedgers:** Hedgers participate in the futures market to eliminate any price risk associated with their existing or expected (natural) positions on the underlying.
- **Speculators (or traders):** Speculators bring liquidity to the futures market. Speculators (unlike hedgers) do not have a natural position in the underlying, so they are exposed to the risk of huge gains or losses from commodity price fluctuations.
- **Arbitrageurs:** Arbitrageurs look to take advantage of pricing inefficiencies in the market to make riskless profits.

DIFFERENCES BETWEEN COMMODITY MARKETS AND OTHER INVESTMENTS

- Commodities are real assets.
- Supply is limited in any given period due to limited availability.
- They are heterogeneous.

Storability: Storability plays an important role when it comes to pricing commodities. A commodity has high storability if (1) it is not perishable and (2) storage costs are low relative to total value.

Renewability: Whether a commodity is renewable or not plays an important role in determining which factors influence price.
- Renewable commodities can theoretically be produced without limitation, but their yearly supply is restricted to the annual harvest.
- The supply of non-renewable commodities in any given period depends on the ability of producers to mine raw material in sufficient quantity and quality.

COMMODITIES AS AN ASSET CLASS OF THEIR OWN

Asset Super Classes

- **Capital assets:** These assets display "continuous performance" such as equities (with their continuous stream of dividends and fixed income securities (with their coupon payments).
- **Store of value assets:** These assets cannot be consumed, nor do they generate any income.
- **Consumable or transferable assets (C/T assets):** These assets do not generate continuous cash flows, but they do have economic value in that they can be consumed or be used as an input in manufacturing. Most commodities belong to the this super class. Commodity prices are primarily influenced by the interaction of demand and supply in specific markets.

PROSPECTS FOR COMMODITY MARKET PARTICIPATION

Buying the physical good: Directly purchasing physical commodities in the spot market.

Advantage:
- It is the obvious, most direct option available to investors.

Disadvantage:
- Direct purchasing does not make practical sense for certain types of commodities (e.g. perishable agricultural goods). While storage and current costs are relatively low for other types of commodities (e.g. precious metals), a commodities portfolio consisting of only those commodities would not be sufficiently diversified.

Commodity stocks: Investing in commodity companies.

Advantage:
- Stock market prices react to developments that affect company value relatively quickly and sensibly.

Disadvantages:
- Does not offer direct exposure to commodities.
- Company stock prices are also influenced by company-specific factors including company strategy, management quality, capital structure, expected profit growth, and risk sensitivity.
- Natural resource companies face additional risks such as operational risks due to technical failures or external events.
- In the energy and metals sectors, there is a paradox in that companies threaten their own longevity by extracting exhaustible resources. A decrease in long-term reserves would result in an increase in current prices (a positive for commodity stocks), but producers suffer from a depletion of resources (a negative for their long-term prospects).
- There is the risk of a total loss if commodity prices fall below production costs as this can lead to the cessation of extraction activities.
- Stock prices can also be influenced by market factors (e.g. stocks with low free floats can exhibit high price volatility when there is a large disconnect between demand and supply for the stock).
- Studies have shown that commodity stocks tend to be only slightly correlated with commodity prices. Historically, returns on commodity stocks have exhibited a lower correlation with commodity futures than even the S&P 500. Further, returns on commodity stocks have been lower than returns on direct commodity investments.

Commodity funds: Investing in commodity mutual funds, which can be actively or passively managed.

Advantages:
- Investors can gain access to a diversified portfolio with moderate transaction costs.
- They can choose among a variety of commodity funds that differ based on management style, allocation strategy, geography, investment horizon and currency.

Disadvantage:
- Investors must ensure that the particular fund they choose matches their desired characteristics.

Commodity futures indexes: These offer investors a passive form of investing in commodities.

Advantage:

- For most investors, an index-oriented approach to investing in commodities is the most reasonable and cost-effective way to attain exposure to commodity investments.

Disadvantage:

- Due to their construction, these indexes can only take positions on short-term futures contracts. Commodity funds on the other hand have flexibility regarding the investment term as they directly invest in commodity futures contracts and are not linked to commodity indexes.

Commodity futures:

Advantages:

- Investors are able to profit from price movements of the underlying commodity without having to worry about the logistical or storage requirements associated with a direct purchase.
- Low capital requirements enable investors to leverage their positions.
- Standardization of contracts results in high liquidity and low transaction costs, allowing investors to quickly and easily take/close positions.
- Investors can profit from rising or declining prices.

Disadvantages:

- The volatility in underlying commodity prices is also reflected in futures prices.
- Rolling can be very costly depending on the forward curve of the futures market.
- Sharp changes in commodity prices can result in frequent margin calls, which can make it difficult and time consuming to manage a portfolio of commodity futures contracts.

Pricing at Commodity Futures Exchanges

Ignoring storage costs, the relationship between the spot price S and the futures price $F(t,T)$ of a commodity at time t with remaining time to maturity T is given as:

$$F_0 = S_0 e^{rT}$$

Spot Futures Arbitrage Relationship/ Spot Futures Parity

$$F_0 = S_0 e^{(r+U)T}$$

Backwardation versus Contango

- Backwardation: This occurs when the term structure curve has a negative slope i.e., futures prices of longer term contracts are lower than the current spot price. In such a case, assuming that there were no changes in the spot price, an investor would earn a profit by holding a long position in the futures contract (as at expiration of the contract, the futures price will converge to the spot price).
- Contango: In a contangoed market, the futures price lies above the spot price and therefore, the forward term structure curve has a positive slope.

Convenience Yield

Convenience yield reflects the utility of holding the physical asset as opposed to holding a contractual agreement calling for delivery of the asset.

After accounting for convenience yield, the futures prices can be computed as:

$$F_0 = S_0 e^{(r+U-Y)T}$$

- For commodities whose convenience yield is lower than storage costs plus the risk-free rate, the futures price will be greater than the spot price so the market will be in contango.
- For commodities whose convenience yield is higher than storage costs plus the risk-free rate, the futures price will be less than the spot price so the market will be in backwardation.

Future Parity

Future parity states that the futures price observed today is an unbiased estimate of the expected spot price at maturity, $E_t[S(T)]$. When future parity does not hold, the market can be in normal backwardation or normal contango.

- When the futures price is lower than the **expected spot price** the market is said to be in normal backwardation.
- When the futures price is greater than the **expected spot price**, the market is said to be in normal contango.

RETURN COMPONENTS OF COMMODITY FUTURES INVESTMENTS

Spot return: This refers to the percentage change in the spot price of the actual underlying commodity

$$RS = \frac{S_t - S_{t-1}}{S_{t-1}}$$

Roll return: This refers to the return earned in the process of switching from a maturing futures contract over to the next shortest futures contract.
- If the futures market is in backwardation the rolling of maturing futures contracts would lead to a positive return.
- If the futures market is in contango the rolling of maturing futures contracts would lead to a negative return.

$$R_r = \frac{F_{t,T} - S_t}{S_t}$$

In this formula, a negative (positive) value represents a positive (negative) roll return, which occurs when the market is in backwardation (contango).

Collateral return: This refers to the interest earned on the cash investment. The collateral return is explicitly considered in a total return index, but not in an excess return index.

Rebalancing return: This component of return arises from the mandatory reallocation of sectors or commodities in a value-weighted commodity index.

MEASURING PERFORMANCE

- The total return index results from the actual futures return (spot return plus roll return) and the collateral return.

- The excess return index captures the spot return and roll return.

  The total return index is based on a fully cash-collateralized commodity investment, while the underlying of the excess return index is assumed to be an **un**collateralized futures instrument.

- The spot return index measures price movements in the futures market (not price movements in the spot market).

Models of Expected Returns

The capital asset pricing model (CAPM): Under this framework, market beta is used to compute expected returns.

The insurance perspective argues that risk premiums are available if producers use commodity futures to hedge price risk.

The hedging pressure hypothesis allows for risk premiums to be earned by going long or short on commodity futures, depending on the balance of hedgers in the market.

The theory of storage argues that there is an inverse relationship between inventory levels of a commodity and its convenience yield i.e., the lower the level of inventory, the higher the convenience yield.

Risk and Performance Characteristics **Vol 5, pg 242**

- Commodities show an equity-like performance over the long run with regards to return and volatility. However, commodity returns exhibit positive skewness, while equity returns exhibit negative skewness (i.e. higher downside risk).
- Over the long-term, commodities have shown low correlation with traditional and other alternative asset classes.

FORWARD RATES
Cross-Reference to CFA Institute Assigned Reading #42

A forward rate is an interest rate that is determined today for a loan that will be initiated in the future. We denote the x-year forward rate y years from today as $_xf_y$. Here, a loan with a term of x years will be initiated y years from today.

- For example, the 3-year forward rate two years from today will be denoted as $_3f_2$.

The Forward Pricing Model

The forward pricing model describes the valuation of forward contracts. It is based on the no-arbitrage argument.

> Forward pricing model: $P(T^* + T) = P(T^*)F(T^*,T)$

Determining Forward Rates from Spot Rates

$$(1+\,_ys_0)^y\,(1+\,_xf_y)^x = (1+\,_{x+y}s_0)^{x+y}$$

Forward Pricing Model

$$P(T^*)\,F(T^*,T) = P(T^*,T)$$

- Forward rates can be extrapolated from spot rates.
- A forward rate can be looked upon as a type of breakeven interest rate.
- A forward rate can also be looked upon as the rate that can be locked in by extending maturity by one year.
- The x-year spot rate today can be expressed as a geometric mean of the 1-year spot rate today, and a series of 1-year forward rates (where the number of 1-year forward rates equals x−1).

Other Important Relationships between Spot and Forward Rates

- If the yield curve is upward-sloping, then the x-year forward rate y years from today, $_xf_y$, will be greater than the long-term spot rate, $_{x+y}s_0$
  - Example: If $_3s_0 > _2s_0 > _1s_0$ then $_2f_1 > _3s_0$
- For an upward-sloping yield curve, the forward rate rises as y (the initiation date) increases.
  - Example: If $_3s_0 > _2s_0 > _1s_0$ then $_1f_2 > _1f_1$

- If the yield curve is downward sloping, then the x-year forward rate y years from today, $_xf_y$, will be lower than the long-term spot rate, $_{x+y}s_0$
  - Example: If $_3s_0 > {_2}s_0 > {_1}s_0$ then $_2f_1 < {_3}s_0$
- For a downward-sloping yield curve, the forward rate declines as y increases.
  - Example: If $_3s_0 > {_2}s_0 > {_2}s_0$ then $_1f_2 < {_1}f_1$
- If the yield curve is flat, all one-year forward rates are equal to the spot rate.

Yield to Maturity in Relation to Spot Rates and Expected and Realized Returns on Bonds

- The yield to maturity (YTM) is calculated as the internal rate of return on a bond's cash flows.
- It only equals the expected rate of return on a bond if (1) the bond is held until maturity, (2) all coupon and principal payments are made in full when due, and (3) all coupons are reinvested at the original YTM. This last condition typically does not hold.
- The YTM is a poor estimate of the expected return on a bond if (1) interest rates are volatile, (2) the yield curve has a steep slope, (3) there is significant risk of default, and (4) the bond contains embedded options.
- Even if we make the assumption that actual future spot rates will turn out to be the same as forward rates (that are based on current spot rates), the expected return on a bond still will not equal its YTM. This is because the YTM implicitly assumes that the yield curve is flat (the same discount rate is applied to each cash flow regardless of its maturity).
- The realized rate of return is the actual return earned by a bond investor over the holding period. It is based on (1) actual reinvestment rates and (2) the yield curve at the end of the holding period.

Yield Curve Movements and the Forward Curve

- If future spot rates evolve as predicted by today's forward curve, forward rates remain unchanged; and since forward rates remain unchanged, so does the forward contract price
- A change in the forward rate (and the forward price) reflects a deviation of the spot curve from that predicted by today's forward curve.
- If a trader expects that the future spot rate will be lower than what is predicted by the prevailing forward rate, he would buy the forward contract because he expects its value to increase.
- If a trader expects that the future spot rate will be greater than what is predicted by the prevailing forward rate, he would sell the forward contract because he expects its value to decrease.

Active Bond Portfolio Management

- The return on bonds of varying maturities over a one-year period is always the one-year rate (the risk-free rate over the one-year period), if spot rates evolve (at the end of the first year) as implied by the current forward curve.
- If a portfolio manager's projected spot curve is above (below) the forward curve and his or her expectation turns out to be true, the return will be less (more) than the one-period risk-free interest rate because the market would have overpriced (underpriced) the forward contract.

Riding the Yield Curve

If the yield curve is upward-sloping, and if a trader is confident that the yield curve will not change its level and shape over her investment horizon, she would buy bonds with a maturity greater than her investment horizon (instead of bonds with maturities that exactly match her investment horizon) to enhance her total return.

THE SWAP RATE CURVE

The yield curve of swap fixed rates is known as the swap rate curve or swap curve. Since it is based on par swaps (the present values of the fixed- and floating-rate legs are equal at swap initiation), the swap curve is a type of par curve.

The swap market is a highly liquid market for two main reasons:

- Swap arrangements offer significant flexibility and customization in contract design.
- Swaps provide a very efficient way to hedge interest rate risk.

The Swap Spread

- The swap spread is defined as the difference between the swap fixed rate on a swap and the rate of the "on-the-run" government security with the same maturity/tenor as the swap.
- The swap spread can be used to measure credit risk and liquidity risk. The higher the swap spread, the higher the compensation demanded by investors for accepting credit and/or liquidity risk. Note, however, that if the bond entails no default risk, then the swap spread could indicate liquidity risk, or it could suggest that the bond is mispriced.
- A more accurate measure (than the swap spread) of credit and liquidity risk is the zero-spread (or z-spread). The z-spread is the constant spread that would be added to the implied spot curve such that the present value of the cash flows of a bond, when discounted at relevant spot rates plus the z-spread, equals its current market price.

Spreads as a Price Quote Convention

- The swap spread represents the difference between the swap rate and the government bond yield (of the same maturity).
  - The swap rate does reflect some counterparty credit risk, while the U.S. Treasuries are considered free from default risk, so the swap rate is typically greater than the corresponding Treasury note rate.
- The TED spread is calculated as the difference between Libor and the yield on a T-bill with the same maturity.
  - The TED spread indicates the perceived level of credit risk in the overall economy.
  - The TED spread can also be thought of as a measure of counterparty credit risk in swap contracts.
- The Libor-OIS spread is calculated as the difference between Libor and the overnight indexed swap (OIS) rate.
  - The Libor–OIS spread is an indicator of the risk and liquidity of money-market securities.
- The I-spread is calculated as the difference between the yield on a corporate bond and the swap rate on a swap with the same tenor as the bond.

TRADITIONAL THEORIES OF THE TERM STRUCTURE OF INTEREST RATES

Unbiased Expectations Theory

The unbiased expectations theory or pure expectations theory states that the forward rate is an unbiased predictor of future spot rates. This implies that bonds of **any** maturity are perfect substitutes for each other. The unbiased expectations theory assumes that investors are risk-neutral. The argument against this theory is that investors tend to be risk-averse.

Local Expectations Theory

The local expectations theory is similar but narrower than the unbiased expectations theory. Instead of asserting that every maturity strategy has the same expected return over a given investment horizon, this theory states that the return over a short-term investment horizon that starts today will be the same (i.e., the risk-free rate) regardless of maturity of the chosen security as long as forward rates are actually realized.

The local expectations theory is economically appealing, but it is often observed that short-term returns on longer-maturity bonds exceed those on shorter-maturity bonds.

Liquidity Preference Theory

The liquidity preference theory accounts for the fact that investors in long-term securities require some compensation for taking higher interest rate risk. This theory asserts that the longer the term to maturity, the greater the price sensitivity (duration) of a bond to changes in interest rates, and the greater the compensation (risk premium) required by investors.

Segmented Markets Theory

The segmented markets theory asserts that the yield for each maturity along the yield curve is determined independently, solely by the supply and demand of funds for the particular maturity, which means that yields do not reflect expected spot rates or liquidity premiums.

The Preferred Habitat Theory

The preferred habitat theory does not assert that yields at different maturities are determined independently of each other. In this theory, both market expectations and the institutional factors emphasized in the segmented markets theory influence the term structure of interest rates.

MODERN TERM STRUCTURE MODELS

Equilibrium Term Structure Models

- Equilibrium term structure models look to describe the dynamics of the term structure using fundamental economic variables that affect interest rates.
- They can be structured as one-factor or multifactor models.
- They make assumptions about the behavior of factors. For example, the model must make an assumption whether the short-term interest rate should be modeled as mean-reverting, or whether it should be modeled to exhibit jumps.
- They typically require estimation of less parameters than arbitrage-free term structure models (described later), but this comes at the cost of less precision in modeling the observed yield curve.

- They typically make an assumption regarding the term premium, i.e., the additional return required by lenders to invest in long-term securities. Arbitrage-free models do not make a term premium assumption.

The Cox-Ingersoll-Ross (CIR) Model

- The CIR model uses one factor, i.e., the short-term rate to determine the entire term structure of interest rates.
- The model has (1) a deterministic component and (2) a stochastic (or random) component.
    - The deterministic component is also called the drift term.
        - Within this deterministic component, the interest rate is modeled as mean-reverting (towards a level b).
        - Another parameter (a) represents the speed at which interest rates revert to the mean. The higher the value of this parameter, the quicker the mean reversion.
    - The stochastic term models risk (volatility).
        - This term makes volatility proportional to the short-term rate, i.e., interest rate volatility increases with the level of interest rates.
        - It also precludes the possibility of negative interest rates.

The Vasicek Model

- The Vasicek model also assumes that interest rates are mean-reverting.
- The model also has the same drift term as the CIR model.
- However, the stochastic component assumes that interest rate volatility is constant.
- The main disadvantage of the model is that it is theoretically possible for interest rates to be negative.

The yield curve estimated with the Vasicek or CIR model may not match the observed yield curve. However, if model parameters are believed to be correct, these models can be used to identify mispricings.

Arbitrage-Free Models

- Arbitrage-free models start with market prices of a reference set of financial instruments. Under the assumption that these instruments are correctly priced, a random process with a drift term and volatility factor is used to generate the yield curve.
- The advantage of arbitrage-free models is the ability to calibrate the model to market data. They exhibit greater accuracy in modeling the market yield curve.
- Arbitrage-free models are also known as partial equilibrium models because they do not attempt to explain the yield curve; instead they take the yield curve as given.

The Ho-Lee Model

- The Ho-Lee model uses the relative valuation concepts of the Black–Scholes–Merton option-pricing model.
- The time-dependent drift term of the model is inferred from market prices, so the model can accurately generate the current term structure.
- This exercise is typically performed via a binomial lattice-based model, which makes use of risk-neutral probabilities.

- The advantage of the model lies in its simplicity, and it can be used to illustrate most of the salient features of arbitrage-free interest rate models.
- Interest rate volatility can be modeled as a function of time in the model.
- The downside is that negative interest rates are theoretically possible.

YIELD CURVE FACTOR MODELS

- The sensitivity of a bond's price to changes in the shape of the yield curve is known as shaping risk.
- Studies that have made use of yield curve factor models have found that yield curve movements are historically well described by three independent movements—level, steepness, and curvature.
  - The level movement refers to upward or downward (parallel) shifts in the yield curve.
  - The steepness movement refers to changes in the slope of the yield curve. These movements are also known as yield curve twists.
  - The curvature movement refers to movements in the three segments of the yield curve. These movements are also known as butterfly shifts.

Managing Yield Curve Risks

Yield curve risk refers to the risk to portfolio value from unanticipated changes in the yield curve. It can be identified and managed using:

- Key rate duration, which measures the change in the value of a portfolio in response to a small change in the yield for a specific maturity.
- A measure based on the factor model, which uses three types of movements—level, steepness, and curvature, to explain changes in the yield curve.

The Maturity Structure of Yield Curve Volatilities

- Interest rate volatility is important for at least two reasons:
  - Changes in the price of a bond results depends on (1) its duration and convexity, i.e., the impact per basis point change in the YTM **and** (2) the magnitude of the change in the YTM, i.e. yield volatility. Therefore, controlling the impact of interest rate volatility on a bond's price volatility is an important part of risk management.
  - Most fixed-income instruments and derivatives contain embedded options, whose values depend on the level of interest rate volatility.
- The term structure of interest rate volatilities is a representation of the yield volatility of a zero coupon bond for a range of maturities. This volatility curve (also known as vol or volatility term structure) measures yield curve risk.
- Interest rate volatility varies across different maturities. Generally speaking, short-term rates tend to be more volatile than long-term rates.
- Interest rate volatility is typically expressed in terms of an annualized standard deviation. For example, if the monthly standard deviation of the 3-month T-bill is 10.15%, then its yield volatility will be expressed as 0.3516 or 35.16% [= $0.1015 \div (1/12)^{0.5}$].

ARBITRAGE-FREE VALUATION
Cross-Reference to CFA Institute Assigned Reading #43

- The law of one price states that two securities or portfolios that will generate identical cash flows in the future, regardless of future events, should have the same price today (in the absence of transaction costs).
- An arbitrage opportunity can be defined as a transaction that involves no cash outlay and results in a risk-less profit. There are two types of arbitrage opportunities.
  - Value additivity, where the value of the whole equals the sum of the values of the parts.
  - Dominance, where one asset offers a greater return for the same level of risk.

Arbitrage-Free Valuation for Fixed-Income Securities

The arbitrage-free valuation approach uses the relevant spot rate (i.e., ytm on the appropriate zero-coupon bond) to discount each individual cash flow from a bond. The sum of the present values of cash flows from a bond, individually discounted at the relevant spot rate, should equal the price of the bond.

INTEREST RATE TREES AND ARBITRAGE-FREE VALUATION

For bonds that contain embedded options, the challenge in developing an arbitrage-free valuation framework is to account for the fact that their expected cash flows are interest rate dependent. An interest rate tree represents the possible future interest rates consistent with the assumed level of volatility. The interest rate tree serves two purposes in the valuation process: (1) it is used to generate cash flows that are dependent on interest rates and (2) it supplies the interest rates that are used to compute present values of cash flows.

The binomial interest rate tree framework assumes that the one-year interest rate can take on one of two possible values in the next period. These two possible interest rates in the next period must be consistent with three conditions:

1. The interest rate model that dictates how interest rates move
2. The assumed level of interest rate volatility
3. The current benchmark yield curve

Backward induction is then used to compute the value of the bond at any given node.

PATH-WISE VALUATION

Path-wise valuation computes the present value of a bond for each possible interest rate path and then computes the average of those values. The resulting price of an option-free bond is the same as the price determined through backward induction. Path-wise valuation entails the following steps:

1. Specify a list of possible paths through a tree.
2. Determine the present value of the bond through each potential path.
3. Compute the average present value across all possible paths.

The number of interest rate paths in the binomial model can be computed using Pascal's Triangle.

MONTE CARLO METHOD

The Monte Carlo method is a method for simulating a sufficiently large number of potential interest rate paths in an effort to discover how a value of a fixed-income security is affected. It is often used when a security's cash flows are path dependent, i.e., when the cash flow to be received in a particular period depends not only on the current level of interest rates, but also on the path interest rates have taken to reach their current level.

OVERVIEW OF EMBEDDED OPTIONS
Cross-Reference to CFA Institute Assigned Reading #44

Callable Bonds

Callable bonds give the **issuer** the right to redeem (or call) all or part of the bond before maturity. This embedded option offers the issuer the ability to take advantage of (1) a decline in market interest rates and/or (2) an improvement in its creditworthiness.

- Callable bonds include different types of call features:
    - An American-style callable bond can be called by the issuer at any time starting with the first call date until maturity.
    - A European-style callable bond can only be called by the issuer at a single date at the end of the lockout period.
    - A Bermudan-style callable bond can be called by the issuer on specified dates following the lockout period.

Putable Bonds and Extendible Bonds

Putable bonds give **bondholders** the right to sell (or put) the bond back to the issuer at a pre-determined price on specified dates. The embedded put option offers bondholders protection against an increase in interest rates, i.e., if interest rates increase (decreasing the value of the straight bond) they can sell the putable bond back to the issuer at the pre-specified price, and then reinvest the principal at (higher) newer interest rates.

- As is the case with callable bonds, putable bonds also typically include lockout periods.
- Most of the time they tend to be European-style and are rarely Bermudan-style, but there are no American-style putable bonds.
- Putable and extendible bonds are equivalent, except that their underlying option-free bonds are different.

Bonds with Other Types of (Complex) Embedded Options

Sometimes the option embedded in a bond may be contingent upon some future event. For example, death-put bonds (which come with an estate put or survivor's option) can be redeemed at par by the heirs of the deceased bondholder. The important thing to note here is that the value of such bonds depends not only on interest rate movements, but also on the holder's life expectancy.

Sinking fund bonds (or sinkers) require the issuer to retire a certain proportion of the issue each year following the lockout period (thereby reducing credit risk). These bonds may also contain additional options, for example:

- Standard call options, which allow the issuer to redeem the entire issue at any point in time following the lockout period.
- Acceleration provisions, which allow the issuer to repurchase more than the mandatory amount of bonds.

- Delivery options, which allow the issuer to satisfy a sinking fund payment by delivering bonds to the trustee instead of cash. If the bonds are trading at less than par, then it is more cost-effective for the issuer to buy back bonds from investors to meet sinking fund requirements than to pay par to redeem them. The delivery options benefit the issuer when interest rates rise.
- A combination of a call option and a delivery option is effectively a long straddle, where the sinking fund benefits the issuer not only if interest rates decline, but also if they rise.

VALUATION OF CALLABLE AND PUTABLE BONDS

Value of callable bond = Value of straight bond − Value of embedded call option

Value of putable bond = Value of straight bond + Value of embedded put option

Effect of Interest Rate Volatility on the Value of Callable and Putable Bonds

All else remaining the same:

- The embedded call option increases in value with higher interest rate volatility. Therefore, the value of a callable bond decreases with higher volatility.
- The embedded put option also increases in value with higher interest rate volatility. Therefore, the value of a putable bond increases with higher volatility.

Effect of Level and Shape of the Yield Curve on the Value of Callable and Putable Bonds

Callable Bonds

All else remaining the same:

- As interest rates decrease, the value of a straight bond increases, and the value of the embedded call option in a callable bond also increases. Since the investor is effectively short on the embedded call option, the value of the callable bond increases less than that of the straight bond, limiting the upside for the investor.
- The value of the embedded call option increases as the yield curve goes from being upward sloping to being flat to downward sloping.
- If the yield curve is upward-sloping at the time of issue and if a callable bond is issued at par, it implies that the embedded call option is out-of-the-money.
- Typically, callable bonds are issued at a large premium. Embedded call options are in-the-money and would be exercised if arbitrage-free forward rates actually prevailed in the future.

Putable Bonds

All else remaining the same:

- As interest rates increase, the value of a straight bond decreases, but the value of the embedded put option in a putable bond increases. Since the investor is effectively long on the embedded call option, the value of the putable bond decreases less than that of the straight bond, offering the investor protection on the downside.
- The value of the embedded put option decreases as the yield curve goes from being upward sloping to being flat to downward sloping.

Valuation of Default-Free Callable and Putable Bonds in the Presence of Interest Rate Volatility

- To value a callable bond, at each node during the call period, the value of the bond must equal the **lower** of (1) the value if the bond is not called (using the backward induction methodology) and (2) the call price.
- To value a putable bond, at every node we use the **higher** of (1) the value determined through backward induction and (2) the put price in the analysis.

Valuing Risky Callable and Putable Bonds: The Option-Adjusted Spread

In order to value bonds with embedded options using an interest rate tree, the option-adjusted spread (OAS) is used instead of the z-spread. The OAS is the constant spread that, when added to all the one-year forward rates in the interest rate tree, makes the arbitrage-free value of the bond equal to its current market price.

- The OAS essentially removes option risk from the z-spread.
- If the OAS for a bond is lower than that for a bond with similar characteristics and credit quality, it suggests that the bond is relatively overpriced (rich).
- If the OAS for a bond is greater than that for a bond with similar characteristics and credit quality, it suggests that the bond is relatively underpriced (cheap).
- If the OAS for a bond is close to that of a bond with similar characteristics and credit quality, the bond looks fairly priced.
- For a given bond price, the lower the interest rate volatility assumed, the lower the option cost and therefore, the higher the OAS for the callable bond given the z-spread.

INTEREST RATE RISK OF BONDS WITH EMBEDDED OPTIONS

Effective Duration

For bonds with embedded options, cash flows can change if the embedded options (which are typically contingent on interest rates) are exercised. Therefore, effective (or option-adjusted) duration, which is a curve duration measure, is the appropriate duration measure for bonds with embedded options.

$$\text{Effective Duration} = \frac{(PV_-) - (PB_+)}{2 \times (\Delta \text{ Curve}) \times PV_0}$$

ΔCurve = the magnitude of the parallel shift in the benchmark yield curve (in decimal).
PV_- = Full price of the bond when the benchmark yield curve is shifted down by ΔCurve.
PV_+ = Full price of the bond when the benchmark yield curve is shifted up by ΔCurve.
PV_0 = Current full price of the bond (i.e., with no shift).

Effective Durations of Callable, Putable, and Straight Bonds

The effective duration of a callable bond cannot exceed that of the straight bond.

- When interest rates are high relative to the bond's coupon, the callable and straight bonds have very similar effective durations.

- When interest rates fall, the limit on the upside of the callable bond due to the presence of the call option reduces the effective duration of the callable bond relative to that of the straight bond.

The effective duration of a putable bond also cannot exceed that of the straight bond.

- When interest rates are low relative to the bond's coupon, the putable bond and straight bond have very similar effective durations.
- When interest rates rise, the price of the putable bond does not fall as much as that of a straight bond as the put price acts as a floor on its value. Therefore, its effective duration is lower than that of the straight bond.

When the embedded option (call or put) is deep in-the-money, the effective duration of the bond with an embedded option resembles that of the straight bond maturing on the upcoming exercise date, reflecting the fact that the bond is highly likely to be called or put on that date.

Also note that:

- The effective duration of an option-free bond changes very little in response to interest rate movements.
- For a putable bond, its effective duration falls when interest rates rise, as the put moves into the money and the bond's price-yield profile flattens out.
- For a callable bond its effective duration falls when interest rates fall, as the call moves into the money and the bond's price-yield profile flattens out.
- Effective duration) is not as effective in capturing the interest rate sensitivity of callable and putable bonds as (1) the price response to up-movements (i.e. one-sided up-duration) and (2) the price response to down-movements (i.e., one-sided down-duration). This is especially true when the embedded option is near-the-money.

Key Rate Duration

Key rate durations (or partial durations) measure the sensitivity of a bond's price to changes in specific maturities on the benchmark yield curve. Key rate durations are used to identify the shaping risk for bonds, i.e., the bond's sensitivity to changes in the shape of the yield curve (steepening and flattening).

- For option-free bonds that are not trading at par, a change in any of the key rate durations has an impact on the price of the bond.
- For option-free bonds that are not trading at par, a change in the key/par rate corresponding to the bond's maturity (10 years) has the greatest impact on price.
- For option-free bonds trading at par, the par rate corresponding to the bond's maturity is the only one that affects its price.
- Key rate durations can sometimes be negative at maturity points that are shorter than the maturity of the bond, if the bond has a very low coupon rate or is a zero-coupon bond.

For option-free bonds, duration is (among other factors) a function of time to maturity. For bonds with embedded options, duration depends on time to maturity and on time to exercise.

Callable Bonds

- When the bond's coupon rate is significantly less than market interest rates, it is highly unlikely to be called. In such a case it is more likely to behave like a straight bond, and the par rate that will have the largest impact on its price will be the rate corresponding to its maturity.
- As the bond's coupon increases relative to the market rate, the likelihood of the bond being called also increases. As a result, the bond's effective duration decreases and gradually, the rate that has the largest impact on the bond's price moves from rate corresponding to its maturity to the rate corresponding to the next call date.

Putable Bonds

- When the bond's coupon rate is significantly higher than market interest rates, it is highly unlikely to be put. In such a case it is more likely to behave like a straight bond, and the par rate that will have the largest impact on its price will be the rate corresponding to its maturity.
- As the bond's coupon decreases relative to the market yield, the likelihood of the bond being put increases. As a result, the bond's effective duration decreases and gradually, the rate that has the largest impact on the bond's price moves from rate corresponding to its maturity to the rate corresponding to the next put date.

Effective Convexity

$$\text{Effective Convexity} = \frac{(PV_-) + (PV_+) - 2(PV_0)}{\left(\Delta \text{Curve}\right)^2 \times PV_0}$$

- Option-free bonds exhibit positive effective convexity. Their prices rise slightly more when interest rates fall than they fall when interest rates rise by the same magnitude.
- For callable bonds:
  - When interest rates are high, they behave like straight bonds.
  - When interest rates fall and the embedded call option is at or near the money, their effective convexity turns negative. This is because their price is effectively capped at the call price.
- For putable bonds:
  - When interest rates are low, they behave like straight bonds.
  - When interest rates increase and the embedded put option is at or near the money, their effective convexity remains positive. At this point, the upside from a decrease in interest rates is far greater than the downside from an increase in interest rates, as the put price effectively serves as a floor on the putable bond's value.
- Therefore, putable bonds have more upside potential than otherwise identical callable bonds when interest rates fall, while callable bonds have more downside potential than otherwise identical putable bonds when interest rates rise.

VALUATION AND ANALYSIS OF CAPPED AND FLOORED FLOATING-RATE BONDS

Valuation of a Capped Floater

Valuing a capped floater using a binomial interest rate tree is different from valuing an option-free bond in the following two ways:

- Since it is a floating-rate security, the coupon payment on the capped floater on the next payment date is based on the interest rate today. Basically, the coupon for the period is determined at the beginning of the period, but paid (in arrears) at the end of the period.
- Since the coupon rate is capped, the coupon at each node must be adjusted to reflect the coupon characteristics of the cap. The effective coupon rate for the upcoming period is the **lower** of (1) the current rate and (2) the cap rate.

  Value of capped floater = Value of uncapped floater – Value of embedded cap.

- The higher the cap rate, the closer the instrument will trade to its par value (as the embedded interest rate call options carry a lower likelihood of exercise, and are therefore less valuable to the issuer).

Valuation of a Floored Floater

A floor provision in a floater prevents the effective coupon rate on the bond from declining below a specified minimum rate. Therefore, it offers investors protection against declining interest rates.

  Value of floored floater = Value of non-floored floater + Value of embedded floor.

- The procedure valuing a floored floater through a binomial interest rate tree is similar to that of valuing a capped floater, except that at each node, the effective coupon rate for the upcoming period is the **higher** of (1) the current rate and (2) the floor rate.

Ratchet Bonds

Ratchet bonds are floating-rate bonds with both investor and issuer options.

- Just like conventional floaters, the coupon rate is periodically reset according to a formula based on a reference rate and credit spread.
- However, the bonds are structured to ensure that at any reset date, the effective coupon rate can only decline; it can never exceed the existing level. As a result, the coupon rate "ratchets down" over time.
- In order to compensate investors for this, the coupon rate on ratchet bonds at the time of issuance is set at a level much higher than that of a standard floater.
- This makes a ratchet bond similar to a conventional callable bond in that when a bond is called, the investor can only purchase a replacement bond carrying a lower (prevailing) coupon rate. A ratchet bond can be thought of as the lifecycle of a callable bond, with one callable bond being replaced by another until the bond's eventual maturity is reached. The appeal for the issuer is that the call decision is on autopilot, and there are no transaction costs.

- Ratchet bonds also contain investor options. At any coupon reset date, the investor has the option to put the bonds back to the issuer at par. Note that this put is actually a "contingent put" as it can only be exercised if the coupon is actually reset.
- Generally speaking, the market price of ratchet bonds remains above par at time of reset unless there has been a deterioration in the credit quality of the issuer.

VALUATION AND ANALYSIS OF CONVERTIBLE BONDS

A convertible bond is a hybrid security that grants the holder the option to convert the security into a predetermined number of common shares of the issuer (so it is essentially a call option on the stock) during a pre-determined conversion period at a pre-determined conversion price.

Convertible bonds offer benefits to the issuer and the investor:

- Investors accept lower coupons on convertible bonds compared to otherwise identical non-convertible bonds because they can participate in the upside of the issuer's equity through the conversion mechanism.
- Issuers benefit from lower coupon rates and from no longer having to repay the debt (if the bonds are converted into equity).

However, note that:

- The issuer's current shareholders face dilution if these securities are converted.
- If the bond is not converted (if the share price remains below the conversion price) the issuer may have to refinance the debt at a higher cost.
- If conversion is not achieved, bondholders would have lost out on interest income relative to an otherwise identical non-convertible bond.

Important Terminology

- The share price at which the investor can convert the convertible bond into ordinary shares is known as the conversion price.
- The number of shares of common stock that the holder of a convertible bond receives from converting the bonds into shares is dictated by the conversion ratio.
- Until they convert their bonds into shares, holders of convertible bonds only receive coupon payments, while common shareholders receive dividend payments.
- Annual dividends below the threshold dividend level have no impact on the conversion price. However, if annual dividends exceed this level, the conversion price is adjusted downward for annual dividend payments to compensate convertible bond holders.
- Almost all convertible bonds are callable and some are also putable.
  - The issuer may call the bond (1) if interest rates have fallen, (2) if its credit rating has improved, or (3) if it believes that its share price will improve significantly in the future.
  - If a convertible bond is callable, the issuer can force conversion if the underlying share price rises beyond the conversion price, in order to avoid making interest payments.
  - The put option may be classified as a hard put (which can only be redeemed for cash) or a soft put (which may be redeemed for cash, common stock, subordinated notes, or a combination of the three).

Analysis of a Convertible Bond

The conversion (or parity) value of a convertible bond indicates the value of the bond if converted at the market price of the shares.

$$\text{Conversion value} = \text{Market price of common stock} \times \text{Conversion ratio}$$

The minimum value of a convertible bond equals the greater of (1) its conversion value (the value if the security is converted into shares immediately) and (2) its straight value (its value without the conversion option). It acts as a moving floor on the value of the security.

The price that an investor effectively pays for common stock if a convertible bond is purchased and then converted into common stock is known as the market conversion price or conversion parity price. It basically reflects the "break-even" price for the investor.

$$\text{Market conversion price} = \frac{\text{Market price of convertible security}}{\text{Conversion ratio}}$$

The market conversion premium per share is the excess amount that an investor pays for acquiring the company's shares by purchasing a convertible bond instead of purchasing them in the open market.

$$\text{Market conversion premium per share} = \text{Market conversion price} - \text{Current market price}$$

The market conversion premium per share can be viewed as the price of the conversion call option. However, there is a difference between (1) buying a stand-alone call option on the issuer's stock and (2) purchasing the call option on the issuer's stock embedded in a convertible bond. The buyer of the stand-alone call option knows the exact dollar amount of downside risk (the call premium), while the buyer of the convertible bond only knows that her maximum loss equals the difference between the price paid for the convertible bond and its straight value. The straight value at any future date is unknown.

The market conversion premium ratio equals the market conversion premium per share divided by the current market price of the company's common stock.

$$\text{Market conversion premium ratio} = \frac{\text{Market conversion premium per share}}{\text{Market price of common stock}}$$

The premium over straight value is sometimes used as a measure for downside risk in a convertible bond. This interpretation, however, is theoretically flawed because the straight value (which serves as a floor on the convertible's price) changes as interest rates/credit spreads change. All other factors remaining the same, the higher the premium over straight value, the less attractive the convertible bond.

$$\text{Premium over straight value} = \frac{\text{Market price of convertible bond}}{\text{Straight value}} - 1$$

The upside potential for a convertible security depends on the prospects for the underlying stock, which are evaluated using techniques for analyzing common stocks.

Valuation of a Convertible Bond

Convertible security value = Straight Value + Value of the call option on the stock

Convertible callable bond value = Straight value + Value of the call option on the stock
− Value of the call option on the bond

Convertible callable and putable bond value = Straight value + Value of the call option on the stock
− Value of the call option on the bond
+ Value of the put option on the bond

Investment Characteristics of a Convertible Security

- If the price of the company's common stock is relatively low, such that the straight value of a convertible bond is significantly greater than the conversion value, the security will trade like a fixed-income security, with factors such as interest rates and credit spreads having a significant impact on its price. In such a situation, the security may be referred to as a fixed income equivalent or a busted convertible. Further, the closer the security is to the end of the conversion period, the more the convertible bond will behave like a fixed-income security, as it becomes increasingly likely that the call option on the stock with expire out of the money.
- If the price of the company's common stock is relatively high, such that the conversion value is significantly greater than the straight value, the security will trade like an equity instrument, with its value heavily influenced by share price movements and relatively immune to interest rate movements. In this case, the security may be referred to as a common stock equivalent. Note that when the embedded call option on the stock is in the money, it is more likely to be exercised when the conversion value exceeds the redemption value of the bond.

- In between these two scenarios, the convertible will trade as a hybrid security with characteristics of both fixed-income and equity instruments.
  - When the underlying share price is below the conversion price and increases toward it, the return on the convertible bond increases significantly, but at a lower rate than the underlying share price. Once the share price exceeds the conversion price, the change in the convertible bond's price increases at the same rate as the underlying share price.
  - When underlying share price is above the conversion price and decreases toward it, the relative change in the convertible bond's price is less than the change in the share price because the convertible bond has a floor on its value.
- Finally, note that except in the case of busted convertibles, the primary driver of a convertible bond's value is the underlying share price. However, large movements in interest rates or the issuer's credit spread continue to affect the value of a convertible bond. For a convertible bond with a fixed coupon, all else being equal:
  - If interest rates rise (fall) significantly, its value would decrease (increase).
  - If the issuer's credit rating were to improve (decline), its value would increase (decrease).

Study Session 15: Fixed Income—Topics in Fixed Income Analysis

CREDIT ANALYSIS MODELS
Cross-Reference to CFA Institute Assigned Reading #45

MEASURES OF CREDIT RISK

Credit risk refers to the risk of loss resulting from a borrower's failure to make full and timely payments of interest and/or principal.

- **Probability of default** (or **default probability**) is the probability of a borrower failing to meet its obligations to make full and timely payments of principal and interest under the terms of the bond indenture.

- **Loss given default** refers to the portion of her **overall position** on the bond (remaining coupon plus principal amount), that an investor would lose if a default actually occurred.
    - The **recovery rate** is the amount of remaining coupon payments and principal repayments that are received or recovered in the event of a default.

- **The expected loss** is calculated as the probability of default multiplied by loss given default.

- The **present value of expected loss** refers to the highest fee (conceptually) that a bondholder would be willing to pay an insurer (or any other third-party) to entirely eliminate the credit risk inherent in a particular bond. Calculating the present value of expected loss requires two modifications to the expected loss:
    - **Risk-neutral probabilities are used** instead of actual probabilities of default that are used to compute the expected loss.
    - **The time value of money is considered** in the calculation.

Note that the combined impact of these two adjustments can result in the present value of expected loss being higher or lower than the expected loss itself.

TRADITIONAL CREDIT MODELS

Credit Scoring

Credit scoring is typically used for small, owner-operated businesses and individuals.

- Credit scores provide an ordinal ranking of credit risk, but not a cardinal ranking
- Credit scores are not explicitly dependent on current economic conditions.
- Credit scores are not percentile rankings of a borrower among a universe of borrowers.
- Lenders typically prefer stability in credit scores over accuracy, and credit bureaus are increasingly trying to take this into account when computing credit scores (which compromises their predictive accuracy).
- Credit scores do not reflect the difference in default probabilities across different types of loans.

Credit Ratings

Credit ratings are generally used for companies, governments (sovereigns), quasi-governments, and asset-backed securities. Similar to credit scores, credit ratings also rank credit risk across borrowers. However, they do not provide an indication of the probability of default.

- Issuers often pay rating agencies to rate their debt, which creates an incentive conflict. Rating agencies may be tempted to give higher-than-justified ratings to companies in order to attain more business.
- Trade-off between stability and accuracy. Rating agencies are tempted to keep ratings unchanged or stable over time to reduce unnecessary volatility in debt market prices. However, actual default probabilities vary with changes in the economic environment.

Strengths of Traditional Credit Ratings

- They summarize an extensive credit analysis of a borrower into a simple statistic.
- They reduce volatility in debt market prices as they tend to remain stable over time and across stages of the business cycle.

Weaknesses of Traditional Credit Ratings

- Since they tend to be stable over time, ratings tend to lose their connection with the actual probability of default of a debt offering.
- They do not vary with the business cycle even though the probability of default depends on the business cycle.
- Conflicts of interest arise when the issuer pays for a credit rating.

STRUCTURAL MODELS

Structural models are built around the economics of a company's liabilities and make use of option pricing theory.

The Option Analogy

Equity Holders' Perspective

The value of equity at time T, S_T, can be expressed as:

- $S_T = A_T - K$ if $A_T \geq K$; or
- $S_T = 0$ if $A_T < K$
- Therefore, $S_T = \text{Max} (A_T - K, 0)$

The position of equity holders is comparable to a holding a European call option on company assets with:

- K as the strike price of the option; and
- T as expiration of the option.

Debt Holders' Perspective

The value of company's debt at time T can be expressed as:

- $D(T,T) = \min(K, A_T)$ OR $D(T,T) = K - \max[K - A_T, 0]$

The position of company debt holders is comparable to (1) holding a riskless bond that pays K with certainty at time T, and at the same time (2) selling a European put option on the assets of the company.

- If the value of the assets is greater than the face value of debt, the put option will be out of the money (and therefore, not be exercised). Debt holders will simply receive the face value.
  - If $A_T \geq K$, then $\max[K - A_T, 0]$
  - Therefore, $K - \max(K - A_T, 0) = K - 0 = K$
- If the value of the assets falls below K, the put option will be in-the-money (and will be exercised). Debt holders will only receive the value of the assets.
  - If $A_T < K$, then $\max[K - A_T, 0] = K - 0 = T$
  - Therefore, $K - \max(K - A_T, 0) = K - (K - A_T) = A_T$

The more the credit risk inherent in the debt, the greater the put option premium (for protection against default), and the lower the value of (risky) debt.

Value of risky debt = Value of risk-free debt − Value of put option on company assets

Note:
- The probability of default at time T reflects the probability of the value of the company's assets at time T (A_T) falling below the face value of debt (K):
  - Probability of default = Probability ($A_T < K$)
- The loss given default equals ($K - A_T$).

Valuation

Make use of the Black-Scholes option pricing model, the value of debt at time t, D(t,T) can be expressed as:

$$D(t,T) = A_t N(-d_1) + Ke^{-r(T-t)} N(d_2)$$

- $A_t N(-d_1)$ represents the present value of the payoff on the company's debt if default occurs.
- $Ke^{-r(T-t)} N(d_2)$ represents the present value of the payoff on the company's debt if default does not occur.
  - $N(d_2)$ represents the risk-neutral probability of no default on debt, or prob($A_T \geq K$).
- The sum of these two terms represents the present value of the company's debt.

Credit Risk Measures

Based on the structural model, we can derive the following formulas for computing various credit risk measures:

- Probability of default = Prob $(A_T < K)$ = $1 -$ Prob $(A_T \geq K)$ = $1 - N(e_2)$

$$e_1 = \frac{\ln\left(\dfrac{A_t}{K}\right) + u(T-t) + \dfrac{1}{2}\sigma^2(T-t)}{\sigma\sqrt{T-t}}$$

$$e_2 = e_1 - \sigma\sqrt{T-t}$$

- Expected loss = $KN(-e_2) - A_t e^{u(T-t)}N(-e_1)$

- Present value of expected loss = $KP(t,T) - D(t,T)$;
  This simplifies to $Ke^{-r(T-t)}N(d_2) - A_t N(-d_1)$

You do not need to know these formulas, just focus on the takeaways

Takeaways

- The present value of the expected loss equals the difference between (1) the value of a riskless zero-coupon bond paying K at maturity and (2) the value of the risky debt, $D(t,T)$
  - Present value of expected loss = $KP(t,T) - D(t,T)$
- The asset's real expected return (u) is used in the calculation of e_1 and e_2 (actual probabilities) which are used in the computation of the expected loss.
- The risk-free rate (r) is used in the calculation of d_1 and d_2 (risk-neutral probabilities), which are used in the computation of the **present value of the expected loss**.
- This should take you back to earlier in the reading when we explained how the actual (or "natural") probabilities of default is used in the computation of expected loss, while risk-neutral probabilities are used in the computation of the present value of expected loss.
- The probability of default depends on the company's assumed liability structure, which is what makes structural models different from the reduced form model.

Analysis of the Difference Between the Expected loss and Present Value of Expected Loss

- The expected loss and the present value of the expected loss includes both (1) a discount for the time value of money and (2) the risk premium required by the market to bear the risk of credit loss.
- In the absence of a (credit) risk premium, the present value of expected loss would always be lower than the expected loss (since it accounts for the time value of money).
- If the present value of the expected loss is greater than the expected loss it implies that the difference between the two is dominated by the risk premium.

Estimation

Historical estimation cannot be used to estimate the parameters in the structural model. This is because the assumption that the company's assets trade in frictionless markets does not hold true.

On the other hand, implicit estimation can be applied to estimate the parameters of the structural model. However, the problem with implicit estimation is that if the model's assumptions are not representative of the market's actual structure, estimated values of the input will be inaccurate, and will result in unreliable estimates for the probability of default, expected loss and the present value of expected loss. Unfortunately, this problem arises when applying implicit estimation to the structural model due to its unrealistic assumptions.

Structural Model Strengths

- It uses an option analogy to make a company's default probability and recovery rate easy to understand.
- It only requires current market prices to be estimated.

Structural Model Weaknesses

- The structure of the balance sheet used to derive the model is unrealistic.
- Only implicit estimation can be used to estimate measures of credit risk because company asset value is an unobservable parameter.
- Use of implicit estimation results in biased estimates of credit risk measures because several unrealistic assumptions are employed in formulating the model.
- Computed credit risk measures do not explicitly consider changes in the business cycle.
- Computation of the probability of default requires an estimate of the market's equity risk premium, and there is no consensus on which model should be used for this exercise.

REDUCED FORM MODELS

Reduced form models overcome one of the biggest weaknesses of structural models (i.e., which unrealistically assume that the company's assets trade in frictionless markets) by assuming instead that only some of the company's debt is traded.

Reduced form models make the following assumptions:

1. The zero-coupon debt of the company trades in frictionless markets that are arbitrage-free.
   - It is important to note here that reduced form models *do not* assume that the company's other liabilities or even its equity trade.
2. The risk-free interest rate is stochastic (basically, it is a random variable).
   - Since interest rates are not assumed constant in these models, they are able to capture the interest rate risk associated with fixed-income securities.
3. A vector of stochastic variables representing macroeconomic factors (e.g. risk-free rate, rate of inflation, level of unemployment, and GDP growth) can be used to describe the state of the economy at time t.
   - This assumption enables the model to capture changing economic conditions.

4. The company defaults at a random time t, where the probability of default over the period (t, t + Δ) when the economy is in state X_t is given by $\lambda(X_t)\Delta$.

- $\lambda(X_t)$ captures what is known as default intensity. Given that the company has not defaulted, default intensity represents the default probability over the next instant (t, t + Δ) when the state of the economy is X_t.
- This allows the model to link default probability with the state of the economy (default probabilities typically rise in recessions and fall during expansions).

5. Given the vector of macroeconomic state variables X_t, a company's default represents idiosyncratic risk.

- To understand the fourth and fifth assumptions consider two companies, GM and Ford. In a recession, the probability of default for both these companies will increase as the macroeconomic factors captured in the model move unfavorably. This represents economy-wide, or systematic risk. Idiosyncratic risk on the other hand, states that whether either of these companies actually defaults given the recession also depends on the company's own actions (e.g. management's strategy) or company-specific risk.

6. In case of default, the percentage loss on the company's debt is $0 \le t(X_t) \le 1$, where $t(X_t)$ represents the loss given default, and $[1 - t(X_t)]$ represents the percentage recovery rate. Notice that in this model, the loss given default depends on economic conditions (X_t), allowing it to be larger in a recession than in a healthy economy.

> Notice that Assumptions 4, 5 and 6 are imposed on the outputs of the model i.e., the probability of default and loss given default.

Valuation

Given the assumption that markets are arbitrage-free, option pricing methodology (with risk-neutral probabilities) can be applied to a reduced form model to come up formulas for the value of a company's debt, the probability of default, the expected loss and the present value of the expected loss. The required inputs include probability distributions for macroeconomic state variables and interest rates.

The reduced form model can also be used to value a zero-coupon bond under the following (simpler) assumptions.

- The default probability is constant i.e., the default probability is not dependent on macroeconomic conditions.
- The dollar value of the loss given default is a constant percentage of the value of the zero-coupon bond just before default.

Estimation

When it comes to reduced form models, both historical and implicit approaches can be used to estimate the model's parameters.

In order to use implicit estimation, all the inputs to the model and the probability distributions of macroeconomic state variables must be completely specified. The problem with this approach however, is that if the assumptions deployed are unrealistic, then resulting estimates will be biased and unreliable. Using historical estimation gets around this problem.

Unlike with structural models, historical estimation can be used in a reduced form model because the economy's macroeconomic state variables and company debt prices are both observable. By applying hazard rate estimation (a technique used for estimating the probability of a binary event, such as default/no default), reduced form credit models are estimated and implemented using discrete time statistical procedures such as logistic regression.

Reduced Form Model Strengths

- The inputs used in the model are observable, allowing the use of historical estimation for credit risk measures.
- Credit risk measures obtained from the model consider changes in the business cycle.
- The model does not impose any assumptions on the company's balance sheet structure.

Reduced Form Model Weaknesses

- In hazard rate estimation, past observations are used to predict the future. Therefore, the model needs to be properly formulated and back-tested.

Comparison of Credit Risk Models

Credit ratings are the least accurate predictors of credit risk. This is because they generally tend to lag changes in an issue's credit risk (due to rating agencies' preference for stability of credit ratings over accuracy).

Reduced form models do better than structural models because they can be computed using historical estimation (hazard rate procedures), while structural models rely on implicit estimation. Hazard rate procedures offer more flexibility in that they are able to incorporate business cycle changes and do not make limiting assumptions on the structure of the balance sheet.

The Term Structure of Credit Spreads

The term structure of credit spreads reflects the relationship between credit spreads and debt maturity, where the credit spread for a given maturity is computed as the difference between yield on a zero-coupon, risky bond (of the same maturity) and a zero-coupon, risk-free bond (of the same maturity).

$$\text{Credit spread} = y_D(t,T) - y_P(t,T)$$
$y_D(t, T) = $ Yield on risky zero-coupon bond.
$y_P(t, T) = $ Yield on default-free zero-coupon bond.

The credit spread is equal to the expected percentage loss per year on the risky zero-coupon bond.

$$\text{Credit spread} = y_D(t,T) - y_P(t,T) = \lambda \Upsilon$$

However, note that the formulas used to draw this conclusion here assume that the default probability and loss given default are constants (which is not true in practice).

Also note that the "actual" credit spread will consist of (1) the expected percentage loss (as in the structural and reduced form models) and (2) a liquidity risk premium.

Asset-backed securities (ABS)

Due to the complexity associated with the cash flows from an ABS, it is better to analyze them as credit derivatives rather than simple bonds. As with any credit derivatives, ABS can be valued using a structural model or a reduced form model. However, this exercise must be performed keeping in mind (1) the composition of the collateral and (2) the distribution waterfall.

Credit risk measures associated with ABS include probability of loss, expected loss and present value of expected loss. Note that since an ABS does not default when an interest payment is missed, the probability of default does not apply, so it is replaced by a probability of loss.

SECURITIZATION
Cross-Reference to CFA Institute Assigned Reading #46

Benefits of Securitization

- It removes the layer between borrowers and investors.
- It allows investors to have a stronger legal claim on the collateral pool of assets.
- Investors can pick and choose the types of securities they want to invest in (in terms of interest rate and credit risk).
- Financial intermediaries are able to originate more loans (by using financing provided by outside investors to originate loans) than they would be able to if they were only able to issue loans that they could finance themselves.
- The increase in the total supply of loanable funds benefits organizations (governments and companies) that need to borrow.
- Since securitized bonds are sold in the public market, they enjoy much better liquidity (lower liquidity risk) than the original loans on bank balance sheets.
- Financial markets are made more efficient.
- Securitization encourages innovation in investment products, which can offer investors access to (otherwise directly unavailable) assets that match their risk, return, and maturity profiles.
- Even large investors, who may be able to purchase real estate loans, automobile loans, or credit card loans directly, would prefer to invest in asset-backed bonds since they would not be required to originate, monitor, and collect payments from the underlying loans themselves.

Parties to a Securitization

Party	Description	Party in Illustration
Seller	Originates the loans and sells loans to the SPV	ABC Company
Issuer/Trust	The SPV that buys the loans from the seller and issues the asset-backed securities	SPV
Servicer	Services the loans	Servicer

In order for a securitization to serve its purpose, the SPV must be a bankruptcy remote entity, i.e., its obligations remain secure even if the parent company goes bankrupt.

RESIDENTIAL MORTGAGE LOANS

- A mortgage loan is a borrowing that is secured by some form of real estate.
- Upon initiation of the mortgage loan, the borrower's equity equals the down payment, but over time, the borrower's equity changes as a result of (1) changes in the market value of the property and (2) payment of periodic mortgage payments (that include a principal component).
- The lower (higher) the LTV ratio, the higher (lower) the borrower's equity, the less (more) likely the borrower is to default, and the more (less) protection the lender has for recovering the amount loaned in case the borrower defaults.

- Most mortgages around the world are structured as amortizing loans.
- A mortgage loan may allow the borrower to prepay (make a principal repayment that exceeds the scheduled repayment for the month) a portion, or the entire amount, of the outstanding mortgage principal at any point during the term of the mortgage.

RESIDENTIAL MORTGAGE-BACKED SECURITIES

- Agency RMBSs are issued by (1) federal agencies (e.g., Ginnie Mae, which is a federally related institution), and (2) quasi-government entities (e.g., Freddie Mac and Fannie Mae, which are government sponsored enterprises or GSEs).
    - There is no credit risk for agency RMBSs issued by Ginnie Mae as they are backed by the full faith and credit of the U.S. Government.
    - There is minimal credit risk for agency RMBSs issued by GSEs as they are guaranteed by the GSEs themselves.
        - Mortgage loans issued by GSEs must satisfy specific underwriting standards established by various government agencies to qualify for the collateral pool backing agency RMBSs issued by GSEs.
- Non-agency RMBSs are issued by private entities.
    - They typically come with credit enhancements to reduce credit risk.
        - There are no restrictions on the types of non-agency mortgage loans that can be used to back non-agency RMBSs.

MORTGAGE PASS-THROUGH SECURITIES

- A mortgage pass-through security is created when shares or participation certificates in a pool of mortgage loans are sold to investors.
- The cash flow collected from the collateral pool includes scheduled principal and interest payments, and prepayments.
- The amount and timing of cash flows paid to investors in the pass-through securities are different from those of the cash flows collected from the collateral pool of mortgages.
- Payments made by borrowers pass through the government agency (and on to investors) net of servicing and guaranteeing fees. Therefore, the pass-through rate (coupon rate on the pass-through security, which is net interest/net coupon) is lower than the mortgage rate on the underlying pool of mortgages.
- Mortgage loans that are securitized to create pass-through securities do not all carry the same mortgage rate and maturity. Therefore, a weighted average coupon rate (WAC) and weighted average maturity (WAM) are calculated to describe the pool of mortgages that serves as collateral for the pass-through securities.
- Market participants use average life (the weighted average time it will take for all the principal payments, i.e., scheduled repayments and projected prepayments, to be received) as a measure of the interest rate risk of a mortgage-backed security.
    - The average life of an RMBS depends on the assumed prepayment speed—the higher the prepayment speed assumed, the shorter the average life of the mortgage backed security.
- The prepayment rate is measured in terms of the single monthly mortality rate (SMM). It is calculated as the amount of prepayment for a month as a percentage of the mortgage balance that was available to be prepaid that month.

Contraction Risk versus Extension Risk

Prepayment risk encompasses contraction risk and extension risk.

Contraction risk occurs when interest rates fall.

- Option-free bond prices increase when interest rates fall. However, for mortgage loans, the issuer (homeowner) has the right to prepay and can easily do so by refinancing her mortgage. This option to prepay is similar to the call option granted to the issuer of a callable bond. When interest rates fall, it becomes feasible for the mortgage issuer/borrower to prepay (just like it becomes feasible for an issuer to call a callable bond), so the upside potential of the pass-through security is limited. It experiences price compression at low interest rates and exhibits negative convexity.
- To make things worse, when interest rates fall, refinancing activity typically increases and leads to an increase in prepayments, reducing or shortening the average life of the pass-through. The (higher-than-expected) cash flows from the pass-through must then be reinvested at current (lower) rates.

Extension risk occurs when interest rates rise.

- The price of a pass-through (just like the price of any bond) will decline when interest rates increase.
- To make things worse, refinancing activity and prepayment rates slow down when interest rates rise, increasing or lengthening the average expected life of the pass-through. Consequently, a greater-than-anticipated amount remains invested in the pass-through at the coupon rate of the instrument, which is lower than current interest rates.

COLLATERALIZED MORTGAGE OBLIGATIONS

Collateralized mortgage obligations (CMOs) redistribute the cash flows from mortgage pass-through securities into packages/classes/tranches with different risk exposures to prepayment risk.

- For CMOs, the mortgage-related products from which cash flows are obtained are considered the collateral, i.e., a pool of mortgage pass-through security serves as the collateral. For mortgage pass-through securities, a pool of mortgage loans serves as collateral.

Sequential-Pay Tranches

- Each class of bond is retired sequentially.
- Interest payments are periodically made to each tranche based on its coupon rate and principal amount outstanding at the beginning of the period.
- Principal payments are first forwarded to Tranche A, then to Tranche B (after Tranche A has been fully paid off) and so on.
- The principal payment pattern for each of the tranches is not known. However, the shorter-term tranches receive protection from extension risk, while the longer-term tranches receive protection from contraction risk.

Planned Amortization Class (PAC) Tranches

- PAC bonds bring increased predictability of cash flows, as they specify a repayment schedule that will be satisfied as long as actual prepayments realized from the collateral fall within a pre-defined band.
- The greater certainty in payments for the PAC tranche comes at the expense of greater uncertainty for the support or companion tranche, which absorbs the prepayment risk.
- The average life of the support tranche fluctuates more wildly than that of the PAC tranche.
- The support tranche provides **two-sided protection** (i.e., protection against extension **and** contraction risk) to the PAC tranche.
- The greater the par value of the support tranche relative to that of the PAC tranche, the greater the prepayment protection for the PAC, the lower the PAC's average life variability, and the greater the support tranche's average life variability.

Floating-Rate Tranches

- Even though the collateral for CMOs carries a fixed rate, it is possible to create a floating-rate tranche (along with an inverse-floater tranche) from any of the fixed-rate tranches in a CMO structure.
- Since the floater varies positively with interest rates, and the inverse floater varies negatively with interest rates, they offset each other.

NON-AGENCY RESIDENTIAL MORTGAGE-BACKED SECURITIES

Non-agency RMBSs are not guaranteed by the government or a GSE, which make the evaluation of credit risk an important consideration when investing in them.

- Cash flows are distributed according to a set of rules that determines the distribution of interest and principal payments to tranches with varying levels of priority/seniority.
- There are also rules for allocating realized losses, with senior tranches having a priority claim over payments and subordinated tranches absorbing losses.
- When it comes to forecasting cash flows on non-agency RMBSs, investors must make assumptions regarding (1) the default rate for the collateral and (2) the recovery rate.

Internal Credit Enhancements

- Reserve funds:
  - Cash reserve funds: The entity seeking to raise the funds deposits some of the proceeds of sale of the loan pool with the SPV. This cash can be used to pay for potential future losses.
  - Excess spread accounts: The excess spread or cash that remains after the payment of net coupon, servicing fees, and all other expenses is kept in reserve to pay for future credit losses on the collateral.
- Overcollateralization: This refers to a situation where the value of the collateral exceeds the par value of the securities issued by the SPV.
  - The amount of overcollateralization for an issue changes over time due to (1) defaults, (2) amortization, and (3) prepayments.

- Senior/subordinate structure: This type of structure has senior bond classes and subordinate bond classes (also known as non-senior/junior bond classes).
  - The structure basically provides credit tranches, as the subordinate bond classes provide credit protection to the senior classes.
  - To provide credit protection to investors in the senior bond classes, a shifting interest mechanism is added to the structure. This mechanism locks out subordinated classes from receiving payments for a period of time if the collateral performs poorly.

External Credit Enhancements

External credit enhancements are third-party guarantees for payments to security holders should the issuer not be able to meet payment requirements.

- Monoline insurers are the most common third-party financial guarantors.

COMMERCIAL MORTGAGE BACKED SECURITIES (CMBSs)

CMBSs are backed by a pool of commercial mortgage loans on income-generating properties (e.g. apartments, warehouses, shopping centres, etc.). In the U.S. (and many other countries), commercial mortgage loans are non-recourse loans. Therefore, evaluation of credit risk for commercial mortgage loans requires examining the income-generating capacity and value of each property on a stand-alone basis.

Two measures are commonly used to evaluate the potential credit performance of a commercial property:

- The debt-service coverage (DSC) ratio is used to evaluate the adequacy of income generated from the property to service the loan. It is calculated as net operating income (NOI) divided by debt service. NOI is calculated as rental income minus cash operating expenses and a non-cash replacement reserve that reflects depreciation of the property over time.
  - A ratio greater than 1 means that cash flow from the property covers debt servicing costs adequately.
  - The higher the ratio, the lower the credit risk
- The loan-to-value ratio equals the loan amount divided by the appraised value of the property.
  - The lower the ratio, the lower the credit risk.

Basic CMBS Structure

- A credit-rating agency determines the level of credit enhancement required for the issue to attain the credit rating desired by the issuer.
- Different bond classes are created with each class having a different priority on cash flows. The various bond classes are retired sequentially with all principal repayments, prepayments, and proceeds from default (from selling repossessed properties) being used to repay the highest-rated tranche first.
- Losses from loan defaults are charged against the lowest-rated tranche first. If this tranche is not rated by credit-rating agencies, it is known as the first-loss piece, residual tranche, or equity tranche.

- The equity tranche typically has no specific interest rate (as it is the residual tranche). Investors price it based on the expected residual rate of return. Actual returns can be better or worse than expected depending on actual future interest rate movements and actual defaults.
- Interest payments are made to all tranches.
- Typically, CMBS investors have significant call protection, which actually results in these securities trading more like corporate bonds than like RMBSs.
  - Call protection at the loan level can come in form of prepayment lockouts, defeasance, prepayment penalties, and yield maintenance charges.
  - Call protection at the structure level comes from credit tranches.
- Most commercial loans that back CMBSs have balloon maturity provisions, i.e., they require a significant amount of principal to be repaid at maturity (as opposed to during the term of the loan). This exposes investors to balloon risk, which is more like extension risk as there is usually a workout period during which the borrower and lender try to modify the original terms of the loan to ensure eventual repayment.

NON-MORTGAGE ASSET-BACKED SECURITIES

The collateral backing asset-backed securities can be classified as either amortizing or non-amortizing assets.

Amortizing loans:

- The periodic cash flows include interest payments, principal repayments (in accordance with an amortization schedule), and (if allowed) prepayments.
- Examples include residential mortgage loans and automobile loans.

Non-amortizing loans:

- These only require a monthly minimum payment with no scheduled principal payment.
- If the payment received is less than the interest amount due, the shortfall is added to the outstanding loan balance.
- If the payment is greater than the interest amount due, the excess serves to reduce the outstanding loan balance.
- Since there is no scheduled principal payment amount, the concept of prepayment does not apply to non-amortizing assets.
- Examples include credit card receivables.

The type of collateral (amortizing versus non-amortizing assets) has a significant effect on the structure of the securitization.

- When amortizing assets are securitized, the total face value (total amount outstanding) declines over time due to scheduled repayments and prepayments, and the number of outstanding loans (composition of the collateral) declines as a result of (1) defaults and (2) full principal repayments or full amortizations.
- On the other hand, securitizations of non-amortizing loans usually take the form of a revolving structure, where the composition of the collateral can change over the term of the securities. This is because principal repayments can either be (1) reinvested by purchasing additional loans, or (2) passed on to security holders.

- During an initial lockout or revolving period (which immediately follows the origination of the transaction), all principal repayments are reinvested in additional loans with a principal amount equal to the total principal amount received. While this can result in a fewer total number of individual loans comprising the collateral, the total face value outstanding remains the same.
- During the principal amortization period (which follows the lockout period), principal repayments are not used to purchase additional loans, but are distributed to security holders.

Auto Loan Receivable-Backed Securities

These securities are backed by auto loan and lease receivables. Cash flows for auto loan-backed securities consist of regularly scheduled monthly interest and principal payments and prepayments.

- Generally speaking, auto loan-backed securitizations come with some form of credit enhancement.
- Typically, the securitizations involve a senior/subordinate structure (to provide credit protection to the senior tranches). Further, some securitizations also involve reserve accounts, overcollateralization, and excess interest on the receivables.

Credit Card Receivable-Backed Securities

- The cash flow from a pool of credit card receivables includes (1) finance charges collected (interest charges on the unpaid balance after the grace period), (2) fees (for late payments and membership), and (3) principal repayment.
- Interest payments are made to security holders periodically (monthly, quarterly, or semiannually). The interest rate may be fixed or floating (typically with no cap).
- During the revolving period (also known as the lockout period), any principal repayments from the pool of receivables are used to purchase additional receivables to maintain the size of the pool. During this period, the cash flow passed on to security holders consists only of (1) finance charges and (2) fees collected from the pool of receivables. Principal repayments are only passed on to security holders once the principal-amortizing period sets in.
- Even though receivables in a revolving structure may not be prepaid (since there is no concept of prepayment here), all the bonds may be retired early if an early or rapid amortization provision is triggered.

COLLATERALIZED DEBT OBLIGATIONS

A CDO is a security that is backed by a diversified pool of securities.

- Like an ABS, a CDO also involves the creation of an SPV.
- A CDO manager (also known as collateral manager) is responsible for managing the collateral portfolio of assets (consisting of debt obligations).
- The funds used to purchase the collateral assets are raised from the issuance of bonds to investors. Bond classes may include senior bonds, mezzanine bonds (with credit ratings between senior and subordinated bonds), and subordinated bonds (also known as the residual or equity class).
- Restrictive covenants are placed on the manager to ensure that the credit ratings assigned to the various tranches at issuance are maintained during the term of the CDO.

- Cash flows from the underlying portfolio of assets include (1) coupon interest payments, (2) proceeds from maturing assets, and (3) proceeds from sale of assets. These cash flows are used to make interest and principal payments to the various bond classes.
- From the asset manager/issuer's perspective, the aim is to earn a rate of return on the collateral pool of assets that is higher than the interest costs of bonds issued. This excess return accrues to the equity holders and the CDO manager. Effectively, issuing a CDO is like undertaking a leveraged transaction where the idea is to use borrowed funds (raised from bonds issued) to generate a return that exceeds the funding cost.
- From the investors' perspective, each class of bonds entails a different level of risk. Senior/mezzanine bond investors may be able to earn a potentially higher return than on a comparably rated corporate bond by gaining exposure to debt products that they may not otherwise be able to purchase. Equity investors can earn an equity-type return by taking the (higher) risk associated with the subordinated class.
- Certain restrictions are placed on the manager (via various tests and limits) to ensure that the senior bond classes are adequately protected and the ratings issued to the bond classes are maintained. Failure to meet these tests may trigger an immediate payoff to the senior bond classes until the tests are satisfied. This payoff would have the effect of deleveraging the CDO (as the asset manager's reliance on its cheapest source of funding, i.e., senior bonds, would be reduced).

The major difference between an ABS and a CDO is that in an ABS the cash flows from the collateral pool are used to pay off bond holders without the active management of collateral. In a CDO, the manager buys and sells debt obligations (assets) to (1) generate the cash flow required to repay bond holders and to (2) earn a competitive return for the equity tranche.

STUDY SESSION 16: DERIVATIVE INVESTMENTS—FORWARDS AND FUTURES

FORWARD MARKETS AND CONTRACTS
Cross-Reference to CFA Institute Assigned Reading #47

Price versus Value of a Forward Contract

The price of a forward contract is the fixed price or rate at which the underlying transaction will occur at contract expiration.

The no-arbitrage price of a forward contract is the price at which the value of the long and short sides equals zero.

- Forward price = $F(0,T) = S_0 (1+r)^T$

The value of a forward contract is the amount that a counterparty would need to pay, or would expect to receive, to get out of the (already-assumed) forward position. Note that a positive (negative) value for the long position implies a negative (positive) value of equal magnitude for the short.

- The value of the long position in a forward contract at contract initiation can be calculated as $V_0(0,T) = S_0 - [F(0,T)/(1 + r)^T]$.
    - To prevent arbitrage opportunities, the value of a forward contract at inception is typically set to zero.

- The value of the long position in a forward contract during the life of the contract can be calculated as $V_t(0,T) = S_t - [F(0,T) / (1 + r)^{T-t}]$.

- The value of the long position in a forward contract at contract expiration can be calculated as $V_T(0,T) = S_T - F(0,T)$.

Pricing and Valuing Equity Forward Contracts

When valuing equity forward contracts we need to adjust for the expected dividend payments from the underlying stock, stock portfolio, or equity index over the life of the contract.

The no-arbitrage price of an equity forward contract can be calculated as:

$$F(0,T) = [S_0 - PV(D,0,T)] (1 + r)^T \text{ or } F(0,T) = S_0 (1 + r)^T - FV(D,0,T)$$

The value of the long position in an equity forward contract on a dividend paying stock can be calculated as:

$$V_t(0,T) = [S_t - PV(D,t,T)] - [F(0,T) / (1 + r)^{T-t}]$$

$PV(D,t,T)$ = PV of dividends expected to be received over the remainder of the contract term (between t and T).

If dividends are assumed to be paid continuously (e.g. for forwards on equity indices):

- The price of an equity forward contract can be calculated as:

$$F(0,T) = S_0 \times e^{(r_c - \delta_c)T}$$

- The value of an equity forward contract can be calculated as:

$$V_t(0,T) = S_t e^{-\delta_c(T-t)} - F(0,T)e^{-r_c(T-t)}$$

Pricing and Valuing Forward Contracts on Fixed-Income Securities

The price of a forward on a fixed income security can be calculated as:

$$F(0,T) = [B_0^C(T+Y) - PV(CI,0,T)] \times (1 + r)^T$$

The value of the long position in a forward contract on a fixed income security prior to expiration can be calculated as:

$$V_t(0,T) = B_t^C(T+Y) - PV(CI,t,T) - F(0,T) / (1 + r)^{T-t}$$

Pricing and Valuing Forward Rate Agreements (FRAs)

The price of an FRA (forward price) represents the interest rate at which the long (short) position has the obligation to borrow (lend) funds for a specified period (term of the underlying hypothetical loan) starting at FRA expiration. Therefore, pricing an FRA is a simple exercise of determining the forward rate consistent with two (given) spot rates. For example, the price of a 1×3 FRA is the 60-day forward rate in 30 days, which is calculated on the basis of 30-day and 90-day spot rates.

- If the actual market interest rate at contract expiration is more (less) than the forward rate, the long (short) benefits and receives a payment from the short (long).

The amount paid to settle an FRA equals the present value of the interest savings on the implied loan. This amount is basically the value of the FRA.

Value of an FRA at contract expiration

- First calculate the implied forward rate (price) based on the spot rates consistent with the FRA. The value of the FRA can then be calculated as notional principal times the difference between the forward rate and the market interest rate at contract expiration (un-annualized).
- The interest savings are discounted at market interest rates over the number of days in the (hypothetical) loan term.

$$\frac{NP \times [(\text{Market interest rate} - \text{Forward rate}) \times (\text{Number of days in the loan term}/360)]}{1 + [\text{Market interest rate} \times (\text{Number of days in the loan term} / 360)]}$$

Value of an FRA prior to expiration

- First calculate the new implied forward rate (price) based on the then-current spot rates consistent with the FRA.
- Calculate the interest savings based on this "new" or "updated" market forward rate.
- Discount these interest savings for a number of days that equals the number of days remaining till FRA expiration plus the number of days in the term of the underlying hypothetical loan. Make sure you use the appropriate discount rate as well.
- The value of the FRA prior to expiration is calculated as:

$$\frac{NP \times \left[\dfrac{(\text{New forward rate} - \text{Original forward rate}) \times \text{No. of days in the loan term}}{360}\right]}{1 + \left\{\text{Current LIBOR} \times \left[\dfrac{(\text{No. of days in the loan term} + \text{No. of days till contract expiration})}{360}\right]\right\}}$$

Pricing and Valuing Currency Forward Contracts

The no-arbitrage price of a unit of foreign currency in terms of the home currency can be calculated as follows:

$$F(0,T) = S_0 \times \frac{(1+R_{DC})^T}{(1+R_{FC})^T}$$

The value of the long position in a currency forward contract at any time prior to maturity can be calculated as:

$$V_t(0,T) = \frac{S_t}{(1+R_{FC})^{(T-t)}} - \frac{F(0,T)}{(1+R_{DC})^{(T-t)}}$$

Assuming continuous interest, the price (F_T) and value (V_t) of currency forward contracts can be calculated as follows:

$$F(0,T) = S_0 \times e^{(r^{cDC} - r^{cFC}) \times T}$$

$$V_t(0,T) = [S_t / e^{r^{cFC} \times (T-t)}] - [F(0,T) / e^{r^{cDC} \times (T-t)}]$$

Credit Risk in Forwards

At any point in time, the value of a forward contract represents the credit risk borne by the party to whom a cash payment would be made to settle the contract at that point in time. Credit risk can increase, decrease or even move over to the other party with changes in the price of the underlying asset over the term of the contract. Credit risk in a forward contract can be mitigated by marking to market periodically to ensure that one party does not become too deeply indebted to the other.

FUTURES MARKETS AND CONTRACTS
Cross-Reference to CFA Institute Assigned Reading #48

Pricing and Valuing Futures Contracts

Futures (like forwards) are priced to have zero value at inception. The no-arbitrage price of a futures contract on an asset that incurs no storage costs and offers no benefits can be calculated as:

$$f_0(T) = S_0 \times (1 + r)^T$$

- If the futures contract is overpriced, traders will be able to earn a riskless profit through cash-and-carry arbitrage. They would borrow money at the risk-free rate, purchase the underlying asset at the spot price and go short on the overpriced futures contract.
- If the futures contract is underpriced, traders will be able to earn arbitrage profits through reverse cash-and-carry arbitrage.

Forwards versus Futures

- Unlike forward contracts, futures contracts are marked-to-market.
- Prices of futures contracts may differ from those of forwards depending on the preference of traders.
  - If asset prices are positively correlated with interest rates, gains generated from mark-to-market adjustments can be reinvested at higher interest rates, while losses can be financed with lower borrowing costs. In such cases, traders prefer futures contracts to forwards and the price of a futures contract will be higher than that of a comparable forward contract.
  - If asset prices are negatively correlated with interest rates, gains generated from mark-to-market adjustments will have to be reinvested at lower interest rates, while losses will have to be financed at higher borrowing costs. In such cases, traders prefer forward contracts to futures and the price of a forward contract will be higher than that of a comparable futures contract.
  - If interest rates are constant, the mark-to-market feature of futures has no impact on trader preferences for forwards or futures.

Futures contracts only accumulate value before they are marked-to-market:

Value of futures contract = Current futures price – Price when previously marked-to-market

Storage Costs and Convenience Yield

Storage costs *increase* the price of a futures contract. Futures price equals the spot price compounded over the term of the contract at the risk-free rate, plus the future value of storage costs over the life of the contract.

$$f_0(T) = S_0(1 + r)^T + FV(SC,0,T)$$

Monetary (dividends and interest) and non-monetary (convenience yield) benefits of holding an asset *decrease* the price of a futures contract. The future value of positive cash flows on the underlying asset over the term of the contract, FV(CF,0,T), is subtracted from the spot price compounded over the term of the contract at the risk-free rate to determine the futures price.

$$f_0(T) = S_0(1 + r)^T - FV(CF,0,T)$$

The future values of costs of storage and benefits from holding the asset are usually netted and denoted by FV(CB,0,T).

$$FV(CB,0,T) = \text{Costs of storage} - \text{Nonmonetary benefits (Convenience yield)}$$

If costs exceed benefits, FV(CB,0,T) is a positive number and is known as cost of carry. In this case, the general futures pricing formula is given as:

$$f_0(T) = S_0(1 + r)^T + FV(CB,0,T)$$

Backwardation and Contango

- If costs of carry (including interest opportunity costs) associated with holding an asset are *lower* than the benefits, then the futures price will be *lower* than the spot price. This situation is referred to as backwardation.

- If costs of carry (including interest opportunity costs) associated with holding an asset are *greater* than the benefits, then the futures price will be *greater* than the spot price. This situation is referred to as contango.

Futures Prices and Expected Spot Prices

- If the futures price is greater than the expected spot price, the situation is referred to as normal contango.

- If the futures price is lower than the expected spot price, the situation is referred to as normal backwardation.

Pricing Eurodollar Futures

In the Eurodollar market, there is a mismatch in the design of spot and futures instruments i.e., Eurodollar futures are structured as discount instruments, while Eurodollar time deposits are actually add-on instruments. This makes Eurodollar futures imperfect hedging instruments, and it is difficult to derive an exact pricing formula (based on the underlying's cost of carry) for them. In the Eurodollar futures market, each tick is worth $25.

Pricing Treasury Bond Futures

When calculating the no-arbitrage price of a Treasury bond futures contract, we must account for coupon payments (monetary benefits) on the underlying bond over the term of the contract. The futures price is calculated as the spot price of the asset compounded at the risk-free rate over the term of the contract minus the future value (as of contract expiration) of reinvested coupons over the term of the contract.

The party going short on a Treasury bond futures contract usually has the option to deliver any one of a number of different bonds. In such cases, each bond is assigned a conversion factor and the no-arbitrage futures price is calculated by dividing the value obtained from the above formula by the conversion factor for the cheapest-to-deliver bond.

$$f_0(T) = \frac{B_0^C(T+Y)[1+r_0(T)]^T - FV(CI,0,T)}{CF(T)}$$

Pricing Stock and Stock Index Futures

When calculating the no-arbitrage price of a futures contract on an individual stock, we must account for the dividends (monetary benefits) on the underlying stock over the term of the contract.

$$f_0(T) = S_0(1+r)^T - FV(D,0,T)$$

With futures contracts on equity portfolios or indices, we assume that dividends are paid continuously. In this case, the no-arbitrage futures price is calculated as:

$$f_0(T) = S_0 \times e^{(r^c - \delta^c)T}$$

Pricing Currency Futures

$$f_0(T) = S_0 \times \frac{(1+R_{DC})^T}{(1+R_{FC})^T}$$

Remember to use a 365-day basis to calculate T if the maturity is given in days.

If interest rates are assumed to be continuously compounded, then the no-arbitrage futures price is calculated as:

$$f_0(T) = S_0 \times e^{(r^{cDC} - r^{cFC}) \times T}$$

STUDY SESSION 17: DERIVATIVE INVESTMENTS—OPTIONS, SWAPS, AND INTEREST RATE AND CREDIT DERIVATIVES

OPTION MARKETS AND CONTRACTS
Cross-Reference to CFA Institute Assigned Reading #49

Put-Call Parity

$$C_0 + X/(1 + r)^T = P_0 + S_0$$

Arbitrage opportunities abound if put-call parity does not hold.

Put-call parity can be used to create synthetic instruments:

- Synthetic call option = Put option + Underlying stock − Risk-free bond
- Synthetic put option = Call option + Risk-free bond − Underlying stock
- Synthetic stock = Call option + Risk-free bond − Put option
- Risk-free bond = Put option + Underlying stock − Call option

Synthetic positions are useful for two reasons:
- They enable us to price options as they produce the same results as options and have known prices.
- They tell us how we can profit from mispricing of options relative to their underlying assets.

American versus European Options

- When the underlying makes no cash payments, the value of an American call equals the value of a European call, all other factors constant.
- When the underlying does make cash payments during the life of the option, it may be beneficial to exercise the American option early, so the value of an American call can exceed the value of a European call, all other factors constant.
- An American put is almost always worth more than a European put, all other factors constant.

The Binomial Model

The binomial model is restrictive in the sense that it assumes discrete time and considers only two possible price changes. However, the model can be extended to encompass all possible outcomes and also allows us to price American options.

One-Period Binomial Model

1. Calculate the option payoffs at expiration in both the up move (u) and the down move (d) scenarios.
2. Calculate the expected value of the option in Period-1 as the weighted average of the payoffs in each scenario.
3. Discount the expected value of the option to the present at the risk-free rate.

$$u = S^+/S \text{ and } d = S^-/S; \text{ and}$$
$$S^+ = Su \text{ and } S^- = Sd$$
$$\pi_u = \frac{(1 + r - d)}{(u - d)}; \quad \pi_d = 1 - \pi_u$$

Two-Period Binomial Model

The two-period binomial model is simply an extension of the one-period model. In this model, the option's price is calculated in the following manner:

1. Calculate the value of the stock in each scenario at the end of the first and the second periods.
2. Calculate the option payoffs in each scenario at the end of the second period.
3. Calculate the value of the option at each node at Year 1 as the present value of the probability-weighted payoffs for the relevant Year 2 nodes.
4. Calculate the value of the option today as the present value of the probability-weighted values at the Year 1 nodes.

Note that the greater the number of periods used in the pricing model, the greater the pricing accuracy obtained.

Two-Period Binomial Model

Important: We are working with a European call option that expires at the end of Period 2. Therefore, the value of the call at the nodes corresponding to Period 1 does not equal the option's intrinsic value (as it cannot be exercised at this point in time). Instead, it equals the probability-weighted present value of the terminal values.

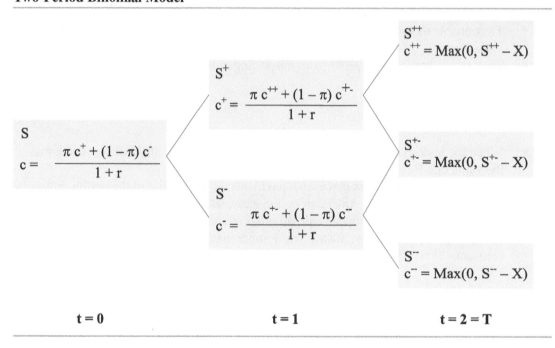

Binomial Interest Rate Option Pricing

Once we have determined the value of the bond at each node that coincides with the expiration of the European option, the value of the option today can be calculated using the following steps:

- Calculate the intrinsic value of the option at each node at maturity of the option.
- Bring these terminal option values back to today. This is where valuing bond or interest rate options is different from valuing equity options.
  - The risk-neutral probability of up and down moves in binomial interest rate models is 50%. With equity options the risk-neutral probabilities (π and $1 - \pi$) depend on u, d and r.

○ The interest rate used to calculate the probability-weighted present values is different for each period in the model (unless the term structure is flat). With equity options, the risk-free rate is constant in all periods in the model.

Valuing Interest Rate Caps and Floors

An interest rate cap places an upper limit on the coupon rate on a floating-rate security. The value of the cap simply equals the sum of the values of the individual caplets (which are basically European interest rate call options) that comprise the cap.

$$\text{Expiration value of a caplet} = \frac{\text{Max}\{0, [(\text{One-year rate} - \text{Cap rate}) \times \text{Notional principal}]\}}{1 + \text{One-year rate}}$$

An interest rate floor places a lower limit on the coupon rate on a floating-rate security. The value of the floor simply equals the sum of the values of the individual floorlets (which are basically European interest rate put options) that comprise the floor.

$$\text{Expiration value of a floorlet} = \frac{\text{Max}\{0, [(\text{Floor rate} - \text{One-year rate}) \times \text{Notional principal}]\}}{1 + \text{One-year rate}}$$

The Black-Scholes-Merton Model

The Black-Scholes-Merton (BSM) model is used when we want to price options in continuous time. The assumptions and limitations associated with this model are listed below:

Assumptions	Limitations
The underlying price follows a lognormal distribution.	No limitation associated with this assumption.
The risk-free rate is constant and known.	The model is difficult to apply for pricing bonds and interest rate options.
The volatility of the underlying asset is constant and known.	The volatility of the underlying asset is rarely known and is generally not constant.
There are no taxes or transaction costs.	This is a simplifying assumption, and can be relaxed.
There are no cash flows from the underlying asset.	The BSM model can be easily altered to relax this assumption.
The options are European.	The model cannot be used to price American options.

Inputs to the Black-Scholes-Merton Model

Input	Call Options	Put Options
The sensitivity of an option's price to the price of the underlying is known as **delta**.	The higher the value of the underlying, the higher the call option's price. Delta is **positive**.	The higher the value of the underlying, the lower the put option's price. Delta is **negative**.
Exercise price	The higher the exercise price, the lower the call option's price.	The higher the exercise price, the higher the put option's price.
The sensitivity of an option's price to the risk-free rate is known as **rho**.	The higher the risk-free rate, the higher the call option's price. Rho is **positive**.	The higher the risk-free rate, the lower the put option's price. Rho is **negative**.
The time decay of an option's price is known as **theta**.	The option's price decreases with the passage of time so theta is **negative**.*	The option's price decreases with the passage of time so theta is **negative**.*
The sensitivity of an option's price to volatility in the underlying is known as **vega**.	The higher the volatility, the higher the call option's price. Vega is **positive**.	The higher the volatility, the higher the put option's price. Vega is **positive**.

* European puts may increase in value as time to expiration decreases (positive theta).

Delta

Delta measures the change in the price of an option for a one-unit change in the price of the underlying.

Delta = Change in option price / Change in underlying

Delta can also be obtained approximately from the Black-Scholes-Merton formula as the value of $N(d_1)$ for call options and $N(d_1) - 1$ for put options. Therefore, approximate changes in prices of call and put options can be calculated for small changes in the price of the underlying as follows:

$$\Delta c \approx N(d_1) \times \Delta S$$
$$\Delta p \approx [N(d_1) - 1] \times \Delta S$$

Call Option Delta

- When a call option is deep out-of-the-money, its delta is close to zero.
- As the price of the underlying increases, call option delta also increases.
- The delta of a call option that is deep in-the-money is close to 1.

Put Option Delta

- When a put option is deep out-of-the-money, its delta is close to zero.
- As the price of the underlying decreases, put option delta also decreases.
- The delta of a put option that is deep in-the-money is close to –1.

A call option's delta can also be used to calculate the number of call options required to be sold short in order to hedge a long position in the underlying. A portfolio that combines a long position in a stock with short positions in call options on the stock is called a delta-neutral portfolio.

Number of call options needed for hedging = Number of shares owned / Call option's delta

It is important to note that a call option's delta changes as the price of the underlying changes and therefore, the portfolio must be continually rebalanced to maintain the hedge.

Gamma

Gamma is a measure of the sensitivity of an option's delta to changes in the price of the underlying.

- Gamma is largest when the option is at-the-money and close to expiration. When gamma is large, delta is very sensitive to changes in the price of the underlying. Consequently, a delta hedge will require more frequent rebalancing.
- Gamma is close to zero when the option is deep in-the-money or deep out-of-the-money. When gamma is small, delta does not change much in response to a change in the price of the underlying.

Effect of Cash Flows on the Underlying

All else equal, cash flows on the underlying asset decrease the value of call options and increase the value of put options. The effect of cash flows on the underlying asset can be incorporated in the put-call parity as follows:

$$C0 + X/(1 + r)^T = P_0 + (S_0 - PVCF)$$

Cash flows from the underlying:
- Decrease the value of call options.
- Increase the value of put options.

Volatility

Volatility may either be calculated by studying past returns, or through the BSM model.

- Historical volatility is calculated as the standard deviation of an asset's continuously compounded returns.
- Volatility calculated using the BSM model is called implied volatility and is based on the assumption that the current market price of an option reflects its true economic value.

Pricing Options on Forwards and Futures

The put-call parity for options on forwards and futures can be stated as:

$$C_0 + [(X - FP)/(1 + r)^T] = P_0$$

Early exercise of an option on a futures contract might be beneficial if it is deep in-the-money as the investor can earn interest income on the cash generated from the positive mark-to-market adjustment. As a result, American options on futures are worth more than European options on futures.

Since forwards are not marked-to market, American options on forwards have the same value as European options on forwards.

The Black Model

The Black model can be used to value European options on futures or forwards. It can also be used to price European interest rate options.

SWAP MARKETS AND CONTRACTS
Cross-Reference to CFA Institute Assigned Reading #50

Price versus Value of Swaps

The price of a swap refers to the fixed rate (and other relevant terms) that will result in a zero value for the swap for both parties at initiation.

The value of a swap refers to its market value based on current market conditions.

Equivalence of Swaps and Other Instruments

Swaps and Assets

- The payoffs of the pay-fixed side of an interest-rate swap can be replicated by issuing a fixed-rate bond and using the proceeds to purchase a floating-rate bond.
- The pay-fixed side of an equity swap may be replicated by issuing a fixed-rate bond and investing the proceeds in a stock or stock index.
- A currency swap is equivalent to issuing a fixed or floating-rate bond in one currency, converting the proceeds into another currency, and using the proceeds to purchase a fixed or floating-rate bond in the other currency.

Swaps and Forward Contracts

A swap can be seen as a combination of several forward contracts. Unless the yield curve is flat, the fixed rates on the different FRAs expiring on each of the swap's settlement dates will be different. As a result, it would be more appropriate to conclude that a swap is a combination of off-market FRAs.

Another subtle difference between swaps and forward contracts is that in an interest rate swap, the payment on the next settlement date is known. For a single forward rate agreement, this is obviously not the case.

Swaps and Futures Contracts

Swaps can be equated to futures contracts only to the extent that futures can be equated to forward contracts. Note that swaps (and forwards) are customized contracts, while futures contracts are standardized.

Swaps and Options

The settlement payments in a swap can also be replicated through combinations of options that expire at the swap settlement dates. For example, the payoffs for the pay-fixed side of an interest rate swap can be replicated by purchasing interest rate calls and writing interest rate puts, where a call and a put expire on each settlement date and the strike price of the options equals the swap fixed rate.

Pricing and Valuing a Plain Vanilla Interest Rate Swap

Pricing an interest rate swap refers to determining the fixed rate that would make the present value of payments expected to be made by either party equal at inception.

$$\text{Swap fixed rate} = \left(\frac{1 - B_0(N)}{B_0(1) + B_0(2) + B_0(3) + \ldots + B_0(N)} \right) \times 100$$

In order to determine the value of a swap at a specific point in time, calculate the present value of the remaining fixed and floating-rate payments.

- The fixed payments at each payment date are calculated using the swap fixed-rate. The value of the fixed-rate bond can be calculated as the sum of the present values (using current market interest rates to discount the cash flows) of all remaining fixed coupon payments and the bond's par value.
- At each payment date, the floating-rate on a bond is set equal to the market interest rate, which makes the bond's value equal to par. To determine the present value of the floating-rate bond, simply discount the sum of the next coupon payment and the par value of the floating-rate bond to the present.

Value (pay-fixed side) = PV (replicating floating-rate bond) – PV (replicating fixed-rate bond)

Value (pay-floating side) = PV (replicating fixed-rate bond) – PV (replicating floating-rate bond)

Note that even though par values (principal amounts) are used to "value" the swap position, the parties in plain-vanilla interest rate swaps do not exchange these principal amounts.

Pricing and Valuing Currency Swaps

The fixed rates on a currency swap are the fixed rates on plain vanilla interest rate swaps in the respective countries.

The value of a currency swap at a specific point in time is determined in the same way as the value of an interest rate swap.

1. Given the notional principal in terms of the domestic currency, calculate the notional principal in foreign currency terms using the exchange rate at swap inception.
2. Calculate the present value of the remaining payments to be made by both parties.
3. Convert the PV of the foreign currency bond's payments into domestic currency using the then-current exchange rate.
- Calculate the value of the swap as the difference between the present values (in domestic currency terms) of the two bonds.

Note that the notional principals of a currency swap (which is based on the exchange rate at swap inception) are exchanged at initiation and then again at the termination of the swap.

Pricing and Valuing Equity Swaps

- The price (fixed rate) and value of the pay-fixed side of an equity swap is determined in the same way as the value of a plain-vanilla interest rate swap.

- The value of the pay-equity return side is determined by multiplying the notional principal by one plus the equity return since the last settlement date.
- The difference between the values of the two counterparties' positions equals the value of the swap.

  - The value of a "pay a fixed rate and receive the return on equity" swap at any point in time is calculated as:

  [(1 + Return on equity) × Notional principal] – PV of the remaining fixed-rate payments

  - The value of a "pay a floating rate and receive the return on equity" swap at any point in time is calculated as:

  [(1 + Return on equity) × Notional principal] – PV (Next coupon payment + Par value)

  - The value of a "pay the return on one equity instrument and receive the return on another equity instrument" swap is calculated as:

  [(1 + Return on Index 2) × NP] – [(1 + Return on Index 1) × NP]

Swaptions

A swaption is an option to enter into a swap.

- A payer swaption is an option to enter into a swap as the fixed-rate payer and floating-rate receiver. A payer swaption will be exercised if the exercise rate is lower than the market swap fixed rate at swaption expiration, so it increases in value when market interest rates increase.

- A receiver swaption is an option to enter into a swap as the fixed-rate receiver and floating-rate payer. A receiver swaption is exercised if the exercise rate is higher than the market swap fixed rate at swaption expiration, so it increases in value when market interest rates decrease.

Valuing Swaptions

The value of a payer swaption can be calculated as:

$$(\text{Market fixed-rate} - \text{Exercise rate}) \times \frac{\text{No. of days in the payment period}}{360} \times \text{Notional principal}$$

The value of a receiver swaption can be calculated as:

$$(\text{Exercise rate} - \text{Market fixed-rate}) \times \frac{\text{No. of days in the payment period}}{360} \times \text{Notional principal}$$

Uses of Swaptions

- To hedge a possible future exposure to fixed or floating-rate interest payments.
- To have the option to terminate a swap.
- To speculate on interest rates.

Relating Swaptions to Options on Bonds

Just like swaps can be related to positions on bonds, swaptions can be related to options on bonds.

- If interest rates have risen since the time of swaption purchase, the payer swaption will be in-the-money. Therefore, a payer swaption can be viewed as a put option on a fixed-rate bond. The value of a put option on a fixed-rate bond also increases when interest rates increase (as the value of the underlying bond falls).

- If interest rates have fallen since the time of swaption purchase, the receiver swaption will be in-the-money. Therefore, a receiver swaption can be viewed as a call option on a fixed-rate bond. The value of a call option on a fixed-rate bond increases when interest rates decrease (as the value of the underlying bond increases).

Credit Risk and Swaps

The party with the positive value in a swap faces credit risk as it holds a net claim against the other party. The party with the negative value is not subject to credit risk.

Current credit risk refers to the risk of the other party failing to meet a payment obligation that is immediately due.

Potential credit risk refers to the possibility that although the other party may currently be able to make payments, it may fail to meet payment obligations in the future.

- Since there are no principal payments in interest rate and equity swaps, the credit risk on these swaps is highest in the middle of their lives.
- Counterparty credit risk is higher in currency swaps as periodic payments are generally not netted and principal amounts are actually exchanged. For a currency swap, credit risk is usually concentrated between the middle and the end of the swap's life.

The swap spread (difference between the swap fixed-rate and the risk-free rate) does not reflect the credit risk in a swap; it measures the general level of credit risk in the global economy.
- An effective way to reduce credit risk is through netting and marking-to-market.

Interest Rate Caps and Floors

- An interest rate cap is an agreement in which one party (in return for an upfront premium) agrees to pay the other at specific points in time if the reference rate *exceeds* a predetermined strike rate.
- An interest rate floor is an agreement in which one party (in return for an upfront premium) agrees to pay the other at specific points in time if the reference rate is *lower* than a predetermined strike rate.

The buyer of an interest rate cap or floor pays an upfront fee which represents the maximum amount that she can lose, or alternatively, the maximum amount that the seller can gain.

The payoff to the buyer of an interest rate cap can be calculated as follows:

$$\text{Payoff} = \text{Max} \left[0, (\text{Market interest-rate} - \text{Cap rate}) \times \frac{\text{No. of days}}{360} \times \text{Notional principal} \right]$$

Similarly, the payoff to the buyer of an interest rate floor can be calculated as follows:

$$\text{Payoff} = \text{Max} \left[0, (\text{Floor rate} - \text{Market interest-rate}) \times \frac{\text{No. of days}}{360} \times \text{Notional principal} \right]$$

Risk-Return Characteristics

Just like in options contracts, the risk involved in interest rate caps and floors is *unilateral*. Only the buyer of an interest rate cap or floor faces counterparty risk (the risk that the seller might not pay). The seller of an interest rate cap or floor does not face any counterparty risk as the buyer has already paid (the option premium) up front.

Interest Rate Caps and Floors as Combinations of Other Instruments

The payments on a cap can be replicated by buying a series of call options on interest rates (caplets). If the market interest rate at expiration of the option is higher than the reference (strike) rate, the call option holder would exercise her option (right to borrow at the lower strike rate) and receive a payment.

The payments on a floor can be replicated by buying a series of put options on interest rates (floorlets). If the market interest rate at expiration of the option lies below the reference (strike) rate, the put option holder would exercise her option (right to lend at the higher strike rate) and receive a payment.

Interest rate caps and floors can be viewed as being equivalent to options on fixed income instruments.
- A call option on a fixed income instrument will benefit if interest rates fall (as the value of the underlying fixed income instrument would rise).
- A put option on a fixed income instrument will benefit if interest rates rise (as the value of the underlying fixed income instrument would fall).

Therefore:

- A long position on a cap is equivalent to a long position on call options on interest rates or a long put option on a fixed income instrument.
- A long position on a floor is equivalent to a long position on put options on interest rates or a long call option on a fixed income instrument.

Interest Rate Collars

An interest rate collar is constructed by a borrower going long on an interest rate cap and writing an interest rate floor. The collar limits the issuer's payments within a range between the cap rate and the floor rate. The net premium paid for the collar is the difference between the premium paid to purchase the cap and the premium received to write the floor.

CREDIT DEFAULT SWAPS
Cross-Reference to CFA Institute Assigned Reading #52

CREDIT DEFAULT SWAPS: BASIC DEFINITIONS AND CONCEPTS

A **credit default swap (CDS)** is a bilateral contract between two parties that transfers the credit risk embedded in a reference obligation from one party to another. It is essentially an insurance contract.

The reference obligation is the fixed-income security on which the protection is written (or whose credit risk is transferred). This is usually a bond, but can also be a loan in some cases.

The protection buyer makes a series of periodic payments (think of them as periodic insurance premium payments) to the protection seller during the term of the CDS. In return for this series of periodic premium payments (known as the CDS fee or CDS spread), the protection buyer obtains protection against default risk embedded in the reference obligation.

The protection seller earns the CDS spread over the term of the CDS in return for assuming the credit risk in the reference obligation. If a credit event occurs, the protection seller is obligated to compensate the protection buyer for credit losses by means of a specified settlement procedure.

CDS are somewhat similar to put options. Put options give the option holder the right to sell (put) the underlying to the put writer if the underlying performs poorly relative to the strike price. The option holder is therefore compensated for poor performance. Similarly, CDS give the protection buyer compensation if the underlying (loan, bond or bond portfolio) performs poorly.

Types of CDS

The reference entity is the entity issuing the reference obligation in a **single-name CDS** (where the CDS is on one borrower). The reference obligation is a particular instrument issued by the reference entity that serves as the designated instrument covered by the CDS. The designated instrument is usually a senior unsecured obligation (which can be referred to as senior CDS), but this instrument is not the only instrument covered by the CDS. Any debt issued by the reference entity that is pari passu (i.e., ranked equivalently in the priority of claims), or higher relative to the reference obligation is covered by the CDS. The payoff to the CDS is determined by the cheapest-to-deliver obligation, which is the instrument that can be purchased and delivered at the lowest cost, but has the same seniority as the reference obligation.

An **index CDS** involves several reference entities (borrowers), which allows market participants to take positions on the credit of a portfolio of companies. Generally speaking, the higher (lower) the correlation of default among index constituents, the higher (lower) the cost of obtaining credit protection on the index CDS.

A **tranche CDS** also covers a portfolio of borrowers, but only to a pre-specified amount of losses (similar to how tranches of asset-backed securities only cover a particular amount of losses).

Important Features of CDS Markets and Instruments

- Like any swap contract, a CDS also specifies a notional principal, which represents the size of the contract.
- The periodic premium paid by the protection buyer in a CDS pays to the protection seller is known as the CDS spread. The CDS spread is a return over LIBOR required to protect against credit risk and is sometimes also referred to as the credit spread.
- In recent years, standard annual coupon rates (basically standard credit spreads) have been established on CDS contracts.
  - Any discrepancy between the standard rate and the actual required credit spread is accounted for via an **upfront premium**.
    - If the standard rate is too low (to capture the credit risk), the protection buyer will pay the seller the upfront premium.
    - If the standard rate is too high, the protection seller will pay the buyer an upfront premium.
- Regardless of which party makes the upfront payment, the value or price of the CDS can change over the contract term due to changes in the credit quality of the reference obligation.
- In the CDS world, since the protection buyer promises to make a series of future payments, she is known as the short and the protection seller is known as the long.
  - The protection buyer, or short, benefits when things go badly i.e., if the credit quality of the underlying instrument declines and CDS spreads increase.
  - The protection seller, or long, benefits when things go well i.e., if the credit quality of the underlying instrument improves and CDS spreads decrease.

Credit and Succession Events

A credit event defines default by the reference entity. It is what triggers a payment from the protection seller on a CDS to the protection buyer. There are three types of credit events:

- Bankruptcy
- Failure to pay
- Restructuring

Determination of whether there has been a credit event is made by a 15-member Determinations Committee (DC) within the ISDA. A supermajority vote of 12 members is required to declare a credit event.

The DC also plays a role in determining whether a succession event has occurred. A succession event occurs when there is a change in the corporate structure of the reference entity (e.g. divesture, spinoff, or merger) such that the ultimate obligor of the reference obligation becomes unclear.

Settlement Protocols

- In a physical settlement, upon declaration of a credit event, the protection buyer delivers the underlying debt instrument to the protection seller. The par value of bonds delivered to the seller must equal the notional amount of the CDS. In return, the protection seller pays the buyer the par value of the debt (which is equal to the CDS notional amount).

- In a **cash settlement**, the idea is that the protection seller should pay the protection buyer an amount of cash equal to the difference between the notional amount and the current value of the bonds. Determining this amount is not an easy task as opinions can vary about how much money has actually been lost (in a default, a portion of the par value is generally recovered).
  - The percentage of the par value that is recovered is known as the recovery rate. This represents the percentage received by the protection buyer relative to the amount owed.
  - The payout ratio (which determines the amount that the protection seller must pay the protection buyer) is an estimate of the expected credit loss. The payout amount equals the payout ratio multiplied by the notional amount.

$$\text{Payout ratio} = 1 - \text{Recovery rate}$$
$$\text{Payout amount} = \text{Payout ratio} \times \text{Notional}$$

Note that actual recovery is a very long process, which can stretch way beyond the settlement date of the CDS. Therefore, to estimate an appropriate recovery rate, there is typically an auction for the defaulted bonds to determine their post-default market value. The protection seller then pays the protection buyer the difference between the par value (which is equal to the CDS notional amount) and the post-default market value of the bonds.

CDS Index Products

CDS indices allow participants to take a position on the credit risk of several companies simultaneously, just like equity indices allow investors to gain exposure to stocks of several companies at the same time. CDS indices are all equally-weighted.

If an entity within an index defaults, it is removed from the index and settled as a single-name CDS (based on its pro-rata share in the index). The index continues to move forward with a smaller notional.

BASICS OF VALUATION AND PRICING

Basic Pricing Concepts

When we talk about pricing CDS, we are interested in determining the CDS spread or in the case of standardized CDS (with 1% or 5% coupon rates) determining the upfront premium.

$$\text{Expected loss} = \text{Loss given default} \times \text{Probability of default}$$

- In the context of valuing CDS, we work with hazard rates that reflect the probability that default will occur given that it has not already occurred.
- The probability of default is calculated as 1 minus the probability of survival.
- The loss given default is computed based on expected recovery rates.

The Protection Leg

The protection leg refers to the contingent payment that the protection seller may have to make to the protection buyer. In order to value the protection leg, we must compute the present value of the contingent obligation of the protection seller to the protection buyer. This is calculated as the difference between:
- The present value of the hypothetical value of the bond if it had no credit risk; and
- The present value of the expected payoff on the (risky) bond, after accounting for the probability, amount and timing of each payment. In order to compute this value:
  - First we compute the expected payoff of each payment on the bond by multiplying the payment adjusted for the expected recovery rate by the probability of survival.
  - Next, we discount the expected payoff of each payment at the appropriate discount rate.
  - Then we sum all these amounts to come up with the expected payoff on the bond.

The difference between these two figures represents credit exposure.

Value of protection leg = Credit risk = Value of risk-free bond – Expected payoff on risky bond

The Premium Leg

The premium leg refers to the series of periodic payments that the protection buyer promises to make to the protection seller. When it comes to valuing the premium leg, things are complicated by the fact that once default occurs, regardless of exactly when it occurs during the term of the CDS, the protection buyer ceases to make payments to the protection seller. As a result, hazard rates must be applied.

The Upfront Payment

The difference in values of the protection leg and premium leg equals the amount of the upfront payment.

Upfront payment = Present value of protection leg – Present value of premium leg

If this difference is positive (negative), the protection buyer (seller) makes the upfront payment to the protection seller (buyer). In order to understand this, note that:
- PV of protection leg represents the value of the contingent payment that the protection seller will make to the buyer.
- PV of premium leg represents the value of expected premium payments that the protection buyer will make to the seller.
- If the value of payments that the seller will make over the term of the CDS is greater, the seller will receive a premium upfront so that overall, both the positions hold equal value at CDS inception.

Upfront premium % $\cong$ (Credit spread – Fixed coupon) × Duration of CDS

Present value of credit spread = Upfront payment + Present value of fixed coupon

Price of CDS per 100 par = 100 – Upfront premium %

The Credit Curve

The credit curve presents credit spreads on a company's debt for a range of maturities. The credit spread refers to the spread on top of LIBOR required by investors to hold the debt instrument. With the evolution and high degree of efficiency in the CDS market, the credit curve for a borrower is essentially determined by CDS rates on its obligations.

One of the factors that influences the credit curve is the hazard rate:
- A constant hazard rate will result in a relatively flat credit curve.
- Upward (downward) sloping credit curves imply a greater (lower) likelihood of default in later years.

Value Changes in CDS during their Lives

Just like any other swap, the value of a CDS also fluctuates during its term. Some of the factors that cause changes in the value of a CDS are:
- Changes in the credit quality or perceived credit quality of the reference entity.
- Changes in duration of the CDS (duration shortens through time).
- Changes in the probability of default, expected loss given default and in the shape of the credit curve.

The change in value of a CDS for a given change in the credit spread can be approximated as:

$$\text{Profit for protection buyer} \cong \text{Change in spread in bps} \times \text{Duration} \times \text{Notional}$$

The percentage price change in the CDS can be computed as:

$$\%\ \text{Change in CDS price} = \text{Change in spread in bps} \times \text{Duration}$$

Monetizing Gains and Losses

- The first method is to enter into a new offsetting CDS.
- A second way to monetize a gain/loss on a CDS position is to exercise or settle the CDS upon default via a cash or physical settlement (discussed earlier).
- A third (least common) method occurs if there is no default. The parties simply hold their positions until maturity. By then, the seller has captured all the premium payments without having to make any payments to the protection buyer.

Applications of CDS

- Manage credit exposures i.e., take on or lay off credit risk in response to changing expectations; and/or
- Take advantage of valuation disparities i.e., differences in the pricing of credit risk in the CDS market relative to another market (e.g., that of the underlying bonds).

Managing Credit Exposures

A party takes a position on a naked credit default swap when it has no underlying exposure to the reference entity.

- In entering a naked CDS as the protection buyer, the investor is taking a position that the entity's credit quality will deteriorate (credit spreads will increase).
- In entering a naked CDS as the protection seller, the investor is taking a position that the entity's credit quality will improve (credit spreads will decline).

In a long/short trade, the party takes a long position in one CDS and a short position in another CDS, where the two swaps are based on **different** reference entities. Such a trade represents a bet that the credit quality of one entity will improve relative to that of the other. The investor would sell protection on the entity whose credit quality it expects to improve (go long on the CDS), and purchase protection on the entity whose credit quality it expects to deteriorate (go short on the CDS).

A curve trade is a type of long/short trade. It involves buying a CDS of one maturity and selling a CDS with a different maturity, where both the CDS are on the **same** reference entity.

With an **upward-sloping** credit curve, a **steepening** (flattening) of the curve means that long-term credit risk has increased (decreased) relative to short-term credit risk.

- An investor who believes that long-term credit risk will increase relative to short-term credit risk (credit curve steepening) will purchase protection (or go short) on a long-term CDS and sell protection (or go long) on a short-term CDS.
  - A curve-steepening trade is bullish for the short run. It implies that the short-term outlook for the reference entity is better than the long-term outlook.
  - An investor who is bearish about a company's short term credit-worthiness will enter into a curve-flattening trade.

The interpretation of the investor's position is the opposite if the credit curve is **currently downward-sloping** (which is rarely the case and generally results from short-term stress in financial markets). In this case, a **flattening** (not steepening) of the curve suggests that long term credit-risk has increased relative to short-term credit risk.

Note that for a given (parallel) change in credit spreads across all maturities, longer-term CDS values will be more affected than shorter-term CDS values (due to their higher durations).

Valuation Differences and Basis Trading

A basis trade aims to profit from the difference in (1) the credit spread implied by the price/yield on a bond, and (2) the credit spread on a CDS on the same reference obligation with the same term to maturity.

Basis trades work on the assumption that any mispricing of credit risk across the bond and CDS markets is likely to be temporary and that credit spreads should converge once the disconnect has been recognized by participants.

In order to determine the profit potential of a basis trade, we must decompose the bond yield into the risk-free rate plus the funding spread plus the credit spread. The risk-free rate plus the funding spread equals LIBOR, so the credit spread equals the excess of the yield on the bond over LIBOR. This credit spread must then be compared to the credit spread on the CDS. If the credit spread on the bond is higher (lower) than in the CDS market, it is said to be a negative (positive) basis.

STUDY SESSION 18: PORTFOLIO MANAGEMENT—CAPITAL MARKET THEORY AND THE PORTFOLIO MANAGEMENT PROCESS

PORTFOLIO CONCEPTS
Cross-Reference to CFA Institute Assigned Reading #53

Assumptions of Mean-Variance Analysis

1. All investors are risk averse.
2. Expected returns for all assets are known.
3. The variances and covariances of all asset returns are known.
4. Investors need only know the expected returns, variances, and covariances of returns to determine optimal portfolios. They can ignore skewness, kurtosis, and other attributes of a distribution.
5. There are no transaction costs or taxes.

Expected return on portfolio of 2 assets

$$E(R_P) = w_1 E(R_1) + w_2 E(R_2)$$

Standard deviation of portfolio of 2 assets

$$\sigma_P = (w_1^2 \sigma_1^2 + w_2^2 \sigma_2^2 + 2w_1 w_2 \rho_{1,2} \sigma_1 \sigma_2)^{1/2}$$

Expected return on portfolio of 3 assets

$$E(R_P) = w_1 E(R_1) + w_2 E(R_2) + w_3 E(R_3)$$

Standard deviation of portfolio of 3 assets

$$\sigma_P = (w_1^2 \sigma_1^2 + w_2^2 \sigma_2^2 + w_3^2 \sigma_3^2 + 2w_1 w_2 \rho_{1,2} \sigma_1 \sigma_2 + 2w_1 w_3 \rho_{1,3} \sigma_1 \sigma_3 + 2w_2 w_3 \rho_{2,3} \sigma_2 \sigma_3)^{1/2}$$

From the formula for calculating the standard deviation of the 2-asset portfolio it is important to understand that:

- The maximum value for portfolio standard deviation will be obtained when the correlation coefficient equals +1.
- Portfolio standard deviation will be minimized when the correlation coefficient equals -1.
- If the correlation coefficient equals zero, the second part of the formula will equal zero and portfolio standard deviation will lie somewhere in between.

Implications of Markowitz Portfolio Theory

- When asset returns are negatively correlated, the final term in the standard deviation formula is negative and serves to *reduce* portfolio standard deviation.

- If the correlation between assets equals zero, portfolio standard deviation is greater than when correlation is negative.
- When the asset returns are positively correlated, the final term is also positive, and portfolio standard deviation is even higher than when the correlation coefficient equals zero. With a correlation coefficient of +1 (perfect positive correlation), there are no diversification benefits.

The risk (standard deviation) of a portfolio of risky assets depends on the asset weights and standard deviations, *and most importantly on the correlation of asset returns.*

- The *higher* the correlation between the individual assets, the *higher* the portfolio's risk.

Effect of Different Weights on Correlation

- When correlation equals +1, the risk-return combinations that result from altering the weights lie along a straight line between the two assets' risk-return profiles.
- As correlation falls, the curvature of this line increases.
- When correlation equals -1, the curve is represented by two straight lines that meet at the vertical axis (zero-risk portfolio) with some combination.

Deriving the Efficient Frontier

- The minimum variance frontier reduces the investment opportunity set to a curve that contains only those portfolios that entail the lowest level of risk for each level of expected return.
- The global minimum variance portfolio is the portfolio of risky assets that entails the lowest level of risk among all portfolios on the minimum variance frontier.
- Investors aim to maximize return for every level of risk. Therefore, all portfolios above and to the right of the global minimum variance portfolio dominate those that lie below and to the right of the global minimum variance portfolio.
- The section of the minimum variance frontier that lies above and to the right of the global minimum variance portfolio is referred to as the Markowitz efficient frontier.

Important:
- The risk-return characteristics of the portfolio are improved as the number of assets in the investment opportunity set increases.
- The composition of the minimum variance portfolio for any level of expected return depends on the expected return of the assets, their variances and correlations, and the number of assets in the portfolio.

Diversification and Portfolio Size

- As more and more assets are added to a portfolio, the contribution of each individual asset's risk to portfolio risk diminishes. The covariance between the assets in the portfolio accounts for the bulk of portfolio risk.

- The *lower* the average correlation between stocks, the *greater* the number of stocks needed in the portfolio to obtain a particular diversification gain.

The Capital Allocation Line (CAL)

- The CAL illustrates the risk-return characteristics of portfolios that combine the risk-free asset with the optimal risky-asset portfolio for an investor.
- If it is assumed that investors do not have homogenous expectations, investors would have different views on expected returns, variance of returns, and correlations between assets and therefore, may have different efficient frontiers, optimal risky asset portfolios and different CALs.
- The optimal risky asset portfolio is achieved at the point where a straight line drawn from the risk-free rate is tangent to the efficient frontier of risky assets. This optimal risky asset portfolio contains none of the risk-free asset.
- If borrowing is only possible at a rate higher than the risk-free rate, the CAL is kinked.
- If borrowing is ruled out altogether, the CAL has a linear portion (to the point of tangency) and a curved portion (the part of the efficient frontier that lies to the right of the point of tangency).

$$CAL : E(R_P) = R_F + \frac{E(R_T) - R_F}{\sigma_{R_T}} \sigma_P$$

The Capital Market Line (CML)

With identical expectations, each investor has the same tangency portfolio and the same CAL. In this case the CAL (that shows the risk-return characteristics of portfolios combining the risk-free asset with the market portfolio) is known as the capital market line (CML).

$$CML : E(R_P) = R_F + \frac{E(R_M) - R_F}{\sigma_M} \times \sigma_P$$

The CML describes the expected returns of only efficient portfolios. The implication of the CML is that all investors (regardless of their tolerance for risk) will invest in a portfolio that combines the risk-free asset with a single risky-asset portfolio (the market portfolio).

The Capital Asset Pricing Model (CAPM)

Assumptions:

- Investors are utility-maximizing, risk-averse, and rational individuals.
- Markets are frictionless, and there are no transaction costs and taxes.
- All investors have the same single period investment horizon.
- Investors have homogenous expectations and therefore, arrive at the same valuation for any given asset.
- All investments are infinitely divisible.
- Investors are price-takers. No investor is large enough to influence security prices.

CAPM equation: $E(R_i) = R_F + \beta_i[E(R_M) - R_F]$

The Security Market Line (SML) is a graphical illustration of the CAPM.

The CAPM basically implies that sensitivity to the market return is the only source of difference in expected returns across assets.

CML versus SML

	CML	SML
Measure of risk	Uses standard deviation (total risk).	Uses systematic risk (non-diversifiable risk).
Application	Tool used to determine the appropriate asset allocation (percentages allocated to the risk-free asset and to the market portfolio) for the investor.	Tool used to determine the appropriate expected (benchmark) returns for securities.
Definition	Graph of the efficient frontier.	Graph of the capital asset pricing model.
Slope	Market portfolio Sharpe ratio.	Market risk premium.

Mean-Variance Portfolio Choice Rules

When comparing two risky portfolios:

- The portfolio with a higher expected return and lower risk will be preferred to one with a lower expected return and higher risk.
- If one portfolio has a higher expected return and higher risk relative to another, the determination of the preferred portfolio depends on the investor's risk tolerance (shape of indifference curve).
- The portfolio with a *higher* Sharpe ratio is preferred.

When determining whether an investment should be added to an existing portfolio:

- Adding the new asset to the portfolio is optimal if the following condition is satisfied:
  - $$\frac{E(R_{new}) - R_F}{\sigma_{new}} > \left(\frac{E(R_p) - R_F}{\sigma_p} \right) Corr(R_{new}, R_p)$$
  - Not only do we consider Sharpe ratios, but also the correlation between the existing portfolio and the new asset.

Practical Issues in Mean-Variance Analysis

Estimating Inputs for Mean-Variance Optimization

1. **Historical Estimates**

   This approach uses historical data to calculate means, variances and correlations between assets. It has two limitations:
   - It requires a large number of estimates for inputs in the calculation (n expected returns, n variances, and $n(n-1)/2$ pairwise covariances).
   - The errors in the estimates of return parameters can be quite large, especially for expected returns and covariances.

2. **The Market Model (Unadjusted Historical Beta)**

   This approach employs regression analysis to estimate the relationship between the returns on an asset and the returns on the market portfolio.

   The market model makes the following predictions:
   - $E(R_i) = \alpha_i + \beta_i E(R_M)$
   - $Var(R_i) = \beta_i^2 \sigma_M^2 + \sigma_{\varepsilon_i}^2$
   - $Cov(R_i, R_j) = \beta_i \beta_j \sigma_M^2$
   - $Corr(R_i, R_j) = \dfrac{\beta_i \beta_j \sigma_M^2}{(\beta_i^2 \sigma_M^2 + \sigma_{\varepsilon_i}^2)^{1/2}(\beta_j^2 \sigma_M^2 + \sigma_{\varepsilon_j}^2)^{1/2}}$

   The advantage of the market model is that it requires estimates of a relatively low number ($3n + 2$) of parameters to construct the minimum-variance frontier. A potential problem lies in determining which portfolio should be used as an appropriate proxy for the market portfolio.

3. **Market Model Estimates (Adjusted Beta)**

   This approach asserts that betas do not follow a random walk (i.e., the best predictor of beta for a particular period is not the beta for the previous period). Betas tend to be mean-reverting (towards 1) so adjusted betas are used to make forecasts of stock returns.
   Adjusted beta = 0.333 + 0.667 (Historical beta)

Instability of the Minimum-Efficient Frontier

Small changes in the risk-return characteristics of individual assets can cause relatively large changes in the minimum variance frontier. The instability can arise from:
- The inputs used in mean-variance optimization, which are subject to random variation.
- The distribution of asset returns, which is not constant over time.

The problem with an unstable minimum-variance frontier is that it becomes misleading and loses its usefulness. Further, the optimization may result in unreasonably large short positions and frequent portfolio rebalancing, which is costly.

Multifactor Models

Multifactor models aim to look for systematic factors that affect the average returns for a large number of different assets. These factors represent priced risk i.e., risk that investors demand an additional return for taking.

1. Macroeconomic Factor Models

   These models use surprises in macroeconomic variables that significantly explain equity returns as factors.

   $R_i = a_i + b_{i_1} F_{INT} + b_{i_2} F_{GDP} + \varepsilon_i$
   R_i = the return to stock i
   a_i = the expected return to stock i
   F_{INT} = the surprise in interest rates
   F_{GDP} = the surprise in GDP growth
   b_{i1} = the sensitivity of the return on stock i to surprises in interest rates.
   b_{i2} = the sensitivity of the return on stock i to surprises in GDP growth.
   ε_i = an error term with a zero mean that represents the portion of the return to stock i that is not explained by the factor model.

   - The model breaks down the return on an asset into three components: the asset's expected return, the unexpected return as a result of surprises, and an error term.
   - The intercept terms reflects the expected return on the asset based on the predicted values of macroeconomic variables.
   - The slope represents the sensitivity of the asset's return to surprises in macroeconomic variables.
   - The error term represents the effect of asset-specific risks on the asset's return.

   Arbitrage Pricing Theory (APT) and the Factor Model

   The assumptions made by the APT are not as strong as those made by the CAPM. APT relies on the following assumptions:

   - A factor model describes asset returns.
   - There are many assets so investors can form well-diversified portfolios that entail zero asset-specific risk.
   - No arbitrage possibilities exist for these well-diversified portfolios.

     APT equation: $E(R_P) = R_F + \lambda_1 \beta_{p,1} + \ldots + \lambda_K \beta_{p,K}$

   - The factor risk premium (i) represents the expected return in excess of the risk-free rate for a portfolio with a sensitivity of 1 to factor i and sensitivity of 0 to all other factors.
   - The expected return on the asset $E(R_P)$ tells us what the intercept term in the multifactor macroeconomic models should be.

2. Fundamental Factor Models

In these models, the factors are stated as returns (rather than return surprises relative to predicted values as is the case with macroeconomic factor models).
- The intercept term and factor sensitivities are interpreted differently from how they are interpreted for macroeconomic factor models.
- For fundamental factor models, the sensitivities are attributes of the security, and are typically standardized.
- Under fundamental factor models, the factor sensitivities or attributes are typically specified first, and then factor returns are estimated through regression analysis. Macroeconomic multifactor models work the other way round.
- Factors of most fundamental factor models for equities can be placed into three broad groups:
  - Company fundamental factors
  - Company share-related factors
  - Macroeconomic factors

3. Statistical Factor Models

In these models, statistical methods are applied to a set of historical returns to determine portfolios that explain historical returns.
- In factor analysis models, the factors are portfolios that explain historical return covariances.
- In principal-components models, the factors are portfolios that best explain historical return variances.

Applications of Multifactor Models

1. Analyzing sources of returns: Multifactor models are used to understand the sources of a manager's returns relative to a benchmark.

$$\text{Active return} = \sum_{j=1}^{K} [(\text{Portfolio sensitivity})_j - (\text{Benchmark sensitivity})_j] \times (\text{Factor return})_j + \text{Asset selection}$$

Active return can be broken into:
- The product of the manager's active factor sensitivities and factor returns, which is called the return from factor tilts.
- The return from individual security (asset) selection.

2. Analyzing sources of risk: Active risk (also known as tracking error) is the standard deviation of active returns.

$$\text{TE} = s(R_p - R_B)$$

The information ratio (IR) is used to evaluate mean active return per unit of active risk.

$$IR = \frac{\bar{R}_p - \bar{R}_B}{s(R_p - R_B)}$$

The higher the information ratio, the better the risk-adjusted performance of the portfolio.

The variance of active risk is referred to as active risk squared.

$$\text{Active risk squared} = TE = s^2\,(R_p - R_B)$$

$$\text{Active risk squared} = \text{Active factor risk} + \text{Active specific risk}$$

- Active factor risk is the contribution to active risk squared of taking different-from-benchmark exposures relative to factors specified in the risk model (factor tilts).
  - Active factor risk can then be computed as the difference between active risk squared and active specific risk.

- Active specific risk or asset selection risk is the contribution to active risk squared of placing different-than-benchmark weights on individual assets after accounting for the differences in factor sensitivities between the portfolio and the benchmark.

  - $$\text{Active specific risk} = \sum_{i=1}^{n} w_i^a \sigma_{\varepsilon_i}^2$$

Factor's Marginal Contribution to Active Risk Squared (FMCAR)

The individual contributions of a portfolio's active factor exposures to active risk squared is measured by computing what is known as the factor's marginal contribution to active risk squared (FMCAR). With k factors, the marginal contribution to active risk squared for a factor, j, is computed as:

$$\text{FMCAR}_j = \frac{b_j^a \sum_{i=1}^{K} b_i^a \text{Cov}(F_j, F_i)}{\text{Active risk squared}}$$

$$\text{FMCAR}_j = \frac{\text{Active factor risk}}{\text{Active risk squared}}$$

where:

b_j^a = The portfolio's active exposure to factor j

$b_j^a \sum_{i=1}^{K} b_i^a\,\text{Cov}(F_j, F_i)$ = The active factor risk for factor j

Factor portfolios

A factor portfolio for a particular factor has a factor sensitivity of 1 for that particular factor and a sensitivity of 0 for all other factors. Factor portfolios are of interest to managers who want to hedge against, or speculate on a particular risk.

Tracking portfolios

A tracking portfolio is a portfolio that has factor sensitivities that are the same as those of a designated benchmark portfolio. They are used by managers who believe they have security selection expertise (and want to deviate from benchmark weights for individual securities) but want to maintain the same factor sensitivities as the benchmark.

RESIDUAL RISK AND RETURN: THE INFORMATION RATIO
Cross-Reference to CFA Institute Assigned Reading #54

The Definition of Alpha

Alpha (also known as **residual return**) is a risk-adjusted measure of the active return (return in excess of the benchmark) on a portfolio.

- **Ex post** (looking backward) alpha is an average of *realized* residual returns.
- **Ex ante** (looking forward) alpha is a *forecast* of residual return.

Ex post alpha for a portfolio is determined by conducting a regression of excess returns on the portfolio against excess returns on the benchmark.

$$r_P(t) = \alpha_P + \beta_P . r_B(t) + \varepsilon_P(t)$$

- The alpha of a portfolio equals the weighted-average of the alphas of the individual assets comprising the portfolio.
- The benchmark portfolio and cash (or the risk-free asset) both have a residual return or alpha of 0.

The Ex Post Information Ratio: A Measure of Achievement

The **information ratio (IR)** is the ratio of annualized residual return or alpha (α) to annualized residual risk (ω).

$$\text{Ex post IR} = \frac{\text{Annualized residual return}}{\text{Annualized residual risk}} = \frac{\alpha}{\omega}$$

Note that:
- The information ratio increases with the time horizon (Y).
  - The numerator, alpha (α) or excess return increases proportionately with time.

  - The denominator, residual risk (ω), or the standard deviation grows as the square root of the time horizon.

  - Therefore, the information ratio will increase with the square root of time.
- The realized information ratio can be negative.
- The information ratio of the benchmark will be 0.

  - $$\text{Ex-post information ratio} = \frac{\text{t-stat of alpha in the regression results}}{\sqrt{\text{Number of years of data used in the regression}}}$$

    $$= \frac{t_\alpha}{\sqrt{Y}}$$

The Ex Ante Information Ratio: A Measure of Opportunity

A managers personal information ratio on Portfolio P is given as:

$$IR_P = \frac{\alpha_P}{\omega_P}$$

For a given investment manager/strategy, the ratio of risk to return remains constant even as the level of risk increases.

The Residual Frontier: The Manager's Opportunity Set

The residual frontier describes the opportunities available to the investment manager. The slope of the residual frontier (expected trade-off between expected residual return, α_P, and expected residual risk, (ω_P) equals the manager's ex ante information ratio (IR).

The manager's information ratio effectively serves as a "budget constraint". She can increase expected residual return only if she accepts a corresponding increase in residual risk.

$$\alpha_P = IR_P \times \omega_P$$

The Active Management Objective

The aim of active management is to maximize the value added from residual return. Value added is measured as:

$$VA_P = \alpha_P - \lambda_R \times \omega_P^2$$

λ_R measures aversion to residual risk.

- An increase in residual return (α_P) increases value added.
- An increase in residual risk ($\omega^2{}_P$) reduces value added.
- An increase in risk aversion (λ_R) magnifies the negative impact of residual risk on value added.

Preferences Meet Opportunities

Given her investment opportunity set (which is determined by her ex ante alpha), the investment manager should try to invest in the portfolio that has the highest value added.

Aggressiveness, Opportunity, and Residual Risk Aversion

$$VA_P = (IR_P \times \omega_P) - \lambda_R \times \omega_P^2$$

This equation expresses value added entirely in terms of risk (ω_P). As risk increases, expected return increases, but so does the penalty for taking risk. Value added initially increases as more risk is taken, but then starts falling once the amount of risk taken exceeds an optimal amount, ω^*.

This optimal level of risk (ω^*) can be determined as:

$$\omega^* = \frac{IR}{2\lambda_R}$$

- The optimal level of risk increases with the manager's investment opportunities (IR).
- The optimal level of risk decreases with the manager's aversion for residual risk λ_R.

Takeaways

- The greater our opportunities (IR) the higher the level of aggressiveness (or optimal risk level).
- The lower our risk aversion level (λ_R) the higher the level of aggressiveness (or optimal risk level).

Reasonable Level of Risk Aversion (λ_R)

$$\lambda_R = \frac{IR}{2 \times \omega^*}$$

Value Added: Risk-Adjusted Residual Return of Optimal Portfolio

$$VA^* = \left(\frac{IR^2}{4\lambda_R} \right)$$

$$VA^* = \frac{(\omega^* \times IR)}{2}$$

The ability of the manager to add value:
- Increases as the square of the information ratio.
- Decreases as the manager become more risk averse (as λ_R increases).

No matter how high or how low our risk aversion level (λ_R) is, we would choose the investment manager with the highest information ratio. Investors will only differ with respect to how aggressively they implement that manager's strategy.

THE FUNDAMENTAL LAW OF ACTIVE MANAGEMENT
Cross-Reference to CFA Institute Assigned Reading #55

The Fundamental Law of Active Management

The fundamental law states that a manager's information ratio can be estimated using two attributes of her strategy- skill and breadth.

- Skill is represented by the manager's information coefficient (IC), which represents the correlation between her residual return forecasts and subsequent results (actual residual returns).
- The breadth (BR) is defined as the number of independent forecasts of exceptional return that a manager makes per year.

$$IR = IC \times \sqrt{BR}$$

According to this formula, if we want to increase our information ratio from 0.3 to 0.6, we can either (1) double our skill (IC), or (2) increase our breadth by a factor of 4.

Impact of Information Coefficient and Breadth on Optimal Level of Residual Risk

$$\omega^* = \left(\frac{IR}{2\lambda_R} \right) = \frac{IC \times \sqrt{BR}}{2\lambda_R}$$

Note that the desired level of aggressiveness (optimal residual risk, ω^*) will increase directly with the skill level (IC) and the square root of the breadth (BR).

- Higher skill increases the probability of success. Since the gains appear to be larger, we would be willing to take more risk.
- Greater breadth allows for more diversification among active bets so the overall level of aggressiveness can increase.

Impact of Information Coefficient and Breadth on Optimal Level of Residual Risk

The value added (VA) by the investment manager (Equation 6 in the previous Reading) can also be expressed in terms of skill and breadth.

$$VA^* = \left(\frac{IR^2}{4\lambda_R} \right) = \frac{IC^2 \times BR}{4\lambda_R}$$

- The value added (risk-adjusted return) by a strategy will increase with the breadth and with the square root of the skill.

ADDITIVITY

The fundamental law is additive in the squared information ratios. Suppose we have two classes of stocks:

- For Class A we have BR_A number of stocks with a skill level IC of IC_A.
- For Class A we have BR_B number of stocks with a skill level IC of IC_B.

The information ratio for the aggregate or combined portfolio can be computed as:

$$IR^2 = BR_A \times IC_A^2 + BR_B \times IC_B^2$$

One of the most important assumptions underlying the fundamental law is that the forecasts should be independent. If γ represents the correlation between the two information sources or managers, the skill level, IC_{COM}, of the combined sources is computed as:

$$IC_{COM} = IC \times \sqrt{\frac{2}{1+\gamma}}$$

- The greater the dependence between the two information sources, the lower the value of incremental information.
- If there is zero correlation between sources ($\gamma = 0$), then $IC_{COM}^2 = 2 + IC^2$ (the two sources will add in their ability to add value).

ASSUMPTIONS OF THE FUNDAMENTAL LAW OF ACTIVE MANAGEMENT

- The manager has an accurate measure of his or her own skills and exploits information in an optimal way.
- The sources of information are independent.
- The skill level (IC) involved in forecasting each active bet (BR) is the same.

Bear in mind that the fundamental law should not be misinterpreted to conclude that improving the information ratio is as simple as increase breadth. More breadth is only better if you can maintain the edge (skill level, IC) as more breadth at the same level of skill allows us to diversify residual risk (and improve the information ratio). Readers must recognize that with more breadth, it becomes more difficult to maintain your edge.

The takeaway from this reading is that you must play often and play well to win at the investment management game. It takes only a modest amount of skill to win as long as the edge (skill) is applied frequently enough.

THE PORTFOLIO MANAGEMENT PROCESS AND THE INVESTMENT POLICY STATEMENT
Cross-Reference to CFA Institute Assigned Reading #56

Importance of the Portfolio Perspective

Risk can either be systematic (diversifiable) or unsystematic (non-diversifiable). Most equity pricing models assume that investors hold diversified portfolios and are only compensated for systematic risk. Therefore, instead of evaluating each investment in isolation, investment managers should take a portfolio perspective when evaluating an investment.

The Portfolio Management Process

Planning

1. Identifying and Specifying the Investor's Objectives and Constraints

   - **Risk Objectives**
     - Risk may be measured in absolute or relative terms.
     - Risk measures include variance, standard deviation and value at risk (VAR).
     - Risk tolerance is a function of the investor's ability and willingness to take risk.
     - Generally speaking, a client with a longer time horizon, high expected income, and greater net worth has a greater ability to bear risk. A client's willingness to bear risk is based on more subjective factors including her psychological makeup, and level of understanding of financial markets.

   - **Return Objectives**
     - Return objectives may also be stated in absolute or relative terms.
     - The return an investor wishes to achieve is called her desired return, while the minimum level of return she needs to achieve is called her required return.
     - A portfolio manager should take the total return perspective.
     - The portfolio manager needs to ensure that the client's return objectives are realistic in light of her tolerance for risk.

   - **Investment Constraints**
     - Liquidity
     - Time
     - Tax concerns
     - Legal and regulatory factors
     - Unique circumstances

2. Creating the Investment Policy Statement

   An IPS includes the following:
   - An introduction that describes the client.
   - A statement of purpose.
   - A statement of duties and responsibilities of all the parties involved.

- A statement of investment goals, objectives, and constraints.
- A schedule for review of investment performance as well as the IPS itself.
- Performance measures and benchmarks to be used in performance evaluation.
- Any considerations to be taken into account in developing the strategic asset allocation.
- Investment strategies and investment style.
- Guidelines for rebalancing the portfolio based on feedback.

An IPS serves the following purposes:
- It helps the investor decide on realistic investment goals after learning about financial markets and associated risks.
- It creates a standard according to which the portfolio manager's performance can be judged.
- It guides the actions of portfolio managers, who should refer to it from time to time to assess the suitability of particular investments for their clients' portfolios.

3. Forming Capital Market Expectations

In this step, the portfolio manager develops long-run risk-return forecasts for various asset classes.

4. Creating the Strategic Asset Allocation

Strategic asset allocation (SAA) refers to the allocation of funds across different asset classes. A portfolio's SAA is important because it is a portfolio's allocation across various asset classes (not its allocation across securities within those asset classes) that is the primary determinant of portfolio returns.

Execution

The execution of the strategy is as important as the planning as it also has a significant impact on portfolio returns. Poorly executed strategies can increase transaction costs hence reducing investment returns. Transaction costs can be both explicit (e.g. commissions, fees, taxes, etc.) and implicit (e.g. missed trade opportunity costs, market price impacts of large trades, etc.).

Feedback

- Monitoring and rebalancing: A portfolio manager must monitor changes in the capital market expectations and investor needs, and rebalance the portfolio accordingly.
- Performance evaluation: Investors should periodically evaluate the performance of the portfolio in light of their investment objectives.

Ethical Responsibilities of Portfolio Managers

Portfolio managers generally have more knowledge regarding capital markets compared to their clients. Their conduct affects the well-being of their clients and many other people. In order to maintain the trust of their clients, portfolio managers should hold themselves to the highest standards of competence and standards of conduct.